GCSE BUSINESS STUDIES

LONGMAN
REVISE
GUIDES

LONGMAN REVISE GUIDES

SERIES EDITORS:
Geoff Black and Stuart Wall

LONGMAN
REVISE
GUIDES

GCSE

BUSINESS STUDIES

Stephen Ison
Keith Pye

Longman

Longman Group UK Limited,
Longman House, Burnt Mill, Harlow,
Essex CM20 2JE, England
and Associated Companies throughout the world.

© Longman Group UK Limited 1988

First published 1988
Fifth Impression 1993

British Library Cataloguing in Publication Data

Ison, Stephenn
   Business studies. – (Longman GCSE revise
   guides).
   1. Business education – England 2. General
   Certificate of Secondary Education – Study
   guides
   I. Title II. Pye, Keith
   658′.0076 HF1141

ISBN 0-582-01573-1

Illustrated by Brian Davis

Set in 10/12pt Century Book Roman

Produced by Longman Singapore Publishers Pte Ltd
Printed in Singapore

C O N T E N T S

EDITORS' PREFACE

Longman Revise Guides are written by experienced examiners and teachers, and aim to give you the best possible foundation for success in examinations and other modes of assessment. Much has been said in recent years about declining standards and disappointing examination results. While this may be somewhat exaggerated, examiners are well aware that the performance of many candidates falls well short of their potential. The books encourage thorough study and a full understanding of the concepts involved and should be seen as course companions and study guides to be used throughout the year. Examiners are in no doubt that a structured approach in preparing for examinations and in presenting coursework can, together with hard work and diligent application, substantially improve performance.

The largely self-contained nature of each chapter gives the book a useful degree of flexibility. After starting with Chapters 1 and 2, all other chapters can be read selectively, in any order appropriate to the stage you have reached in your course. We believe that this book, and the series as a whole, will help you establish a solid platform of basic knowledge and examination technique on which to build.

Geoff Black and Stuart Wall

ACKNOWLEDGEMENTS

We are indebted to the following examination groups for permission to reproduce their questions. The answers given are entirely the responsibility of the authors.

University of London Examinations and Assessment Council
Midland Examining Group
Northern Examinations and Assessment Board
Northern Ireland Schools Examinations and Assessment Council.
Southern Examining Group.
Welsh Joint Education Committee.

We are also indebted to the Controller of Her Majesty's Stationery Office for permission to use extracts of the National Criteria and certain tables, to Warrington & Runcorn Development Corporation for the use of the advertisement in figure 6.9 and to Sarah Chappell, Joanna Foxcroft and Ursula Jacobs for providing student answers. We also thank the various Business Studies students who reviewed the draft chapters.

Our thanks also go to our wives for their constant encouragement and help and to David Lines, Geoff Black and Stuart Wall for their advice and comments.

Stephen Ison and Keith Pye

ACKNOWLEDGEMENTS

The publishers are grateful to the following schools and colleges for their co-operation: Bishop Fox's School, Taunton; Chase High School, Malvern; Derby Tertiary College, Mackworth; Impington Village College, Cambridge; Poole Grammar School; Pope Pius Comprehensive School, Rotherham; Queensbury School, Bradford; Rugby School; St Helena School, Chesterfield; St Christopher School, Letchworth; St Mary's High School, Cheshunt; Shildon Sunnydale Comprehensive School; Sir William Perkins's School, Chertsey; South Park Sixth Form College, Middlesbrough; Thrybergh Comprehensive School, Rotherham; Waddesdon Church of England Secondary School, Aylesbury; Wollaston School, Wellingborough.

CHAPTER

1

THE EXAMINATIONS AND ASSESSED COURSEWORK

SHORT ANSWER QUESTIONS
DATA RESPONSE QUESTIONS
CASE STUDIES

GCSE IN BUSINESS STUDIES

Each GCSE subject must conform to a set of *National Criteria* which have been established for that subject. If you study the National Criteria for *Business Studies* you will note that the aims of GCSE courses in Business Studies are:

1. to develop knowledge and understanding of the environment within which business activity takes place and of the way in which changes in that environment influence business behaviour;
2. to develop knowledge and understanding of the major groups and organisations within and outside business and consider ways in which they are able to influence business objectives, decisions and activities;
3. to develop understanding of the roles and purposes of business activity in both the public and the private sectors and of competition and monopoly;
4. to develop knowledge and understanding of how the main types of business and commercial institutions are organised, financed and operated and how their relations with other organisations, consumers, employees, owners and society are regulated;
5. to develop appreciation of the factor inputs and product outputs of businesses and the forces which help to determine and control them;
6. to promote knowledge and appreciation of the working world and of the cooperation and interdependence which participation in society entails and to encourage the confidence and awareness of students in their approach to such participation, particularly through group activity within the classroom and direct experience outside it;
7. to develop knowledge and understanding of the language, concepts, techniques and decision-making procedures in business behaviour appropriate to a specific course of study;
8. to develop skills of numeracy; literacy; discovery; selection and employment of relevant sources of information; presentation and interpretation;
9. to develop an awareness of the nature and significance of innovation and change within the context of business activities.

Only courses which satisfy these *aims* in full are allowed to use the title 'Business Studies'.

C O R E   C O N T E N T

The six examination groups must also develop syllabuses which cover *five* main topic areas. These have been called the *core-content* headings, namely:
1. External environment of the business
2. Business structure and organisation
3. Business behaviour
4. People in business
5. Aiding and controlling business

This book aims to follow closely these five core-content headings as you can see from the Table of Contents (p. v). Table 1.1 helps you see which chapters and topic areas are relevant to your particular syllabus.

Chapter and Topic	ULEAC	MEG	NEAB Syllabus A	NISEAC	SEG	WJEC
3. Background to business	●	●	●	●	●	●
4. Types of business	●	●	●	●	●	●
5. Management	●	●	●	●	●	●
6. Location, size and growth	●	●	●	●	●	●
7. Finance for business	●	●	●	●	●	●
8. Purchasing and production	●	●	●	●	●	●
9. Marketing	●	●	●	●	●	●
10. International trade	●	●	●	●	●	●
11. Business accounts	●	●	●	●	●	●
12. Business documents	●				●	●
13. Population	●	●	●	●	●	●
14. Recruitment, selection and training	●	●	●	●	●	●
15. Motivation	●	●	●	●	●	●
16. Communication	●	●	●	●	●	●
17. Industrial relations	●	●	●	●	●	●
18. Aiding and controlling business	●	●	●	●	●	●
19. Business in a changing world	●	●	●	●	●	●

Table 1.1

T H E   E X A M I N A T I O N S

Table 1.2 will give you an idea of the different examination papers you can expect from the six Examination Groups.

Examination Group	Paper	Time (hours)	Marks* %	Candidates	Questions
University of London Examinations and Assessment Council	1	2	70	Taken by ALL candidates. Grades available C, D, E, F, and G	There will be a series of compulsory stimulus data response questions: Section A: One question. Section B: A series of questions.
	2	1½	70	Taken by candidates likely to attain grades A or B. Grades available A, B, and C	An unseen case study.
				Candidates who take the higher level (Paper 2 and Coursework) will be awarded the grade attained at this level only if a Grade C or D is attained at the foundation level (Paper 1 and Coursework). Candidates ungraded at the higher level will be awarded the grade attained at the foundation level.	
Midland Examining Group	1	2	50	Common core paper	A paper containing a number of compulsory questions.
	2,3,4,5	1	20	Optional papers 2. Accounting 3. Business and Change 4. Commerce 5. Technology and Change Candidates must enter for one of 2–5.	Each paper contains a number of compulsory questions.
Northern Examinations and Assessment Board Syllabus A.	1	1½	35	Common paper	Three structured questions based on case studies or other stimulus material.
	2	1½	35	Common paper	One extended case study.
Northern Ireland Schools Examinations and Assessment Council	2	1½	40	Common paper	A number of compulsory questions.
	1	1½	40	For those wishing to be considered for an award on limited level range 7–4 inclusive	Section A: ten compulsory short answer questions. Section B: three compulsory structured questions.
	OR				
	3	1½	40	For those wishing to be considered for an award on limited range of levels 10–6	Three compulsory structured questions.
Southern Examining Group	1	1½	42	Common paper	Consist of about 40 compulsory questions based on a case study to be given to candidates 6 weeks before the examination.
	2	¾	18	Options: A. Business Studies (Business and Change) B. Information Technology C. Commerce D. Finance and Accounting E. Enterprise F. Modern Languages	A–D and F consist of between 2 and 5 compulsory questions based on same case study as in Paper 1 but additional material relevant to option may be included. Option E: Takes form of a report or reports written during the course. Option B: Paper will require some practical tasks.
Welsh Joint Education Committee	1	2	70	Common paper	Compulsory structured questions.

* % marks do not total 100 as the remaining marks are for assessed coursework.

Table 1.2 **Business Studies GCSE – The examinations.**

As you will see there are *four* main types of examination questions, although every Examination Group does not necessarily use all four.

These test specific areas of the Business Studies syllabus. If your Examination Group uses this technique, then you could be asked questions such as, 'In what ways do producer and consumer goods differ?'. You will then be given one or two lines in which to answer the question.

2 ▷ DATA RESPONSE QUESTIONS

These present a short passage, table, graph or some other form of data, and use it to develop a number of questions. In answering the questions you will find some of the relevant information in the data. Data response questions aim to test whether you can relate what you know to particular situations or pieces of information. Some of the Examination Groups will use the term *structured questions* for what are essentially data response questions.

3 ▷ CASE STUDIES

Case studies are used as part of the assessment process. The case studies form one whole paper and are based on a particular theme. That theme might be the experience of a particular company over a number of years. Questions might concern, for example, the company's financial problems, its methods of recruitment, its management, structure, and locational decisions. Also, you might be called upon to give your own advice. The SEG allows the case study to be given to the candidates six weeks before the date of the examination.

C O U R S E W O R K

As part of the assessment process you will be required to undertake compulsory coursework. Table 1.3 gives a summary of what is expected and the percentage of marks available from the six Examination Groups. The coursework is not meant to be simply a desk exercise. Instead you will be expected to relate your 'classroom' Business Studies to the local environment. It is suggested that you *yourself* should be involved in collecting and assembling the information to be used in the assignments. More detail on the preparation and presentation of coursework can be found in Chapter 2.

Examination Group	Marks %	Coursework
London	30	Each year the examining group will prescribe six assignments from which you will have to select two. Each assignment is worth 30% and should not exceed more than 1000 words.
Midland Examining Group	30	One assignment of no more than 2500 words, representing about 10 hours on all elements of the task.
Northern Examinations and Assessment Board	30	You are to submit between one and three assignments. If only one is submitted then it should be no more than 3000 words. On the other hand if two are submitted then each assignment should be no more than 1500 words, and if three, then not more than 1000 words. This is an approximate guide.
Northern Ireland Schools Examinations and Assessment Council	20	Two assignments should be submitted, selected from different areas of the syllabus.
Southern Examining Group	40	A file of work produced over the course (32%), group work assessment (8%)
Welsh Joint Education Committee	30	Two of four assignments should be undertaken. Approximately 30 hours of student-centred activity should be undertaken.

Table 1.3 **Business Studies GCSE – Assessed coursework**

G R A D E S

If you study Table 1.2 you will note that there are different examination papers. For each Examination Group there is a ***common*** paper undertaken by all candidates. Then, unless you are a candidate with the NEAB (which has a second common paper), you will undertake one of two alternative papers. The decision as to which paper you sit will depend on the grade you are likely to obtain. Your teacher or lecturer may be actively involved in this choice. To give you some idea of the standards you would have to achieve to be awarded a particular grade, the National Criteria state the following:

1 Grade F
Candidates will normally have demonstrated:
1.1   some ability to recall knowledge from areas of the syllabus;
1.2   some ability to select and apply commonly used methods, techniques and procedures;
1.3   familiarity with vocabulary central to the course and ability to make simple calculations;
1.4   some ability to apply data to the solution of simple problems;
1.5   some ability to communicate effectively.

2 Grade C
Candidates will normally have demonstrated:
2.1   ability to recall and use knowledge from the whole range of the syllabus;
2.2   ability to select and apply appropriate methods, techniques and procedures;
2.3   familiarity with the vocabulary and theory appropriate to the syllabus and ability to use numerical methods;
2.4   ability to organise and apply data to a variety of problems;
2.5   some ability to analyse and discuss;
2.6   ability to communicate effectively in writing.

CHAPTER

2

THE EXAMINATION AND ASSESSED WORK TECHNIQUES

REVISION
COURSEWORK
    REQUIREMENTS
PLANNING AND RESEARCH
PRESENTATION

GETTING STARTED

Everyone will have their own method of preparing for examinations and your teachers may give you lots of helpful advice on the best methods to adopt. There is no one best approach, each of us is different and what works for one person may not work for you. However, this chapter suggests a number of useful techniques you might consider when planning your revision and taking your examinations. It also considers how to present coursework, which we have seen is an increasingly important part of the GCSE in Business Studies.

PREPARATION FOR THE EXAMINATION

The first, and perhaps most obvious, point to make is that there is no substitute for hard work. Having worked steadily throughout the course you must carefully organise your time in the last three or four months before the examination so that you gain your proper reward for that work. Do not, therefore, leave your revision until the last minute.

1 ▷ REVISION

Instead, work out a revision timetable well before the examination. On a blank piece of paper, construct a chart, as in Fig. 2.1.

Day	am 9	10	11	noon 12	1	2	3	4	pm 5	6	7	8	9
Monday													
Tuesday													
Wednesday													
Thursday													
Friday													
Saturday													
Sunday													

Figure 2.1

You will not be able to work every single hour, so block out the times when you usually have meals, go to school or college and enjoy leisure time. Over the period of your revision for the examinations you might, of course, reduce your usual amount of leisure time. Going out with friends should fit around your revision, rather than your revision fit around going out with your friends! Once you have done this, you can then allocate the time you have left to revise.

In doing this, you will have to take into account the number of subjects you have to revise. Try to give roughly the same time each week to each of your subjects. Making a timetable should indicate why it is a good idea to start revising early, although it is never too late to do something. Once you have a study timetable it is important to stick to it.

In Business Studies you should try to cover the whole syllabus as there are *integrated questions* (see Ch. 20) which test your knowledge over a range of topics.

Before revising you need to decide where will be the best *place* to revise. It may be your bedroom, the school library or even the local town library. Wherever you choose, it will need to be fairly quiet, have sufficient lighting and be comfortable. You may even find sitting on your bed is the best place provided you do not fall asleep! Above all you need to be organised.

Once you have prepared a revision timetable or organised a programme which suits you, then you have to settle down and actually revise the various areas or topics within the subject.

An aim of this book is to aid you in that revision. When revising bear in mind the format of the examination papers of the examining body for which you are entered. We have seen that the six Examining Bodies mentioned in Chapter 1 use a mixture of question *types*, namely compulsory structured questions, integrated case studies, short questions and task-related questions, such as designing a job application form. Try to be familiar with each type of question used by your Examining Body. Practise answering such questions in this book. Only the London and East Anglian Group offers a choice with their essay-type questions. With questions being compulsory and integrated, this again makes it important that you revise the *whole* syllabus.

For a number of Examining Bodies the examination paper acts as an *answer book* with blank lines left for you to answer the questions. Each Examination Group will produce papers which are slightly different in format, so it is important that you obtain copies of past papers or specimen papers. At the end of each chapter you will find examination questions from the various examination groups, together with tutor's outline answers. Although you should not view these answers as being anything other than suggestions, they should help you gain some idea of what the examiner expects of you. Chapter 20 also gives a number of **integrated questions**, that is questions which cover more than one area of the syllabus. You may find it useful to use this chapter after you have finished the course. Each chapter concentrates on a particular topic and has sub-headings which help highlight the main elements within that topic. If this is your own book and not a school/college book, then you may like to use the margins to add your own notes and comments as you revise. One good way to revise is to read your class notes on a topic, then to read the relevant chapter in this book and attempt the questions at the end of the chapter.

You may like to enlist the help of others in your revision, for example by getting a member of your family to test you. It is not worthwhile doing this, however, until you have revised the topic by yourself.

We suggest that you read over the essays written in class or for homework. Carefully note any comments made by the teacher or lecturer as this will reduce the possibility of you making the same mistakes in the examination. The work you have undertaken for assignments should also prove useful revision material. You are likely to be at some disadvantage if your **written English** is not very good, so you may have to spend some time trying to improve this area. At the very least, learn to spell the more important terms used in Business Studies; words such as 'interest' and even 'business' are often incorrectly spelt.

TAKING THE EXAMINATION

You need to get to bed early on the night before the examination. Late-night revision is often counter-productive, especially if it makes you tired during the examination itself. Make sure you have set the alarm clock, particularly if the examination is in the morning. Teachers find every year that some students enter the exam room late. You will not normally be allowed any extra time. Make sure you have checked and double checked where the examination is, as well as the time it starts. You might even visit the place where the examinations will be held before the day they start, so that you get a feel for the atmosphere. Also make sure you have the necessary equipment, namely two pens (black or blue), a ruler, two pencils (HB), a rubber, pencil sharpener and a watch.

You may not have a choice of desk in the exam room. However, if you can choose, sit away from the windows, particularly if it is a hot day. Also, avoid desks near the doors as these could be noisy due to candidates arriving late and leaving early.

Spend some time **reading through the instructions** on the examination paper. Make sure you notice which questions, if any, are compulsory and then think about the questions, perhaps jotting down some ideas in rough. You will gain no marks for irrelevant information. The examination is not about writing down everything you know, so avoid waffle.

Write as **neatly** and as **clearly** as you can. Try not to use slang language such as 'high interest rates will make firms go bust'. Avoid giving opinions, such as 'I think that . . .'. Try to justify your points, for instance, you might write 'There are three reasons why it could be argued that . . .'

Use **all the time you have available** rather than leaving the examination room early. You will not be able to change anything you have written once you have left the room. In **checking** over your work you could spot mistakes or think of other points to add. You should always aim to leave time at the end of the examination to read through your answers.

Each exam paper will allocate marks to each question. These can be found on the right-hand side of each question. They should allow you to calculate the **marks per minute** and so the amount of time you should spend on each question. If, for example, the examination paper is to take one and a quarter hours and there are 30 marks to be awarded on the paper, then roughly two and a half minutes should be spent on each mark. Only use this as a rough guide, and remember to set a little time aside for reading through the question paper carefully and checking your work. However, working out the marks per question should help you to avoid spending 10 minutes on a question worth only 2 marks whilst spending 2 minutes on a question worth 10 marks.

There is always the temptation after the exam to chat with others who have taken the same paper. This kind of 'post mortem' should be avoided if possible. What is done is done! Those you talk to may only depress you by convincing you that you could have written more, answered different questions or even answered the same questions in a better way. It is far better to forget the exam paper you have finished and start thinking about the next one.

C O U R S E W O R K

As you will have noted from Table 1.3 in Ch. 1, the six Examination Groups have a *compulsory coursework element* which accounts for 20 to 30% of the overall assessment. This section gives you some guidance on how to prepare and present coursework assignments.

1 ▶ REQUIREMENTS

The starting point is to find out exactly what the Examining Groups' *requirements for coursework* are; Table 1.3 will give you a general outline. For instance how many assignments do you have to undertake? Are there any guidelines on length?

You must next decide on the topic area for each assignment. The topic must, of course, be part of the Business Studies syllabus of your Examining Group. You may choose a particular area for study because you are interested in it. For example, you may eventually want to work in marketing and so decide to undertake an assignment in that area.

An alternative guide to use when deciding on an area for study is to think of someone you know who could provide you with information. Perhaps a member of your family works in a local business and could obtain information or even arrange an interview for you. It could be that you work on a Saturday and could therefore base an assignment around that work. In any event, the coursework is designed to be undertaken outside the classroom, so that you relate what you have learnt in your Business Studies course to the local business environment.

At the end of each chapter of this book you will find a section entitled 'Coursework'. This gives you one or two assignments which you may find useful for that topic area. You might want to adapt them to suit your own interests or situation. In any event, they could be used as a guideline.

2 ▶ PLANNING AND RESEARCH

When *planning* your coursework make sure you are aware of all the possible *sources of information*: you could visit the local library to find information on your town, or city, or the company you are investigating; you might visit (by appointment) a local business to obtain information and perhaps to interview some of the staff; or you might construct a questionnaire to be used with a particular group of people. You should make every effort to avoid the assignment coming straight out of a book. Make sure that you keep a careful *record* of all the interviews (plus dates), phone calls and information which you have obtained. It is very easy to misplace information and to forget what you have been told in an interview. You will need to organise your study, perhaps keeping a file which contains all the material relevant to your assignment. The best assignments follow an integrated approach. If you are looking at why a particular firm has grown in your area, it may be that all the five 'core' content headings (see p. 2) will be relevant.

3 ▶ PRESENTATION

You will have to make sure that each assignment is neatly and clearly presented. If your writing is difficult to read you may feel it is worth getting it typed (if possible). There are different approaches to the presentation of assignments. One method may be to use the following format:
▶ The Title and Contents.
▶ Introduction. What are you aiming to do? How are you going to do this? You could give a brief outline of these points which would then form an introduction.
▶ Case Study: your own findings on the topic you have chosen.

► Conclusions.
► Sources of information used such as newspapers, interviews, and books.

In presenting your assignment you may want to use not only written information but also diagrams, tables, graphs, etc. Remember to draw these clearly and to fully label all axes, and other features. Keep a note in your file of the date the assignment has to be handed in or, better still, write it on the front of your file. Your teacher/lecturer will no doubt remind you, but it will be safer to have the date close at hand. Try to plan your work on the assignment so that you finish it in good time. You do not want to leave it until the last minute. It is nearly always possible to tell those assignments which have been rushed because of a lack of time.

GETTING STARTED

If you look around your home you can hardly fail to notice the influence which business has on your life. The goods you possess, whether for immediate consumption such as food, or to give you satisfaction over a longer time period such as a television, will have been produced by a *business*. If you watch independent television you will not be able to escape advertisements making you aware of the goods and services which businesses provide. If your household purchases a national daily newspaper you will also notice that this includes advertisements of goods and services on offer. Your local newspaper will also include advertisements for employment vacancies, which may be of importance to you if you are considering leaving school in the near future or if you are looking for part-time work. One of the aims of a course in Business Studies is to develop your knowledge and understanding of *business and its environment*. This applies at the local, national and international levels of business.

This chapter sets out the background to business. Why do businesses produce goods and services? What resources do they use in the production of these goods and services? What is meant by production? Within what kind of economic system do these businesses operate? Do they all set themselves the same objectives?

**SCARCITY AND CHOICE
OPPORTUNITY COST
RESOURCES
MEETING OUR NEEDS
TYPES OF ECONOMIC
    SYSTEM
THE MARKET ECONOMY
THE PLANNED ECONOMY
THE MIXED ECONOMY
BUSINESS OBJECTIVES**

E S S E N T I A L   P R I N C I P L E S

1 ▶ SCARCITY AND CHOICE

Individuals, as *consumers* within an economy, require a large number of goods and services. Businesses aim at producing these with a view to making a profit.

Most individuals are restricted in what they can buy because of the size of their income. Some will, therefore, spend much more of their income on *basic necessities*, such as food, drink and housing. Others will have more income and therefore be able to buy *luxuries*, such as microwave ovens, compact-disc players and video recorders. If you think about your own situation as a student, then there will be many goods and services you would like to buy. Goods, such as one of the latest top-twenty records, a book or a new pair of shoes; or services, such as a haircut, an evening out at the cinema or a football match. You will not be able to buy all the goods and services you would like to because of the limited amount of *resources* you have. These limited resources will, in your case, be the money you obtain each week either as pocket money or for doing particular jobs. This being so you will have to make *choices*. Some of the goods and services you want you will be able to buy but others you will not. This need to choose follows from the fact that although you have *unlimited wants*, you have *limited resources*, in other words your resources are *scarce*.

In the same way, businesses will have to choose how they use their limited resources. Do they use their limited funds to extend their factory or buy a new machine? Do they spend money on developing a new product or do they spend more on advertising the products they are already producing? A business must continually make these and many more decisions.

Governments also have to make choices as to how to spend the money they obtain from taxpayers. If more is spent on providing educational services, this might be at the expense of the National Health Service.

2 ▶ OPPORTUNITY COST

> **Make sure you state that opportunity cost is the *next best* alternative foregone, not just any alternative!**

As mentioned above, as a student you may have unlimited wants but limited resources, so that you will have to make choices. These choices will involve *opportunity cost*. If, for example, you use your money to go to a football match, then you will not be able to use that money to go to the cinema. In making your choice you will have a *scale of preferences*; perhaps football is first, the cinema second and swimming third. The cinema would then be the next best alternative you have had to do without, as a result of spending your money on a football match. The next best alternative you have foregone is called the opportunity cost. The opportunity cost of your visit to the football match is then the visit to the cinema which you have had to give up. The concept of opportunity cost is just as relevant to business and the Government. A business which chooses to buy, say, a new fleet of lorries, will forego what it sees as the next best alternative. This might have been to build a new warehouse in which to store its finished products. In this case, the opportunity cost of buying the new fleet of lorries is the new warehouse. Governments will also have similar choices to make involving opportunity cost. For example an extra £1 billion on school buildings may mean less new hospitals in the country.

3 ▶ RESOURCES

The resources of an economy which can be used to produce goods and services can be divided into four categories (called the *factors of production*):
▶ Land
▶ Labour
▶ Capital
▶ Enterprise

A. LAND

> **Do not forget that land also includes the resources on or below the surface.**

You may feel that land is simply the surface of the earth on which factories and offices can be built. It is this, but it is also the material resources, which are on or below the surface. It therefore includes agricultural products; mineral deposits, such as coal, iron ore, tin and oil; and the resources obtained from the sea, rivers and lakes.

B. LABOUR

If land is classed as a natural resource then labour is classed as a human resource. Labour is not just the physical or manual work which individuals undertake in providing goods and services. It is also the mental and intellectual skills which individuals use in the course of production.

C. CAPITAL

Unlike land and labour, capital is a manufactured resource. It includes factories and a wide variety of machinery and technology, such as computers. Capital can take a number of forms:

Fixed capital

This is made up of such things as factories and machinery. Fixed capital is needed by a firm before it can start producing.

Circulating capital

This is sometimes called working capital and includes the stocks of raw materials which the business will need to manufacture its products. It will also include partly finished products which are not yet ready to be sold and finished goods which are not yet sold.

D. ENTERPRISE

Land, labour and capital are used to produce goods or services but they need to be organised. Enterprise brings the factors of production together. The person who does the organising is called the Entrepreneur or Businessperson.

4 ▶ MEETING OUR NEEDS

A. PRODUCTION

Businesses have to meet the needs of their customers whether they provide goods or services. If they fail to meet those needs they will very quickly go out of business. Businesses must therefore carefully consider what the consumer requires and how the consumers tastes are changing over time.

When you go into a shop and buy a product such as a loaf of bread then you are completing a whole *chain of production*. This has started with the farmer planting the grain and ended with you buying the bread from a retailer. You may think that production is just the process of manufacturing the bread. This is not, however, the whole picture because production is also made up of the provision of the raw materials; in the case of the loaf of bread, this would be flour, salt, yeast and water. The chain of production will also include the services which ensure that the finished product finds its way to the consumer. These services include the transport of bread to the shops, the selling (retail) of bread from the shops and the attempt to make you buy that type of bread (advertising).

It is possible to divide production into three broad areas, namely primary, secondary and tertiary production, as can be seen in Fig. 3.1.

Types of production

i. Primary production.   Companies in this area of production are involved in the extraction of raw materials, whether above or below the earth's surface. This means that primary production covers farming, forestry and fishing as well as mining, quarrying and drilling for such raw materials as coal, limestone and oil.

> 66 It can be difficult to learn a great deal of information. Sometimes a diagram, such as figure 3.1, is useful in giving you the important points. 99

ii. Secondary production.   Secondary production involves the manufacture of goods, that is the process of turning the raw materials into products. You can, perhaps, make a list of such companies in your town or city. These companies may manufacture finished products which are ready for the end-user to buy or semi-finished products which will go towards making other products. If you refer to Fig. 3.1 you will also notice Construction, which involves the building industry and the Public Utilities, including the industries of gas, electricity and water.

As seen in Fig. 3.1, the manufacture of goods can be separated into two types, namely consumer goods and producer goods. You may be more familiar with *consumer*

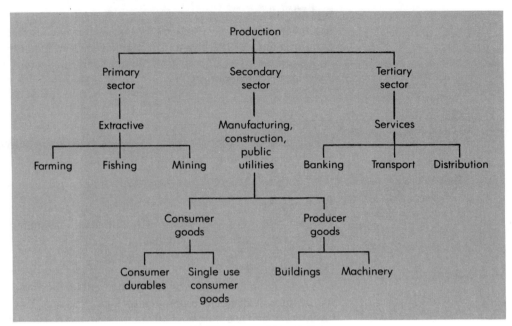

Fig.3.1. Types of Production

goods as you will find many examples in your home. The single-use consumer goods are items which are used only once, such as food and matches. *Consumer durables* on the other hand are long-lasting and can be used again and again, such as the washing machine, refrigerator or television. *Producer goods* are used by companies and individuals in the manufacture of other goods (which could in turn be consumer goods). Producer goods include such items as lathes, drills and computers and they can also be called *investment goods* or *capital goods*.

iii. Tertiary production. Once the goods have been manufactured, that is by no means the end of the chain. A number of activities will still have to occur before the goods reach the consumer. They will have to be transported, advertised and distributed through wholesale and retail outlets. Banking and financial services will be involved in insuring the finished product and, even before manufacture, in raising the money to begin production (see p. 64). *Tertiary* production, therefore, involves all these service activities such as banking, transport, and distribution. Services are sometimes classed as *intangible goods*, as they meet our needs in much the same way as goods do.

B. SPECIALISATION

In early society, individuals would themselves produce all the products they needed. If they produced a surplus of any product, then they would exchange some of that surplus for the other products in short supply. This is known as a system of *barter*. Perhaps you could think of the problems barter would create (see Ch. 7)!

The introduction of money (see also Ch. 7) solved one of the problems of barter, in that it allowed individuals to specialise. They were now able to produce the goods, or to provide the services, that they were better at. With the money they obtained they could then buy the goods and services they needed. Specialisation has developed to a point where individuals can now specialise in one small part of a productive process. You should be able to note many examples of specialisation in the area in which you live. Think particularly of the manufacturing business where the process of producing the goods may be divided into a large number of small steps, many undertaken on a production line. This is known as the *division of labour*.

C. THE INTERDEPENDENCE OF BUSINESS

Figure 3.1 gives some idea of the *interdependence* of business. All the members of society involved in *production* are also *consumers*, as are those who are not directly involved in some aspect of production. *Individuals* would find it difficult to exist by their own efforts in modern society as they rely on others to specialise and produce the goods and services they require. In other words individuals are **interdependent**. So too, are **businesses**. Take the case of a chocolate manufacturer, which must rely on **primary producers** to supply its raw material, namely cocoa beans. The beans have then to be imported so a chocolate manufacturer must also depend on the **tertiary sector**, namely the transport services of road and sea.

The business will also require a skilled workforce capable of producing the chocolate products. In return, the employees will be dependent upon the manufacturer to provide employment and the income which goes with it. With that income, the employees of the chocolate manufacturer can become the consumers of the goods and services of other businesses.

Once the chocolate has been produced the manufacturer must seek to sell it. This may require the services of an advertising agency to bring the product to the notice of the consumer. Wholesale distributors may purchase the product in bulk from the manufacturer. Retail outlets will then purchase the product for consumers. The manufacturer is, of course, reliant on the consumer whether in the UK or abroad. If the demand is inadequate then the business will not survive.

Other services will also be important for the chocolate manufacturer. Extra finance may be required to expand the factory, to obtain new machinery or to buy a new fleet of lorries. For this reason the services of the local bank may be needed. Also, the banks will have a whole range of additional facilities to help the manufacturer in importing and exporting the product (see Ch. 7). The business will need to insure the products, particularly when they are in transit, as there may be a risk of damage or accident. The manufacturer will also be dependent upon communications of all types – not just the work of the advertising agency but also the provision made by the postal and telecommunications services (see Ch. 16).

Finally, there will be an interdependence between the manufacturing company and the Government. The Government will require the company to pay corporation tax on the profits made from the production of goods and services, and the company's employees will also be subject to income tax. In return, there are a number of benefits the Government will provide for the company. The company may be in an area of the UK which receives grants and subsidies as part of the Government Regional Policy. Even if it is not, Central and Local Government will have helped provide the infrastructure, namely roads, schools, energy supplies and health care, all of which benefit the company.

5 TYPES OF ECONOMIC SYSTEM

Make sure you do not get the different economic systems mixed up!

So far we have looked at the major purpose of business activity, that is to provide the goods and services which meet our needs. This involves the areas of primary, secondary and tertiary production, and varying degrees of specialisation by those in employment. All this productive activity will be undertaken in a particular type of economic system, which is largely determined by political factors. There are three main types of economic system:
▶ the market economy
▶ the planned economy
▶ the mixed economy

6 THE MARKET ECONOMY

In an extreme ('pure') market economy there would be no government involvement at all. What is produced would depend solely on what business views as profitable and what the consumer demands. The pure market economy can be seen to have certain features;

i Private enterprise
There is no state ownership of businesses hence no nationalisation takes place. All businesses are either owned by an individual (sole trader) or by a group of individuals (partners or shareholders). The resources in the economy are owned by private enterprise and their use depends on the 'signals' provided by the market mechanism (see page 16).

ii Freedom of choice
The owners of land and capital are able to use their resources in whatever way they

regard as most beneficial to them (e.g. giving the highest profit!). Consumers can spend their income as they wish and workers can undertake the type of employment they prefer.

iii Competition

This is an important feature of a market economy. It is usually argued that a large number of businesses competing with each other will produce a cheaper product of better quality. In other words competition will promote greater efficiency.

The market economies are sometimes called free enterprise, laissez-faire or capitalist economies. There is perhaps no economy which quite meets the idealised form of a pure market economy, although some countries, like the USA, are quite close.

A. THE MARKET MECHANISM

We have seen that an economy has resources of land, labour, capital and enterprise. Decisions have to be made as to how to use these resources. We see below that in the planned economy it is the Government which decides how these resources should be allocated and the prices which should be charged for the goods and services they produce. In the market economy however, these decisions are left to private businesses and are the result of the market mechanism.

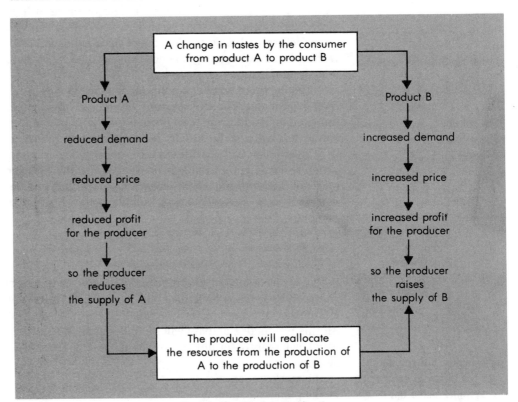

Fig.3.2. The Market Mechanism

Figure 3.2 outlines how the market mechanism operates. When you buy goods or services, you are signalling to the producer that you have a preference for their product. The more 'signals' of this type that producers obtain from other consumers, the more they will produce of that product. The reason for this is that, other things being equal, the greater the demand for their product, the higher the price they will be able to charge, and therefore the higher the profit level they will obtain. When you spend your money on a product it is like voting. In this case you are voting for a particular company's goods or services. The more income you have then the more 'votes' you possess.

A change in the price acts as a signal to the producer to alter supply, as we can see in Fig. 3.2. The producer will move resources away from the production of those products which have a falling demand, to the production of those products which have a rising demand. In the case of Fig. 3.2 the move would be away from product A and towards product B.

B. ADVANTAGES OF THE MARKET ECONOMY

1. The market mechanism allocates resources automatically without any need for government intervention.
2. Businesses compete with each other. This should result in increased efficiency and a better range and quality of product, from all of which the consumer can benefit.
3. All individuals within the economy have freedom of choice.

C. DISADVANTAGES OF THE MARKET ECONOMY

1. Businesses will charge the price that most consumers are willing to pay. This could mean that certain individuals will be unable to obtain the goods and service they require.
2. Competition may not in fact take place. Larger businesses may take over the smaller firms or squeeze them out of existence. What is called a monopoly situation may then occur. This may be against the interests of the consumer. The monopoly may charge higher prices, knowing that no alternative sources of supply are available.
3. With no government intervention, businesses will only take account of their own private costs of production, namely the cost of the raw materials they use, and the wages, rent, rates and interest they pay. They will not take account of the social costs they impose on others as they produce. For instance the firm may cause pollution, perhaps of the air or rivers, or bring about congestion as its vehicles use local roads. It might increase noise levels by operating its machinery or cause visual intrusion by building a factory which overlooks local houses. These costs to society as a whole, as a result of the firm's production, are called social costs, and are likely to go unchecked in the market economy without government intervention.

7   THE PLANNED ECONOMY

The planned economy uses its resources in a way decided by the government or state. A planned economy includes these features:

i. Resources are owned by the state

In the case of businesses the profits are used for the benefit of the economy and not for the owners/shareholders as in the market economy, the view being that this creates a more equal society.

ii The production of goods and services is determined by the state

Resources will be allocated according to the government or planning authorities view as to the desires of the consumers and not by the profit motive or self interest. However, they may wrongly predict those desires. They may find that there is an overproduction of certain goods and services that the consumer does not want and an underproduction of other goods and services which are in high demand.

   The planned economy is sometimes called the command or controlled economy. You may not think of Britain as a planned economy but during the Second War the Government did take control of the economic resources of the nation so that they could be used to meet the war effort.

A. ADVANTAGES OF A PLANNED ECONOMY

1. All businesses are state owned so that it is not possible for a private monopoly to develop.
2. The state decides what is to be produced so that any wasteful competition can be avoided.
3. The state can take account of the social costs and the social benefits in deciding what to produce.

B. DISADVANTAGES OF A PLANNED ECONOMY

1. The government decides what is to be produced. If it misjudges the requirements of the consumer, then shortages or gluts of certain goods and services can occur. Shortages result in long queues for products whilst gluts lead to large stockpiles of unwanted products.

2. Since the state owns all the factors of production this may reduce the incentives to work harder. There is no opportunity for individuals to own their own businesses and to make profits.
3. There will be a lack of competition between businesses and a lack of variety for the consumer. Private monopoly may merely be replaced by public monopoly.
4. In the market economy resources will be allocated automatically through the market mechanism. In the planned economy there will be state planning. This may involve a lot of resources and lead to large planning bureaucracies which are slow to take decisions.

This type of economic system sets out to combine the advantages of both the market economy and the planned economy. In fact, most economies in the world can be viewed as mixed economies although, as Fig. 3.3 shows, some are closer to the market economy and others to the planned economy.

Fig.3.3. Market, Planned and Mixed Economies

In the mixed economy resources are owned partly by private individuals and enterprises, and partly by the state; they are allocated partly by the market mechanism and partly by government intervention. In the UK over the last few years the economy has moved more in the direction of the market economy with certain nationally owned enterprises being privatised, such as British Telecom, British Gas and British Airways (see Ch. 4).

As a student you may set yourself objectives. At present your main objective may be to obtain high grades in your GCSE examinations. Businesses will also have objectives and these will normally be formulated by the management of the Company, the Board of Directors. By business objectives we mean the targets that the company is aiming to achieve. Businesses may have more than one objective, but profit is likely to be one of them. A business may set out to maximise its profits, that is, make as much profit as possible. This is an objective which the **owners** of the business are likely to prefer, whether sole traders, members of a partnership or shareholders (see Ch. 4). In a medium or large company the shareholder may have less say in the running of the company. Effective control of the company may be in the hands of the top management. Management may have different objectives in mind than shareholders. The managers may seek, as their main objective, to sell as much of the firm's output as possible. In other words, to maximise the volume of sales. The managers' status or promotional prospects may depend more on the sales revenue or size of the company than on the profit performance of the company. Lastly, a business may view the growth of its productive capacity as its main objective. It may set out to achieve this by taking over other businesses.

MANAGEMENT OBJECTIVES

The top managers of a business may set other objectives, which benefit themselves directly rather than the company. One such objective could be an improvement of their own status. This could be achieved by increasing the size of their own department or the number of staff they are in charge of. On the other hand, the objective of management may be a 'quiet life', avoiding unnecessary risks. Some businesses may not set objectives which maximise anything, whether it be profits, sales revenue or growth. They may simply aim to do the best they can in the circumstances. This could be seen as a satisficing rather than a maximising objective.

The objectives throughout the business may be different. For example, the overall objective set by a company may be to maximise profits, whereas a particular department's objective may be to maximise its quota of employees or its sales performance. Objectives may also change through time, sometimes as a result of conflict. Suppose a business pursues sales maximisation without too much thought for the profit objective, its shareholders are then likely to be concerned, and at the Annual General Meeting may challenge (and change) the direction of the company.

Certain companies are not profit-making private businesses. Nationalised Industries may, for example, have as their main objective the provision of a satisfactory service to the community, i.e. a social objective. They may have added to this a further objective of making a certain level of profit or of at least breaking even.

EXAMINATION QUESTIONS

QUESTION 1

"Britain is a good example of a 'mixed economy' "
(a)   State briefly what is meant by a mixed economy. (2 lines provided)   **(2 marks)**

(b)   Name two other kinds of national economies and give a brief description of each. (4 lines provided)   **(4 marks)**

Specimen question: Northern Ireland Schools Examinations Council

QUESTION 2

An economy's resources are used by businesses in the production of goods and services. The goods produced can be either producer goods or consumer goods. The consumer goods may be either single use or durable and they directly satisfy the wants of the consumer.
(i)   What is meant by the term resources mentioned in the above passage:
(2 lines provided)   **(2 marks)**
(ii)   In what way do producer goods and consumer goods differ? (4 lines provided)
   (4 marks)
(iii)   Give 2 examples of both single use consumer goods and consumer durables. (2 lines provided)   **(4 marks)**

QUESTION 3

Study the following data and answer the questions printed below.

Distribution of Employment 1965–1985 in the county of Midshire			
% of Employment in:	1965	1975	1985
Primary	20	?	10
Secondary	50	45	?
Tertiary	30	40	50
Unemployment %	4	6	10
Working Population (000's)	300	320	350

(a)   Give **TWO** different examples of **jobs** that might be classified as
   (i)   tertiary activities. (one line for each example)   **(2 marks)**
   (ii)   primary activities (one line for each example)   **(2 marks)**
(b)   What percentages of the workforce were employed in
   (i)   primary activities in 1975? (one line)   **(2 marks)**
   (ii)   secondary activities in 1985? (one line)   **(2 marks)**
(c)   How many people worked in tertiary activities in 1985.
   (Show your working.)   **(3 marks)**

(d)   Using the figures from the table, ***state*** and ***explain TWO*** main changes that have taken place in employment over the last 20 years.   **(4 marks)**
    1.   (3 lines provided)
    2.   (3 lines provided)

(e)   How many people were unemployed in Midshire in 1985?
    (3 lines provided)   **(2 marks)**

(f)   State and explain **TWO** ways in which the State can help people who are unemployed.
    1.   (3 lines provided)
    2.   (3 lines provided)   **(4 marks)**

Reproduced by permission of the Midland Examining Group (MEG)

A TUTOR'S ANSWER TO QUESTION 1

QUESTION 1

(a)   A mixed economy includes elements of both the free market and the planned economy. This means that resources, namely land, labour, capital and enterprise, are allocated partly by the market mechanism and partly by the government (or planning authority). These resources are both privately and publicly owned.

(b)   The free market and the planned economy

The ***free market economy*** relies on the market mechanism (supply and demand) to allocate resources rather than on government intervention. The market determines the price of the products and the price acts as a signal to producers and consumers. For example a high price will encourage more production and discourage some consumption. The market will eventually settle on a price that brings 'harmony' between producers and consumers. All the resources are privately owned by individuals or businesses. In the ***planned economy*** resources are owned by the state and the planning authority within the state decides what is to be produced. Planners may produce more than consumers wish to buy, in other words there will be overproduction. The extra output will then have to be held in storage. Wrong decisions by planners can therefore cause serious problems.

STUDENT'S ANSWER – EXAMINER'S COMMENTS

QUESTION

An economy's resources are used by businesses in the production of goods and services. The goods produced can be either producer goods or consumer goods. The consumer goods may be either single use or durable and they directly satisfy the wants of the consumer.

(i)   What is meant by the term resources mentioned in the above passage?

(ii)   In what way do producer goods and consumer goods differ?

(iii)   Give 2 examples of both single use consumer goods and consumer durables?

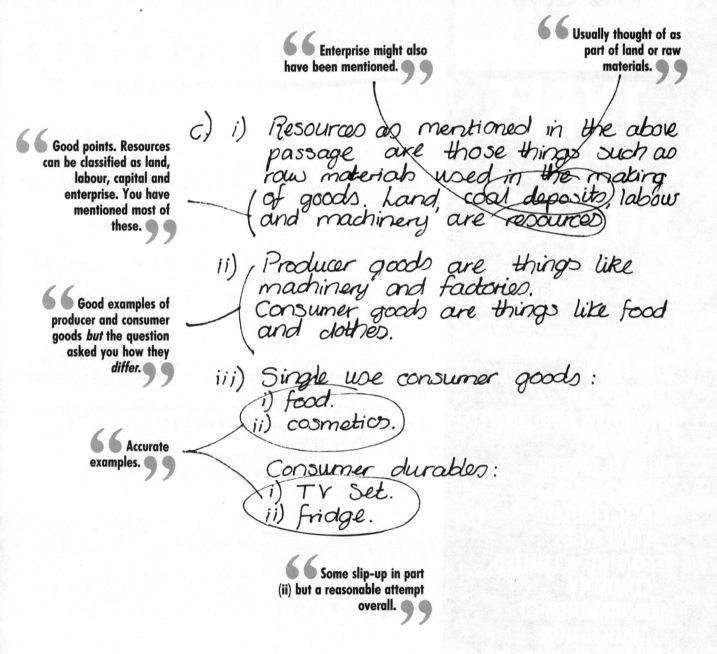

Enterprise might also have been mentioned.

Usually thought of as part of land or raw materials.

Good points. Resources can be classified as land, labour, capital and enterprise. You have mentioned most of these.

c) i) Resources as mentioned in the above passage are those things such as raw materials used in the making of goods. Land, coal deposits, labour and machinery are resources

ii) Producer goods are things like machinery and factories.
Consumer goods are things like food and clothes.

Good examples of producer and consumer goods *but* the question asked you how they differ.

iii) Single use consumer goods :
i) food.
ii) cosmetics.

Consumer durables :
i) TV set.
ii) fridge.

Accurate examples.

Some slip-up in part (ii) but a reasonable attempt overall.

CHAPTER 4

TYPES OF BUSINESS

SOLE TRADER
PARTNERSHIPS
UNLIMITED AND LIMITED
  LIABILITY
PRIVATE LIMITED
  COMPANIES
PUBLIC LIMITED
  COMPANIES
BECOMING A LIMITED
  COMPANY
MEMORANDUM OF
  ASSOCIATION
ARTICLES OF ASSOCIATION
PUBLIC SECTOR
  COMPANIES
PRIVATISATION
CO-OPERATIVES

GETTING STARTED

In your local town or city you will be able to find examples of the different types of business. It is important in any Business Studies course to obtain a clear understanding of the different forms of business organisation which exist. As Fig. 4.1 shows, there are three broad types of business:

▶ Private sector companies
▶ Public sector companies
▶ Co-operatives

There is a distinction between these businesses in terms of *ownership:*

  1. Private sector companies are owned and controlled by individuals. They may vary from one person businesses to large companies with many owners (shareholders).

  2. *Public sector companies* are said to be owned by the state on behalf of the general public, and include the nationalised industries.

  3. *Co-operatives* are either owned by the people who work in them (producers' co-operative) or by the consumers who purchase from them (retail co-operative).

  As well as the *ownership* distinction there is the *legal* distinction. For this you will need to understand a little of:

  (a) The Companies Act
  (b) The Industrial and Provident Societies Acts

and how they affect the business organisation.

E S S E N T I A L   P R I N C I P L E S

1 ▷ SOLE TRADER

Consider the following business: SMITH'S PLUMBING ENGINEERS.

Dave Smith started out working for himself as a plumber 5 years ago. He thought the name Smith's Plumbing Engineers sounded good and having advertised himself in the *Yellow Pages* he has never been short of work.

> ❝ **Make sure you understand the main differences between the various types of business. This knowledge is the basis for answering many types of question.** ❞

A. OWNERSHIP AND FINANCE

▶ As the name suggests the sole trader is a *one person* business where the individual may have been responsible for starting off the business.

▶ It is very easy to set up a business like this for there are *no legal formalities* and for this reason they are the most common form of enterprise.

▶ The sole trader will need to provide the *capital* of the business. This could be from personal savings or a loan from a bank. Dave obtained a loan which he used to purchase a van, specialist plumbing tools and an advertisement in the *Yellow Pages*.

B. ADVANTAGES OF SOLE TRADER

1. Dave Smith (the owner) is working for himself, so he has an incentive to run the business as *efficiently* as possible.
2. Only a relatively *small amount of capital* is necessary to start up the business.
3. Dave Smith is in sole charge and therefore can *take decisions quickly* because no one has to be consulted.
4. Dave Smith does not have to *share the profits* with anyone.

C. DISADVANTAGES OF SOLE TRADER

1. If the business loses money then his personal belongings are at risk because he has *unlimited liability* (see page 24).
2. If the owner dies or is ill it is *difficult to keep continuity* within the business.
3. The owner may have *difficulty in obtaining extra capital* for expansion.
4. The business may not do as well as it could because the owner may *lack new ideas*, as a result of working in isolation.

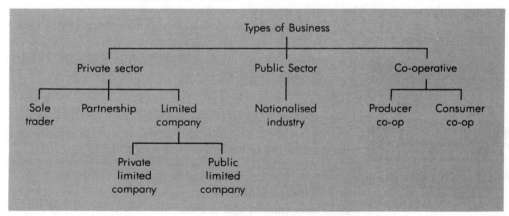

Fig.4.1. Types of Business

2 ▷ PARTNERSHIPS

The sole trader can get round a number of the problems he faces by forming a *partnership*. Dave Smith may decide to go into partnership with a friend of his, Jim Collier. Jim has experience in installing central heating systems. He is also willing to put £5,000 into the business. After some discussion they decide to call the partnership SMITH AND COLLIER PLUMBING AND HEATING ENGINEERS.

A. OWNERSHIP AND FINANCE

▶ They are covered by the ***Partnership Act 1890*** which defines a partnership as 'the relation which subsists between persons carrying on a business in common with a view of profit'. Which means a partnership is made up of members who are in business and whose aim is to make profits. So a charity could not be a partnership.

▶ Partnerships are allowed to have 2–20 members – although there are exceptions. This is the case with Banks which, if they are a partnership, are not allowed more than 10 partners, and also with firms such as accountants and solicitors who are allowed to have more than 20.

▶ Many partnerships can be set up ***without a contract*** between the partners. However a written agreement is preferable since it will help to solve any disagreements which may occur. Dave and Jim do not have a written agreement, and this could create problems if they find they can not work with each other.

▶ All the partners are equally responsible for the debts of the partnership; they have ***unlimited liability*** (see below).

▶ A partner may simply provide capital for the partnership but take no active part in the day to day running of the business. This partner is known as the ***dormant*** (or ***sleeping***) partner.

B. ADVANTAGES OF PARTNERSHIP

1. ***More capital*** will be available for the business to expand. In our example, £5,000 more.
2. Partners will bring ***different ideas*** to the business.
3. ***Specialisation*** (see page 14) can occur with the individual partners concentrating on those areas of the business at which they are most efficient. Jim is the central heating specialist as well as being able to do the accounts, whereas Dave specialises in the general plumbing but also orders the raw materials required.
4. All partners are entitled, unless they decide otherwise, to an ***equal share*** of the profits and must contribute equally to the losses.

C. DISADVANTAGES OF PARTNERSHIP

1. Like a sole trader the partners still have ***unlimited liability***.
2. There could be ***disagreements*** amongst the partners which, unlike in the case of a limited Company which is a separate legal entity from the owners, could lead to the total break-up of the partnership.
3. The actions of one partner are ***binding*** on the others. So it is important that the partners are chosen with care.
4. There may be problems when one of the partners dies, particularly if that person's capital is taken out of the business by the family of the deceased. In this case the partnership may have to be dissolved (ended) and a new partnership made up of the remaining partners.

3 ▶ UNLIMITED AND LIMITED LIABILITY

Before dealing with public and private limited companies it is important to explain what is meant by the terms ***unlimited and limited liability***.

A. UNLIMITED LIABILITY

Both sole traders and partnerships have ***unlimited liability***. This means that if the business cannot pay its creditors (individuals or firms it owes money to) then the owners may be declared bankrupt. If this is the case then the owner's personal possessions, such as home and car, can be taken and used to pay for the debts of the business.

Students often get the two mixed up. So beware!

B. LIMITED LIABILITY

With ***limited liability*** the owners' (the shareholders) responsibilities for the debts of the company are limited to how many shares they have in the company. For example, a shareholder with £100 of shares will only lose the £100 if the company goes into liquidation and not all his or her personal possessions. The benefit of this is that potential shareholders will not be put off by the possibility of losing everything they own.

4 ▷ PRIVATE LIMITED COMPANIES

A sole trader or partnership may wish to remove the risk of unlimited liability by forming a private limited company. This would mean that the sole trader would need at least one other person, who more than likely would be a member of the sole trader's family. Dave and Jim decide on such a course of action, as outlined later in this chapter. Dave and Jim's company will be called CAMBRIDGE PLUMBING AND HEATING ENGINEERS LIMITED and it will have its own legal personality, being separate from its owners.

A. OWNERSHIP AND FINANCE

▶ A private limited company, identified by *Ltd* after the company's name, may have a number of owners from 2 to no upper limit, called shareholders.

▶ The owners obtain shares which entitle them to a share of the profits in proportion to the number and type of shares possessed.

▶ Certain restrictions are placed on private limited companies. The shares cannot be sold on the Stock Exchange and cannot be advertised for sale publicly through newspapers, etc., so they have to be sold privately (thus '*private* limited company') with the agreement of the other shareholders. Shares may first have to be offered to existing shareholders.

▶ Private limited companies are likely to obtain the majority of their finance by issuing shares but may also borrow money from a bank.

▶ The shares are not allowed to be sold to the general public and this has the effect of limiting the amount that can be raised.

B. ADVANTAGES OF PRIVATE LIMITED COMPANIES

1. *More capital* is available as there are more owners.
2. *The owners are protected from losing their personal possessions* by limited liability. To those trading with a limited company the word *limited* serves as a warning in that if the company goes into liquidation then the owners are not responsible for any debt beyond their own shareholding in the company.
3. The company will have its *own legal identity* so that, unlike a partnership, it can carry on in business unaffected by a shareholder's death.
4. They have only to publish their accounts in a summarised form. They are able, therefore, to retain some privacy. However, the accounts have to be available to the public if the public asks for them.

C. DISADVANTAGES OF PRIVATE LIMITED COMPANIES

1. In becoming a Private Limited Company the sole trader or partnership will *lose some control* over the running of the business and will be accountable to the shareholders who have voting rights. This can be avoided to some extent by the founder member or members owning the majority of the shares.
2. Although more capital can be raised than by a sole trader or by a partnership there is still the problem that *shares cannot be sold to the general public* on the open market.

5 ▷ PUBLIC LIMITED COMPANIES (PLCs)

These are the largest type of business in the private sector and they are identified by the letters plc after the name of the company, eg. Cadbury Schweppes plc.

> **You may need to *name* an example of a large company in manufacturing or construction which is in the private sector. This will normally be a plc such as ICI plc.**

A. OWNERSHIP AND FINANCE

▶ The number of shareholders can range from 2 upwards.

▶ The shares can be sold to members of the general public initially, through advertising in the national newspapers. The shareholders then become part-owners of the company and have certain rights:

    (i)   to receive the company's annual reports/accounts

    (ii) to attend, vote and speak at the company's Annual General Meeting (AGM)

    (iii) To elect the Board of Directors and the Chairman of the Board.

▶ As many plc's have their shares traded on the Stock Exchange, the shareholder can sell the shares (now second-hand) to anyone who is willing to buy them (see Ch. 7).

B. ADVANTAGES OF PUBLIC LIMITED COMPANIES

1. As with a private limited company the shareholders have *limited liability*.
2. More capital can be raised than by a private limited company because *shares can be sold to the general public*.
3. The growth of a public limited company allows it to take advantage of *internal economies of scale* (see Ch. 6).

C. DISADVANTAGES OF PUBLIC LIMITED COMPANIES

1. As the company grows in size it may experience *diseconomies of scale* (again see Ch. 6).
2. There may be *communication problems* between the management and workforce.
3. Shares can be transferred easily by the shareholders of a public limited company and they could be *bought by a company intent on a takeover bid*.
4. The company's *full annual accounts have to be published.*

It is unlikely that Cambridge Plumbing and Heating Engineers Limited will ever make moves to become a plc. Only if the company decides, for example, to manufacture its own central heating systems would it consider 'going public'. In that case it would sell shares on the open market in order to obtain the finance to start manufacturing the system.

6. BECOMING A LIMITED COMPANY

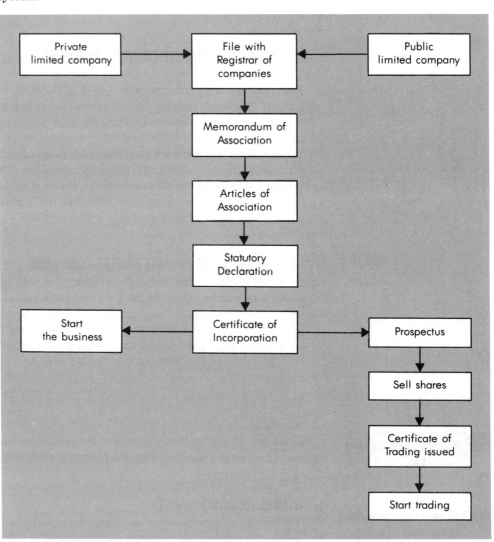

Fig.4.2. The procedure for becoming a limited company

It may be useful to learn how to draw figure 4.2.

If the business wants to become a limited or public limited company then it will have to be registered. Figure 4.2 lays down the procedure which Dave and Jim will have to comply with if they want their business to become a private limited company. Figure 4.2 also outlines the procedure for becoming a public limited company.

The founders of the company have to file the relevant documents with the Registrar of Companies.

This deals with the company's relationship with the outside world. The main contents of the memorandum are:

A. THE COMPANY'S NAME

This allows the Registrar to make sure that no two companies are using the same name. A private limited company's name must contain the word 'limited' (or the letters Ltd) and a public limited company's name must contain the letters 'plc'. Dave and Jim will not be able to use the name 'Cambridge Plumbing and Heating Engineers Limited' if any other company has already registered the name.

You will need to understand the Memorandum and Articles of Association. You are often questioned on these.

B. THE COMPANY'S ADDRESS

This shows where the company has its registered office. Dave and Jim may have premises on a trading estate which includes an office. The address being: 52 The Estate, Highfield, Cambridge CB3 7EQ.

C. THE OBJECTS OF THE COMPANY

This states the purposes for which the company is formed, such as for the manufacture of chocolate or, as in our example, to provide a plumbing and heating service. Future shareholders, therefore, have some idea of what they are devoting their funds to. In practice, such 'objects' clauses usually outline many different types of activity in order to cover any future change which the business might wish to pursue.

D. A STATEMENT

A statement that the liability of the shareholders is limited.

E. THE AMOUNT OF CAPITAL

The amount of capital to be raised by issuing shares and the type of shares, e.g. £100,000 divided into £1 shares. A public company must have at least £50,000 of share capital.

F. AN AGREEMENT

An agreement of those who sign the memorandum that they wish to form a limited company and that they agree to purchase the stated number of shares.

This deals with the internal relationship of the company, that is the day-to-day running of the company.

The Articles cover:
1. The procedure for calling a general meeting
2. The methods of electing directors
3. The rights and duties of directors
4. The borrowing power of the company
5. Rules about the transfer of shares
6. The division of profits

As regards point 5, for a limited company the Articles of Association will contain a restriction on the right to transfer shares.

Once these two documents have been completed they are sent to the Registrar of Companies along with the *Statutory Declaration*. This states that the promoters of the company have complied with the requirements of the Companies Act. The Registrar of Companies will then check the details and make sure everything is in order before issuing a *Certificate of Incorporation.* This sets up the company as a legal entity. It is the 'birth certificate' of the company. The *private* limited company can now commence business.

A *public* limited company also needs a *Certificate of Trading*. This is issued by the Registrar of Companies when he is satisfied the company has raised sufficient finance to cover its proposed plans. The company will have to advertise the sale of its shares, decide on how they are to be issued and then start trading (see Ch. 7).

9 ▶ PUBLIC SECTOR COMPANIES

These are concerns which are owned by the Government on behalf of the general public and are of two types:

Public Corporations such as the BBC. They are a special sort of public enterprise which are set up by a special document called a Royal Charter.

Nationalised Industries such as British Rail and British Coal.

> **Make sure you understand the main differences between private and public sector companies.**

1. Unlike private limited companies and public limited companies which are owned by the shareholders, public corporations and nationalised industries are owned by the state and there are no shareholders.

2. Each nationalised industry is set up by an Act of Parliament and has a separate legal identity from the Government.

3. Nationalised industries are influenced by four groups:
   (a) The Government, which is responsible for the general policy of the nationalised industry.
   (b) A Minister or Secretary of State within the Government is responsible for the interests of the nationalised industry within Parliament and for ensuring that the industry operates in the interests of the public.
   (c) The Board of Directors are responsible for the day-to-day running of the industry. The Government appoints the Chairman.
   (d) Consumer Consultation Councils which monitor the activities of nationalised industry, eg. British Rail – Transport Users' Consultative Committee. They act as a *watchdog*. (See Ch. 18 for an explanation of Consumer Protection.)

4. Nationalised industries must aim to 'at least' break even financially, although the interest of the public may lead them to make losses.

THE REASONS FOR NATIONALISATION

1. Certain industries are *natural monopolies*, which means they can be better organised nationally to take advantage of economies of scale (see Ch. 6). The argument here is that anything less than a national monopoly would be 'inefficient'.

2. Certain industries are *costly to set up and run*. Unless the early investment is paid for by the Government, they might not begin operations at all. For example, the Channel Tunnel Group has faced large problems in raising finance; if it had been a nationalised concern the State could have provided the initial finance.

3. Certain industries have been brought under government control for *strategic reasons*. Rolls Royce engines are important to Western defence, which was one of the reasons why the company was nationalised when it faced problems in 1971. (The company was returned to private ownership in 1987.)

4. Certain industries *would have gone bankrupt* if they had not been nationalised and this would have resulted in high job losses, e.g. British Leyland in the early 1970s.

5. Certain industries have been nationalised to *avoid the duplication of services*, e.g. British Rail.

6. Certain industries are under national ownership for *safety reasons*, e.g. British Nuclear Fuel.

10 ▶ PRIVATISATION

Since the election of the Conservative Government in 1979 a number of nationalised industries have been *privatised* or *denationalised*. This means that they have been transferred from the status of nationalised industries to that of plc's. Examples include:

> **Try to be aware of any other companies that are likely to be privatised.**

- ▶ British Aerospace
- ▶ National Freight Corporation
- ▶ British Airways
- ▶ British Telecom
- ▶ British Gas
- ▶ Water
- ▶ Electricity
- ▶ British Airports Authority
- ▶ Sealink
- ▶ Jaguar

THE REASONS FOR PRIVATISATION

The main *reasons* put forward for privatisation are:

1. *Greater competition* between businesses leading to increased efficiency, better quality, lower prices and greater choice for the consumer. This is because firms will need to improve the goods and services they provide if they are to sell more than their competitors.

2. It *allows the management to manage* rather than to face interference from the Government, which may be against the interests of the company.

3. If the company makes a profit, then the benefits will go to improving the company or as dividends to the shareholders. If the company makes losses, then the company will have to carry the consequences. This could lead to the company being *better organised* because the management will not have the Government to fall back on to 'bail them out'.

4. It is hoped that more of the general public will be able to own shares as nationalised industries like British Telecom and British Gas are privatised. In other words there will be *greater public participation* in the running of British industry.

---

11 ▶ CO-OPERATIVES

Co-operatives are a different kind of business organisation and fall into two categories:
▶ Retail co-operatives
▶ Producer co-operatives

A. RETAIL CO-OPERATIVES (Co-operative Retail Societies)

The retail co-operative movement was started in 1844 by a number of weavers in Rochdale who became known as the 'Rochdale Pioneers'. You will know the consumer co-operatives as retail shops, 'Co-ops', which can be found in the main shopping areas of most towns.

Ownership and Finance

> 66 **The differences between retail and producer co-operatives can often create problems. Make sure you know the differences.** 99

1. Retail co-operatives are not covered by company law but draw their legal personality from the Industrial and Provident Societies Acts.

2. Anyone can buy shares, which cost £1.00 each with an upper limit of £10,000.

3. The shareholders or members, as they are called, have ONE VOTE no matter how many shares they have; this is unlike a plc where the shareholders have votes at the Annual General Meeting in relation to the number of shares owned.

4. Although they possess limited liability the shares do not increase in value and cannot be sold on the Stock Exchange. If the owner wants to dispose of the shares they have to be sold back to the co-operative society.

5. The members share the profits. This could be in the form of:
    (a) a rate of interest paid on the basis of share owned; or
    (b) reduced prices in the shops as a result of the profit being ploughed back into the business.

6. The members elect a management committee who are responsible for the day-to-day running of the society.

7. Retail societies are members of the Co-operative Wholesale Society (CWS) from which they purchase their stock.

B. PRODUCER CO-OPERATIVES

There is no strict definition of a producer co-operative. Many are small, perhaps 10 or 11 workers, but they can be much larger.

Ownership and Finance

1. The aim of producer co-operatives is one of equity, equality and mutual self-help. The idea is that they are run on democratic lines with each member of the co-operative having one vote on decisions that have to be taken, irrespective of the amount of capital they have put into the business or of how hard they work.

2. They register with the Registrar of Friendly Societies. This can create a problem in that a minimum of 7 members is needed and so a prospective co-operative may take a number of non-working founder members who may have only a limited knowledge of the ideas of the co-operative movement.

3. The finance is provided by the members of the co-operative, who have an equal claim to a share of the profits. A certain amount of the profit will be ploughed back into the co-operative.

4. Extra finance can be obtained by expanding the co-operative through accepting more members. Problems can occur with a larger co-operative in that it may take longer to arrive at decisions and more disagreements may occur.

EXAMINATION QUESTIONS

QUESTION 1
State two reasons for the Memorandum of Association. (2 lines provided)   **(2 marks)**

QUESTION 2
Explain what is meant by 'Unlimited Liability'? (2 lines provided)   **(2 marks)**

QUESTION 3
"The private sector and the public sector are different ways of achieving the same thing."

(a) Explain the essential difference between the private sector and the public sector. (6 lines provided)   **(4 marks)**

(b) Give an example in each case of a large organisation engaged in secondary production
    (i)   in the private sector _____
    (ii) in the public sector _____
                                                                       (2 marks)

(c) What is the 'same thing' that both are supposed to be achieving? (2 lines provided)   **(3 marks)**

Specimen question: Northern Ireland Schools Examinations Council

QUESTION 4
Jeni Farnhill started to design and make wedding dresses five years ago in her home. The business has expanded and now she has four people working for her in small premises in her local town. At present she is a *sole trader* but Jeni is in the process of *registering* her business as a *private limited company* with the name Gala Dresses Ltd.

1. Outline the main features of a private limited company (3 lines provided) **(3 marks)**

2. State three reasons why Jeni Farnhill may have decided to become a Private Limited Company. (3 lines provided)   **3 marks)**

3. In becoming a Private Limited Company why are the Memorandum of Association and the Articles of Association important to the shareholders? (5 lines provided)   **(4 marks)**

TUTOR'S ANSWER TO QUESTION 3

(a) The private sector is made up of businesses which are either owned by an individual or a group of individuals. This sector includes the sole trader, partnerships, private and public limited companies and co-operatives. In the case of private and public limited companies the owners are the shareholders. The public sector includes businesses which are owned by the Government, whether it be central or local Government.

(b) (i) Here you need to name an example of a large company in manufacturing or construction which is in the private sector. This will normally be a plc such as ICI plc.

   (ii) British Nuclear Fuels. Make sure you read the question carefully because it asks you for examples of *secondary production* not primary or tertiary.

(c) Both the private and public sector are supposed to be achieving the production of goods and services in order to satisfy human needs. In other words they are different ways of organising production, i.e. of bringing together the resources of land, labour and capital.

C O U R S E W O R K

ASSIGNMENT

1. In your *local area* choose a type of business organisation. It can be either
   (a) a sole trader – it could be a local corner shop.
   (b) a partnership – it could be a local firm of solicitors.
   (c) a private limited company (Ltd) – it could be a small family business but make sure it has Ltd after its name.
   (d) a public limited company (plc) – your local area should have a plc, which will normally be a well known company name.

2. Make arrangements to go and visit the business of your choice.
   (a) What type of business organisation is it?
   (b) What size is the business? (e.g. in terms of the number of people employed)
   (c) What are the advantages and disadvantages the business faces by being the type of organisation it is?
       Example: If it is a *sole trader* does it face difficulties raising funds?
             Would it like to expand?
             Has the owner ever thought about taking a partner? (If not, why not?)
             If it is a *partnership* how many partners are there?
             What are the benefits of having that number of partners?
   (d) Are there any plans for the organisation you have chosen to change its legal form?
       Example: Does the sole trader plan in the future to become a private limited company?
   (e) If the company is a plc then perhaps you could obtain some information on its Memorandum and Articles of Association. You could match up what the text book has to say with the company's Memorandum and Articles.

3. Write up your findings in the way outlined in Chapter 2.

STUDENT'S ANSWER – EXAMINER'S COMMENTS

The following is a student's answer to question 4, page 30.

4. i)   A private limited company, otherwise known as Ltd., is one which offers shares, but the share-holding is restricted. Shares tend to belong to members of the family or employees and cannot be sold through the stock exchange to the general public. Liability is limited, that is, in case of bankruptcy the shareholder is only liable to lose what he has put into the company (price of the shares) and not his personal assets. Ltd. company must be registered (in the) memorandum of Association and the Articles of Association. In these the name and address of the company must be given, its aims and objectives; in the Articles of Association details are given about the general running of the company such as shareholders' meetings.

> **66** Registered with the Registrar of Companies using the Memorandum of Association and the Articles of Association. **99**

> **66** Before you start an examination question make sure that you read *all* parts of the question. Too much has been written about the Memorandum and Articles of Association in part (i), given that these are in part (iii). This is not wrong, but it does waste time! **99**

ii)   Jeni Farnhill may have decided to become a Ltd. because it has limited liability, capital is increased and membership is restricted to private individuals.

> **66** These are good points. **99**

iii)   The memorandum of Association and the Articles of Association are important to the share holders because they provide information about the company such as its name and address, the capital (profit) it intends to make and a statement that liability of the shareholders is limited; and it gives details of how shareholders meetings are to be conducted and the rights of the members.

> **66** This is a good answer in terms of the space provided on the examination paper. It is well worth making sure that you understand all there is to know about the Memorandum and Articles of Association, as questions are often set on these. **99**

CHAPTER

5

MANAGEMENT

GETTING STARTED

It is difficult to define the term 'management' for there is no single definition. It is easier to define what management is by explaining what a manager does.

Any business, whether it is small or large, will have to be organised. Consider your school: the teachers are usually divided into departments based on subject areas and there are also ancillary or support staff, such as cleaners and cooks. The Headmaster will be involved in managing the school, perhaps helped by a Deputy Headmaster and by the Heads of the various departments. If we take the example of a company called Chocolate Delight plc, a confectionary manufacturer, the staff there specialise in particular types of work and there are managers in charge of making sure that the work is completed. These managers can be seen as leaders who try to make sure that the business is running smoothly. There is a managing director responsible for the overall running of the company.

You will need to have an understanding of how management is organised, what management does, and how they distribute work to the staff they are responsible for.

The **owners** of limited companies are the shareholders who entrust the **control** of limited companies to the directors they have **elected.** The directors, who are the top management, will **appoint** the middle management of the company who are then **employees** of the company as are the rest of the staff. (See Fig. 5.1.)

FUNCTIONS OF
   MANAGEMENT
THE ORGANISATION OF
   MANAGEMENT
MANAGEMENT
   STRUCTURES
DEPARTMENTAL
   FUNCTIONS
FORMAL AND INFORMAL
   ORGANISATION
TYPES OF LEADERSHIP
SPAN OF CONTROL
CHAIN OF COMMAND
DELEGATION

ESSENTIAL PRINCIPLES

❝ It is easy to confuse the various functions of management, so be careful! ❞

A. PLANNING

The managers of Chocolate Delight plc, or in fact any business, will have to make decisions which will affect the running of the company. Decisions such as where to locate the factory, what products should be manufactured, how those products should be made, who should be responsible to whom and how the company's resources are to be used to achieve the best results.

The more skilled the management is in planning, the more successful the company is likely to be.

B. CONTROLLING

Once the plans for the company have been established there must be supervision and checking of those responsible for carrying out the plans.

The management must ensure that their instructions are being carried out and that the company is achieving its objectives.

C. CO-ORDINATING

The management are responsible for the activities of those who work for the company. They must make sure that departments are aware of each other's activities and of the decisions taken, so that there is no duplication, friction or lack of understanding. Co-ordinating really refers to ensuring the smooth operation of the company.

Fig.5.1. The relationship between shareholders, directors and managers

D. MOTIVATING

For any company to be efficient it must have a staff which is motivated. This can be achieved partly through the wages paid, through fringe benefits and a share of the profits, and also by the ability of the management to promote job satisfaction. The whole area of motivation is dealt with in Ch. 15.

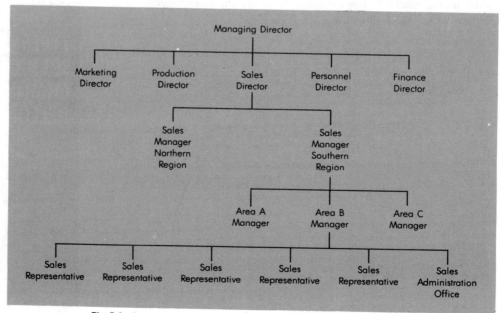

Fig.5.2. Organisation chart for a typical manufacturing company

The structure of a business is shown by an *organisation chart*. Figure 5.2 shows such a chart which could refer to Chocolate Delight plc or a typical manufacturing company. If this referred to a wholesaler then there would be no production department but perhaps a buying department.

The chart is like a family tree which shows:

(i)   The responsibilities of the management of Chocolate Delight.

(ii)   The status of the various levels of management.

(iii)   The lines of communication within the company.

No chart can show all the complex parts of a company's management structure but it does give some idea of how the management of a business is organised.

A. PYRAMIDAL

Chocolate Delight might have a Sales Department organised in the traditional way as in Fig. 5.3.

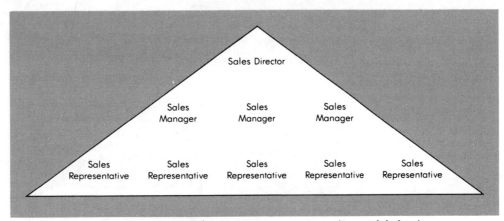

Fig.5.3. Hierarchical management structure (Pyramidal chart)

This is sometimes called a *hierarchical* structure and it shows the direct lines of authority in a *pyramidal* shape. The three Sales Managers are responsible to the Sales Director, and the Sales Representatives are responsible to the Sales Managers. Hierarchical structures are clear and easy to understand for those working in them, but they have the disadvantage that people become 'departmentalised'.

B. HORIZONTAL

Chocolate Delight may choose another way of showing structure which tries to avoid the idea of levels of superiority. This is the idea behind the *horizontal* chart which is read from left to right with the most senior management on the left as in Fig. 5.4.

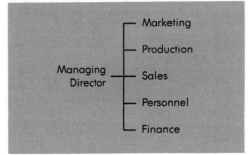

Fig.5.4. Horizontal management chart

C. CONCENTRIC

This is yet another way of showing the pyramidal structure. This is by using a *concentric* chart which, like the horizontal chart, seeks to avoid emphasising the various levels of authority. The Managing Director will be in the innermost circle and the other management team will be arranged in concentric circles moving out from the centre, as in Fig. 5.5.

D. MATRIX MANAGEMENT

A business could be organised on a project-based approach as in Fig. 5.6. This type of structure is often referred to as a *matrix*. It is often found in businesses which are developing new products, which in the case of Chocolate Delight could be a new

Fig.5.5. Concentric management chart

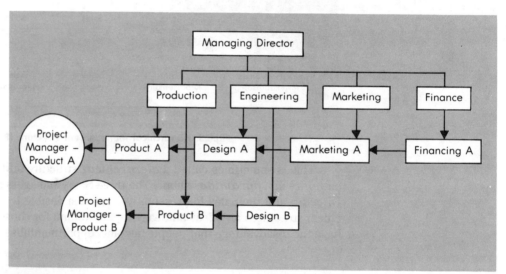

Fig.5.6. Matrix management chart

chocolate bar. Instead of being accountable to their immediate superior, as is the case in the pyramidal structure, staff are responsible to a project manager who would have to make sure that the project being worked on is completed on time and is up to standard.

In developing a new chocolate bar, production, engineering, marketing and finance staff could be involved along the lines of Fig. 5.6. Together they could bring their different skills and experience to the particular project, namely the type of chocolate bar the consumer requires, and decide on the machinery needed, how the bars should be made and whether the company has sufficient funds to finance the production of a new product. The benefit of this structure is that the individuals working on the project could operate as a team, and so be easier to organise and motivate. The disadvantage is that the project members may feel insecure because the project will only be for a period of time.

4 ▶ DEPARTMENTAL FUNCTIONS

Companies will usually split their management into a number of **departments**. As Fig. 5.2 shows, Chocolate Delight has marketing, production, sales, personnel and finance departments.

The **advantages** of a departmental organisation are that:
(a) it allows **specialisation** to take place, with individual managers undertaking the duties they are best at.
(b) the company can be **better organised** if the various functions of the company are divided into different departments.

> **Do not get the management functions and the departmental functions confused with each other.**

(c)   each department has its *area of responsibility*, which is clearly set out and is relatively easy to understand.

A. MARKETING

In the case of Chocolate Delight, market research assesses the type of chocolate product the consumers desire and how much they are prepared to pay. They must bear in mind the machinery, manpower and raw materials that the company has available. The development of new products or services will also require extra finance and advertising in order that production can take place and that the consumer be made aware of the new products or services available. It will be necessary to distribute the products, so different forms of transport will have to be considered, taking into account cost, convenience and reliability. The marketing function will be dealt with in more detail in Chapter 9.

B. PRODUCTION

The production department will be responsible for changing the raw materials or assembling the components into finished products. 'Production' can involve both the manufacture of goods and the provision of services such as banking and insurance although these 'service' companies may not have a production department as such.

The production department of Chocolate Delight must take into account the type of factory and machinery they have at their disposal and the level of skilled labour they require. Usually they are also responsible for ensuring that the finished chocolate bars are properly stored and that the stocks do not become too large.

C. PURCHASING

The purchasing department is responsible for buying the raw materials and anything else the company needs. In fact everything from office supplies to production machinery.

D. SALES

The sales department is closely linked to the marketing department. Its function is to form a link between the company and the customer and it is concerned with selling the product or service. The department will employ sales representatives who will build up a network of customers. With Chocolate Delight this will range from large superstores to small corner shops and newspaper kiosks. The representatives may pass on to the marketing department (see Ch. 9) vital information about the new products that competitors are introducing and any changes in the tastes of consumers.

E. PERSONNEL

The personnel department is responsible for the human resources of the company. Its aim is to recruit the right people for the firm's departments, to help organise them and to make sure there is adequate staff development. This covers areas such as staff training, staff appraisal, promotions and routine matters like employees' taxation forms, sickness benefit, holiday pay and pensions. The rates of pay, salary structure and all negotiations with the staff over such matters as working conditions and dismissals will be dealt with by this department (see Ch. 14 and 15).

F. FINANCE

The finance department deals with all the monetary aspects of the company. This involves monitoring the inflow and outflow of payments, such as the invoices sent for confectionery sold and for the costs of raw materials, new machinery and wages.

There may be other departments, such as research and development and design. The activities of all these departments will be overseen by the managing director and the board of directors.

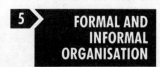

5 ▷ FORMAL AND INFORMAL ORGANISATION

How Chocolate Delight organises its staff is very important. If they are badly organised, decision-making will be more difficult and the company will not achieve the best results. An organisation chart is shown on page 34 but more generally any organisation really has two separate structures. Not only its formal organisation, but also its informal organisation.

A. FORMAL ORGANISATION

This consists of the channels of communication set up officially within a company. As can be seen from the chain of command in Fig. 5.7, the production worker is responsible to, and takes orders from, the production foreman; the production foreman in turn is responsible to, and takes orders from, the production manager, and so on.

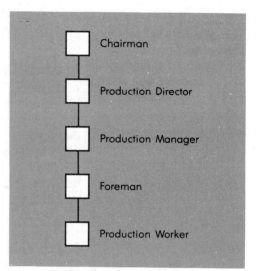

Fig.5.7. The Chain of Command

B. INFORMAL ORGANISATION

The informal organisation cannot be shown in the organisation chart. It operates as workers at various levels throughout the company develop their own ideas and even take their orders from each other or perhaps from their union leader. It is always necessary to consider the informal structure when trying to see how a company really operates. For example, the managing director's secretary may be a junior member of the company but might have a great deal of power and influence over what goes on. The formal organisation of the company is established by the management but the informal organisation develops amongst the whole staff depending on personalities, tradition and many other factors.

6 ▸ TYPES OF LEADERSHIP

The term *leadership* refers to the role taken by an individual or a group in organising other members of staff. There are essentially three types of leadership:

A. THE AUTOCRATIC LEADER

The leaders with an autocratic style decide on all areas within the business, whether it be what is to be produced, how it is to be produced or who should do which job. In Chocolate Delight this style could be adopted at certain times or in certain situations. In a crisis, such as having to produce a particular amount of confectionery to satisfy an urgent export order, the workforce could be told what to do, without any discussion. With an autocratic leadership style there is little or no communication between the leaders and the staff they are responsible for. The advantage of this style is that decisions can be taken more speedily, but there may then be a need for greater supervision. The staff are also likely to grumble and suffer from a lack of job satisfaction because they are rarely consulted.

B. DEMOCRATIC LEADER

The leadership of Chocolate Delight may be one which encourages the workers to participate in the decisions of the company. The democratic leader tries to foster a more friendly, co-operative working environment, where the staff may put forward ideas for new products or new ways of producing existing products. This can promote greater job satisfaction amongst staff, and bring about new and unexpected improvements as a result of staff involvement. If there is a disadvantage with this style, it could be that it takes longer to arrive at decisions because of the amount of discussion which takes place between the leaders and staff. Output might then be lower than necessary in the period before the decision is actually taken.

C. LAISSEZ-FAIRE LEADER

The laissez-faire style of leadership is one which leaves the workforce to its own devices, with little control being exercised over it. At certain times Chocolate Delight could use this type of leadership in order to maximise the flexibility of the organisation and to encourage the workers to make their own decisions.

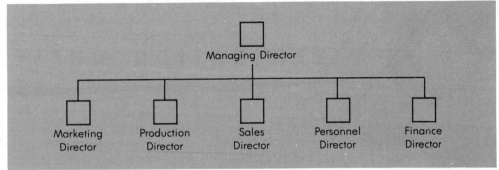

Fig.5.8. The Span of Control

Figure 5.8 illustrates part of the organisation chart of Chocolate Delight plc. As you will see, the managing director is at the head of the whole company but he or she can only directly control the work of the five directors. The Area B sales manager in Fig. 5.2 can be seen to directly control the work of six sales representatives.

The span of control is the number of workers a person can directly control and this will vary depending on:

(i)   the type of work, whether it is repetitive, such as putting chocolates into boxes, or highly skilled, requiring a great deal of supervision.

(ii)   the ability and the amount of training of those being controlled.

If the span of control is too wide then supervision will be very difficult. If the span of control is too narrow then subordinates may fail to develop their own ideas.

> **Students often confuse the 'span of control' with the 'chain of command' so be careful!**

8 CHAIN OF COMMAND

The chain of command within Chocolate Delight is from the managing director and board of directors to the sales manager, then on to the area manager and finally the sales representatives. Decisions will be passed down the chain as shown in Fig. 5.7. A short chain of command may be the most desirable because, the fewer links there are in the chain, the easier it is for the management and workforce to communicate.

9 DELEGATION

The board of directors will not be able to do all the work themselves within the company so they will have to delegate the day-to-day running of the company to others. In Fig. 5.2 the sales director will delegate to the two sales managers who cover the northern and southern regions of the UK. They may be given the authority to do the job but the final responsibility will still remain with the board of directors. Delegation may take place because the managers may not have time to do the job themselves.

The management of Chocolate Delight may, however, be a management who are afraid to delegate, perhaps because:

(i)   they fear the job will not be done properly. This could be because the workers of the business are not capable.

(ii)   delegation may make the managers span of control difficult to monitor.

If authority is not delegated then it is said to be ***centralised***. This means that there is a great deal of control from the top (whether it be from the managing director or board of directors).

Where authority ***is*** delegated then it is said to be ***decentralised***, with decisions being taken at all levels of the company. If there was complete decentralisation then the manager would no longer have a job.

You cannot determine decentralisation from an organisation chart. The chart does not show the ***degree*** to which authority and responsibility are delegated, which is the key factor in determining the extent of centralisation. Instead, the ***decisions taken*** have to be looked at. For example, if sales manager Southern Region on Chocolate Delight's organisation chart frequently took important decisions which the sales director deliberately never checked, then this would be decentralisation. Decentralisation would be greater if:

(i)   many important decisions have to be made at all levels;

(ii)   the company has many divisions which may even run themselves, making their own decisions;

(iii)   there are a large number of good staff at all levels of the company.

EXAMINATION QUESTIONS

QUESTION 1

The incomplete chart shown below indicates how various work functions may be performed by specialised departments.

(a)   Complete the chart by filling in the blank boxes which have been indicated with a question mark.   **(3 marks)**

(b)   Give two reasons why a firm might organise itself on a departmental basis.
(3 lines for answer)   **(4 marks)**

(c)   Describe two functions of the marketing department of a firm.
(4 lines for answer)   **(4 marks)**

(d)   How and why should a sales target set by the Marketing Executive be communicated to a production worker on the shop floor. (3 lines for answer).   **(4 marks)**

Specimen question: Northern Ireland Schools Examinations Council

QUESTION 2

A. Griffiths Ltd is involved in the manufacture of sportswear. The company is divided into 5 departments, marketing, production, personnel, finance and sales, and it employs 300 staff. Each of the departments has a director and A. Griffiths is the Managing Director. At a recent Board of Directors meeting it was decided to develop a new range of tracksuits.

(i)   (a)   State what is meant by the Board of Directors.
(2 lines for answer).   **(2 marks)**

(b)   How important will the marketing department be in the development of the new range of tracksuits. (3 lines for answer)   **(3 marks)**

(ii)   A Griffiths has been Managing Director of the business for a number of years and is seen to have an autocratic style of leadership. Is this likely to prove beneficial in the development of the new tracksuits? (4 lines for answer)   **(4 marks)**

(iii) How important will it be to have an effective chain of command in the development of new products. (2 lines for answer)   **(1 mark)**

TUTOR'S ANSWER TO QUESTION 2

(i)   (a)   The Board of Directors is a group of individuals who are elected by the shareholders to whom they are accountable. Their purpose is to run the company. This will involve, above all else, deciding what the company policy is going to be.

(b)   The marketing department will have the important task of finding out what type of tracksuit is popular with the customer. This may involve design, colour, and range, as well as how much the consumer is prepared to pay. It may use questionnaires or conduct sample surveys in trying to perform this task. The marketing department will therefore be important in the early stages of development of the new range of tracksuits. It may also try to establish how many tracksuits the company can expect to sell and to what groups of consumers.

(ii) *You will first need to briefly state what an autocratic style of leadership is*. This style of leadership is one with little or no communication between the leader(s) and the staff for which they are responsible. This style could prove beneficial in the development of a new range of tracksuits simply because decisions can be more speedily taken, without time-consuming discussions between the management and the rest of the staff. The product could be developed and put on the market far quicker, which may be an advantage if the company has competitors who are also developing new products in the same field.

The disadvantage may be that, because there is limited discussion within the company, the product may not be as good as it might have been if a more democratic approach to leadership had existed.

(iii)   An effective chain of command is vital if a new product is being developed. The decision taken at the Board meeting to produce a new range of track suits has to be communicated to the staff within the company. If the chain is faulty then the development could be delayed or the orders misinterpreted by the workforce.

C O U R S E W O R K

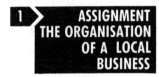

1 ▷ ASSIGNMENT THE ORGANISATION OF A LOCAL BUSINESS

1. Choose a business in the area where you live. Size is not important but it should not be too small as you are trying to obtain information on its organisation structure. The choice of business might be made in one of the following ways:
   ▶ A member of your family or a family friend works for the business.
   ▶ A local business interests you; possibly a business you want to work for.
   ▶ You may have a part time job working for a business, perhaps on a Saturday, and therefore know someone who could help you.
2. Contact the business either by telephone or by post and arrange to meet them. The personnel department is the one which is most likely to help.
3. The first thing to find out is the make-up of their organisation chart. You could set out your questions in a questionnaire covering areas such as:
   ▶ How many departments are there?
   ▶ How has the chart changed as the company has grown?
   ▶ Who is responsible to whom?
   Once this information has been obtained it should be possible to build up an organisation chart.
4. It may be possible to find out other information such as:
   ▶ Is the management leadership autocratic, democratic or laissez-faire?
   ▶ Is the span of control too wide or the chain of command too long?
   ▶ Does the management of the business delegate? (if not, why not?)
5. Set out the assignment in the way outlined in Chapter 2.
6. In your conclusion clearly state whether the business in your opinion is organised in an efficient way. Perhaps you could indicate areas where the business could improve its organisation.

STUDENT'S ANSWER – EXAMINER'S COMMENTS

The following is a student's answer to question 1, page 40.

A good point – but if the span of control is to be mentioned, it must be clearly explained.

1. a) Distribution

    Production executive.

A good answer. The student could also have mentioned the benefits of specialisation, with each person doing what they are best at. Using departments also allows individual areas of responsibility to be seen.

b) 1) To help communication. One manager per department so communication flows easily up and down.

   2) To prevent having a large span of control. With more departments, there are smaller spans of control.

A good answer. You could also mention that the marketing department tries to make sure that the firm produces the goods that the consumer wants.

c) 1) Advertising the product by choosing the best medias, and the best presentation of the product to the general public.

   2) To carry out the most accurate market research, by collecting relevant information on the product.

The Production Executive is likely to get the Production Manager to pass the information to the production workers.

d) The marketing executive should tell the production executive who should pass the information to the production workers on the shop floor. This is to increase workers' motivation, so they understand why they are doing the job and it's purpose.

This is a good point. Motivation is likely to increase if the workers know what is happening within the firm.

LOCATION
SIZE
AND
GROWTH

GETTING STARTED

All businesses will have to make important decisions, many of which will affect how successful they are for many years to come; decisions such as where to locate, what size to operate at and whether or not to take over another firm. There are important benefits to be obtained from choosing correctly. A wrong decision could lead to the business making losses or even going out of business.

ESSENTIAL PRINCIPLES

1 > LOCATION

The decision of where to **locate** a business is a very important one. It is perhaps the first decision for the manager or management of a new business to make, whether it is a small one-person business or a large public limited company (see Ch. 4). If the location chosen is a poor one then the business may be less competitive and therefore less profitable than it could be. For example, a filling station located on a road that does not have much traffic will be less profitable than one located on a main road with heavy through traffic.

Most sites will have advantages and disadvantages but the best site will normally be the one with the lowest costs for producing the goods and services and for distributing them to the consumer.

For certain firms the choice of location is limited. Shipbuilding firms will need to be on the coast and will need to have a deep water estuary. Other firms may be **footloose**, that is be able to set up anywhere. But even these firms will benefit by searching for the best possible site.

2 > INFLUENCES ON LOCATION

There are a number of factors which will **influence** a firm's location as shown in Fig 6.1.

> As a quick revision tip you might learn figure 6.1.

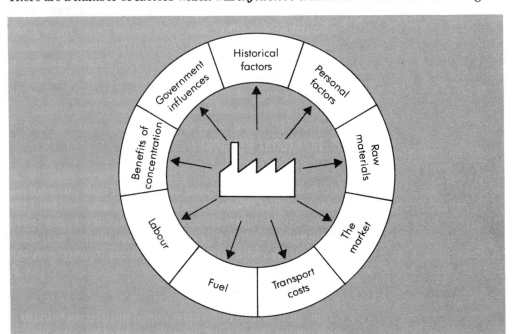

Fig.6.1. The factors influencing the business location

A. HISTORICAL FACTORS

In the Industrial Revolution many businesses were drawn to the sources of raw materials and power. The pottery industry developed in Stoke-on-Trent because of the proximity of clay, and the brewing of beer in Burton-on-Trent because of the type of water there. Water power was used in driving machinery, so that fast flowing streams attracted firms such as Richard Arkwright's textile factory at Cromford in Derbyshire. These factors are less important today but do help explain why certain businesses are in their present location.

B. PERSONAL FACTORS

Certain firms may have located in an area just because the individual who set up the company lived in that area. Henry Rowntree was one such person who founded Rowntrees (now part of Cadbury Schweppes plc) in York. Boots the chemists of Nottingham and Morris the car producer at Cowley were also founded in these particular areas because the person who started the company lived here.

C. RAW MATERIAL

Some industries are tied completely to the location of the raw materials themselves, such as the coal- and tin-mining industries. In other industries the location of the raw materials has an important influence on the place of production. Iron and steel mills initially located near the raw material source because, during the refining of the iron ore, the product lost weight (ore refining is a bulk decreasing industry) and became easier and cheaper to transport. These **bulk decreasing** businesses are likely to locate near their raw material supplies as this will make transport and distribution costs cheaper.

We have seen (above) that a firm may continue to locate itself in an area long after the original reasons for locating have gone, in the case of our example even after the exhaustion of iron ore. This is called **industrial inertia**.

D. THE MARKET

If the goods being produced are **weight** or **bulk increasing** products then it may be worthwhile locating the firm close to the market, as this may reduce transport costs. The location of the market is one of the most important factors affecting the location of firms which produce goods which are expensive to transport. For example furniture manufacturers are generally located near to where the furniture is to be sold.

E. TRANSPORT NETWORKS

Historically, being close to an efficient transport network has been very important. Water transport was cheap and reliable, if rather slow. Nevertheless, the canals had an important influence on the location of firms during the eighteenth and nineteenth centuries. The development of railways in the nineteenth century allowed businesses to locate over a wider area with access to a major terminal important for many firms. The railways became less important with the improvements in the road network, particularly after the advent of the motorway system in the 1960s. Extending the motorway system is one of the ways by which the Government hopes to attract industry into areas of high unemployment. Easy access to the motorway system is an important factor in locating factories for many firms.

F. FUEL

Many businesses in the nineteenth century located near to the main source of fuel, usually coal. Much of manufacturing industry was, therefore, set up in the areas of major coalfields. However, with the advent of gas and electricity and with the introduction of a national distribution system, location near to a fuel supply was no longer that important.

G. LABOUR

To produce any goods or services labour is needed. The problem is that sometimes the right type of labour is very scarce. It can also be difficult to get workers to move from one area to another. A firm may be attracted to an area because of the availability of skilled labour and the fact that the area may have a tradition in a particular industry, such as the textile industry in West Yorkshire. On the other hand a location may be avoided because it has a reputation for strikes and absenteeism.

H. BENEFITS OF CONCENTRATION

As businesses develop in an area it is likely that they will attract other businesses, leading to a concentration of firms in a particular area. As a result that area will adapt itself to the needs of those businesses.

Local colleges of education will develop courses relevant to the firms' needs and small specialist firms will set up to provide the main firms with components or to dispose of their waste products. The local banks and insurance companies are also likely to become expert in the needs of their local industry, being able therefore to offer them specialist treatment. All these are known as **economies of concentration**.

I. GOVERNMENT INFLUENCES

Since 1934 the Government has aimed to intervene directly in the location of business, restricting the location of firms in certain areas and encouraging their location in other areas. New Towns, such as Welwyn Garden City, Stevenage and Milton Keynes, were established and also Assisted Areas. There are two types of assisted areas:

(i)   Development Areas

(ii) Intermediate Areas

Both types are areas of high unemployment, and businesses setting up there obtain financial incentives of one form or another. Of the two there is a greater level of financial assistance available in Development Areas. In 1980 the Government also introduced 'Enterprise Zones'. Here firms received assistance such as ten years exemption from rent and rates.

3 ▶ NATURAL AND ACQUIRED ADVANTAGES

The advantages of a particular location can be seen in terms of natural or acquired advantages. *Natural* advantages include the possession of raw materials, (e.g. coal, iron ore), the availability of sources of power, (e.g. water, coal), nearness to major markets and having an appropriate climate. (In the case of the textile industry a damp climate meant thread was less likely to break.) All these natural advantages have been of historical importance to location. *Acquired* advantages have more to do with the benefits gained from the *concentration* of firms in the locality, rather than with the characteristics of the locality itself.

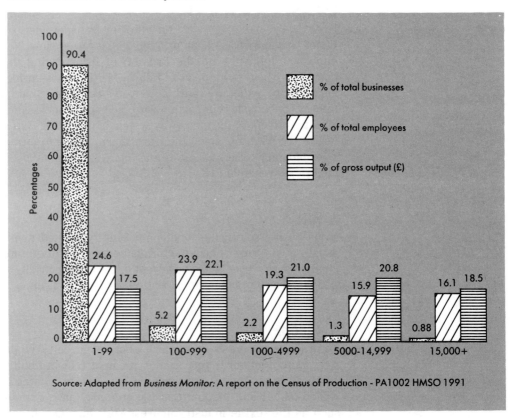

Source: Adapted from *Business Monitor:* A report on the Census of Production - PA1002 HMSO 1991

Fig. 6.2 UK manufacturing - by size 1989

4 ▶ SIZE

A. IMPORTANCE OF SIZE IN THE UK

Once located, a business needs to consider the *size* at which it is going to operate. In all industrialised economies businesses will vary in size. Some will be very small, employing one or two workers, whereas others will be large public limited companies (see p. 25), employing thousands of workers. As can be seen from Fig. 6.2 over 90% of UK firms employ less than 99 workers. In other words most UK firms are small to medium in size. But these firms only account for 24% of the total number of persons employed, and only 17% of gross output. If however you look at those firms employing between 5,000 and 14,999 workers, they account for only 1.3% in number of firms, but 15.9% in number of persons employed and 20.8% of gross output. It is the large firms which, though relatively few in number, dominate UK employment and output.

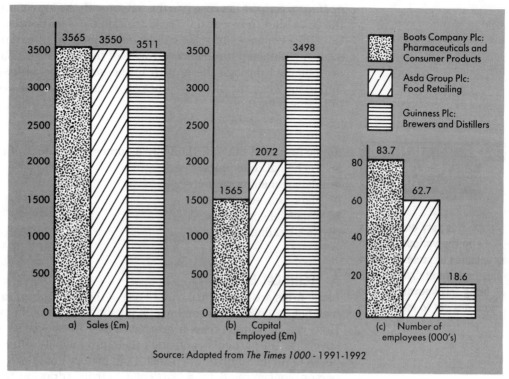

Fig. 6.3 measuring the size of firms

B. MEASURING SIZE

When ***measuring*** the size of individual firms we come up against a problem, namely what measure do we use? The ***Times 1,000*** looks at the world's top companies, using total turnover (sales) as its main measure (see fig. 6.3 (a)). Using this measure Boots Co. plc is seen as the 136th largest company with Asda Group 139th and Guinness 140th. If, however, capital employed or number of employees is used as a measure then a different picture is obtained (see Fig. 6.3 (b) and (c)).

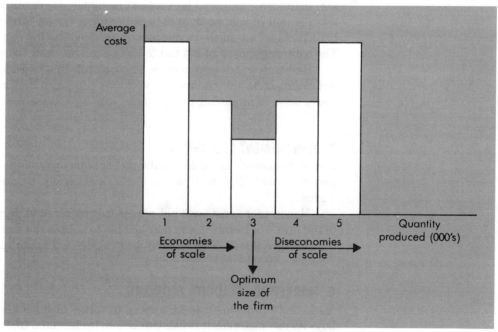

Fig.6.4. The optimum size of the firm.

C. ECONOMIES OF SCALE

Larger firms are seen as being more efficient in that they can produce their goods more cheaply and sell them at a lower price. These reduced costs are a direct result of the increased size of the firm and are called ***economies of scale*** (benefits of size).

As you can see from Fig. 6.4 the firm's costs start to fall with increased production and they are at the lowest in this case when 3,000 units are produced. This is called the *optimum output* because it is the output with the lowest average cost. After this output the costs start to rise again. These are called *diseconomies of scale*.

The economies of scale can be either internal or external. *Internal* economies of scale are obtained through the growth of the *firm* itself. *External* economies of scale are obtained through the growth in the size of the *industry as a whole*. They are important when the industry is heavily concentrated and are outside the direct control of business itself.

5 ▷   INTERNAL ECONOMIES OF SCALE

❝ It is very easy to mix up the various internal economies of scale so revise this topic carefully! You can bring this knowledge into your answer to many types of question. ❞

As the firm grows in size, there are a number of sources of internal economies:
► Technical economies
► Management economies
► Marketing economies
► Financial economies
► Risk-bearing economies

A. TECHNICAL ECONOMIES

Large firms are able to make more use of the *division of labour*; with a small output it may not be possible to employ one person wholly on one process or part of a process. However, as output rises a greater degree of specialisation is possible. As workers specialise on particular activities their productivity often increases, 'practice makes perfect'. Adam Smith showed that a pin factory could produce many more pins if each person concentrated on a particular activity (drawing the wire, cutting the wire or sharpening the head) rather than trying to undertake all the various activities. It is this specialisation which is called the division of labour.

The firm can also make more use of *machinery*. For example, a machine may only be used for two hours per day in a small firm, but may be fully used in a large firm. This will save the 'cost' of having expensive machinery lie idle. Larger specialised machinery can be used which produces more output per hour. It may even be possible for the whole process to be undertaken in the form of a production line (mass production). This would not usually be economically possible in a smaller firm.

Benefits can be made from increased *volume*, for example, if a container is doubled in size its surface area increases four times but its volume increases eight times. There are, therefore, savings to be made in using larger containers which will cost relatively less per unit of volume than the smaller ones. Larger lorries (juggernauts), aircraft and blast furnaces are further examples of the benefits that can be obtained from extra size. The 'runnings costs' of a 4 tonne lorry are less than twice those of a 2 tonne lorry.

Research and development is also possible in a larger firm and this could lead to an improvement in the quality of the goods produced and a reduction in costs through better ways of producing the goods.

B. MANAGEMENT ECONOMIES

Larger businesses are able to take on (appoint) qualified staff who are specialists in a particular area. The small firm is likely, of necessity, to have a work force of 'jack of all trades'.

Management costs will not necessarily increase in proportion to the growth in size of the firm. For instance, you may be able to double the size of the firm without doubling the managerial staff. This will reduce management costs per unit of output.

C. MARKETING (TRADING) ECONOMIES

Marketing economies can be viewed in terms of buying and selling. When a business buys its raw materials it is likely to obtain preferential treatment, perhaps in the form of a discount, if it is making a *bulk* purchase. A larger business is in a stronger position to secure good discounts because it could threaten to go elsewhere if it was not satisfied with the terms, and this threat would be a financially powerful one because of the size of its order. When selling the product, specialist sales personnel can be appointed, who can often obtain larger orders with no extra time and effort than that needed to obtain a smaller order. Administration, transport, advertising and packaging costs can also be spread over large orders. For example the packaging costs per item are likely to be less for 1,000 items than if 10 items were packed.

D. FINANCIAL ECONOMIES

Most firms need to borrow money to finance their business (see Ch. 7). Large firms are able to obtain their finance from banks more easily, borrowing at lower interest rates. A bank will more readily give a loan to a well-known company, than to Joe Bloggs who is just starting up a window cleaning business. The larger firm is also likely to have more assets that it can offer to the bank as security for the loan.

E. RISK-BEARING ECONOMIES

Large producers can spread their risk so that they do not have all their 'eggs in one basket'. They can obtain their supply of raw materials from different sources and this will allow them to safeguard against shortages. Larger firms can also produce a wide range of products; for example, Hillsdown plc owns Ross Poultry, Smedley's Canned Vegetables, Needler's Sweets as well as stationery, furniture and travel companies. If there is a fall in the demand for one of the products, losses can be offset by profits from sales of the others.

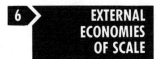

6   EXTERNAL ECONOMIES OF SCALE

There are economies to the firm which result from the industry as a whole growing in size. Sources include:
▶ Economies of disintegration
▶ Economies of concentration
▶ Economies of information

A. ECONOMIES OF DISINTEGRATION

As the industry in an area grows, it may mean that certain processes can be done better by a specialist (ancillary) firm. In the West Yorkshire woollen industry, firms specialised in a particular process such as spinning, weaving, and dyeing. Other firms specialised in making textile machinery. The same specialisation has occurred in the motor vehicle industry; for example, Lucas has specialised in the production of car lamps and electronics for the major car assemblers in the Midlands. The individual firm can often get cheaper and better quality components and services from these specialist firms.

B. ECONOMIES OF CONCENTRATION

An industry may develop in a particular area, enabling individual firms to gain such advantages as:
▶ Better training: as local colleges offer courses for the main industry of the area, a pool of skilled labour will eventually develop, to the benefit of individual firms.
▶ Better transport: the road and rail networks often improve as an industry develops in an area. These improvements are designed to serve the industries' needs, but of course benefit each other.
▶ Better commercial services, such as banks and insurance companies: these will become expert, having special knowledge of an industry's needs.
All of these will be of mutual advantage to particular firms in the area.

C. ECONOMIES OF INFORMATION

Similar firms in an area will require up-to-date information on such things as raw material supplies and foreign government regulations. There may be a free flow of such information between firms. Firms may also group together to make a joint contribution to research and development, whereas they may not be able to undertake independent research. This will save individual firms both time and money.

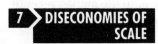

7   DISECONOMIES OF SCALE

We have seen that as a business grows in size, it will obtain certain benefits known as economies of scale. However, a business may grow *too* large. As you can see from figure 6.4, its costs will start to rise after a certain level of output. This happens mainly because the larger firm becomes more difficult to manage, to organise and to control. The reasons for this are:

A. DECISIONS TAKE LONGER

This is because there will be a large number of individual views and ideas to take into account. This is often the case where firms have merged and where there are two management teams. There will be an extended chain of command. A sole trader with perhaps two people working for him/her will be able to take decisions on the spot. It may take a large public limited company days or even weeks, with many board meetings, to arrive at a decision. That decision will then have to filter down to the workers on the shop floor.

B. NO PERSONAL LINKS

The large firm may be remote, with no personal links with its customers.

C. NO LINKS WITH THE WORKFORCE

As well as being remote from its customers, the management in a large company may be remote from its workforce. This may cause low morale and industrial relations problems, (see Ch. 17). There is evidence to suggest that as firms increase in size, so do the number of strikes. This may be for a number of reasons:
► Workers may feel as though they are not part of the firm and that their views are not taken into account.
► The work may be very tedious in large firms where mass production methods are used.
► There may be a lack of understanding between the management and the workers; a 'them and us' situation may develop.

8 ▶ OPTIMUM SIZE OF A BUSINESS

Having looked at the economies and diseconomies of scale it can be seen that there must be some *optimum* (best possible) size, such that if the firm grows any more the disadvantages will outweigh the advantages. The optimum size is that point where the firm can produce most efficiently. In figure 6.4 this is the point of lowest average cost (3,000 units). It may be difficult for a firm to know when it has reached its optimum production level but it is something of which the firm should always be aware.

9 ▶ GROWTH

Firms will seek to *grow* for a number of reasons:
► In order to reduce their average costs by obtaining economies of scale.
► So that they can produce a wider range of products. By diversifying in this way, the firms will have the other products to fall back on if one of their products fails or goes out of favour. This is called 'spreading the risk'.
► A larger firm will give the owner or management more power and status. An extreme example of this is provided by the TV programme *Dallas* in which the characters strive to build an industrial empire and with it to increase their power and status.

HOW DO FIRMS GROW?

Many firms start off as small one-person businesses (see Ch. 4) and remain like this for a variety of reasons. Others, however, will grow into large companies employing thousands of workers. How do they grow into these large companies?

1. New Products

Firms are always looking for new products or new ideas which will sell, so allowing the company to grow. Before 1976 Rowntree did not produce a solid milk chocolate bar. They noted however that all the other solid milk chocolate bars on the market were thin. They therefore decided to produce a thick, chunky bar – so the 'Yorkie' bar was born. You can perhaps think of several new products that have come onto the market recently and are selling well. Many will allow the company to make more profit.

2. The Market

Over time the demand for certain goods and services will increase, whereas for others it will decrease. Over the last ten years there has been a growth in the popularity of computers for commercial, industrial and home use. This expansion in the demand has led to a growth in the computer industry. The same could be said of the motor car industry which grew rapidly over the thirty to forty years up to the 1970s. If the demand for goods or services is high and growing then the firms producing those goods or services are likely to grow.

3. Integration

It takes time to develop new products and to wait for the demand for the product to grow. As a result, firms have, in recent times, increased their size by merging or by amalgamating with other firms. This is known as *integration* (the joining together of two or more firms). An example is the firm Cadbury Schweppes plc. There are *three* types of integration:

▶ vertical integration
▶ horizontal integration
▶ conglomerate integration

A vertical merger takes place between firms which are at different stages of production.

Fig.6.5. Backward Vertical Integration

Fig.6.6. Forward Vertical Integration

A. BACKWARD VERTICAL INTEGRATION

Is where a firm merges with an organisation supplying its raw material requirements (see (a) and (b) in Fig. 6.5).

The benefits of this are:

▶ the firm can control the quality and quantity of these raw materials instead of relying on other firms.
▶ the firm can cut out the raw material suppliers' profit.
▶ the firm can make sure delivery is on time.
▶ the firm may be able to obtain certain economies of scale (see p. 47).

> 66 In explaining the different types of integration it is always useful to use real-world examples. 99

B. FORWARD VERTICAL INTEGRATION

Is where a firm takes over the retail outlet (see Fig. 6.6). The benefits of this are:

▶ the standard of the outlet can be controlled. This is particularly important as the manufacturer may be spending millions of pounds on advertising and will therefore want the product sold in the right conditions at the 'point of sale'.
▶ the outlet is tied to the manufacturer's product and this may help that product and hinder the product of competitors.
▶ the firm may be able to obtain certain economies of scale.

A horizontal merger takes place between firms at the same stage of production. The chocolate manufacturers Rowntree and Mackintosh merged in 1969 (see Fig. 6.7). There are obvious advantages from this:

▶ Economies of scale can be obtained. These may include technical economies as the enlarged firm increases the size of manufacturing plant, in the course of rationalizing production. More specialisation of labour and machinery can now take place. Also the other internal economies of scale may be available.

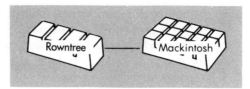

Fig.6.7. Horizontal Integration

▶ The two firms together will now have more influence on the market (market power) as the merger reduces the number of competitors.

12 ▸ CONGLOMERATE INTEGRATION

A conglomerate merger occurs when the firms amalgamate which produce goods or services that are not directly related. The main advantages of this are:
▶ to diversify production in order to spread risks.
▶ to combat market 'saturation': a situation where there is little room for further growth in the firm's output as the demand is already fully satisfied. Therefore, the firm can only grow by joining existing firms rather than by producing and selling extra output.
▶ Larger firms are able to obtain economies of scale.
Purely financial organisations often appear at the head of conglomerates in order to co-ordinate managerial and financial services. These are sometimes called *holding companies*.

The policy of the Government towards mergers has varied from time to time. If it is thought that a merger could lead to a monopoly developing then it may be referred to the *Monopolies and Mergers Commission*.

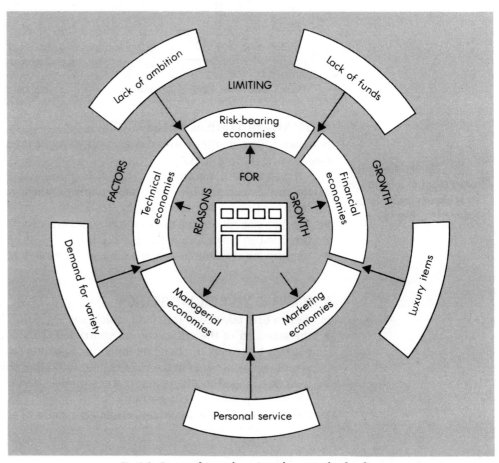

Fig.6.8. Factors for and against the growth of a firm

13 ▸ THE SURVIVAL OF SMALL FIRMS

If there are so many benefits to be made from firms growing in size, then why are there so many small firms in existence?

A. DEMAND FOR VARIETY

For certain products demand will fluctuate, with the consumer demanding a wide variety of styles. Firms will then need to change production methods quickly and easily and this can be done more readily if the firm is small. A small firm can produce in 'batches' and move from one type of production to another as demand changes. The mass production technique assumes a constant and high volume of output, in order to set up a full assembly line.

B. INABILITY TO OBTAIN ECONOMIES OF SCALE

For the production of certain goods and services there will be little scope for obtaining economies of scale and so the firm will remain small.

C. PERSONAL SERVICES

Certain services need personal attention, such as hairdressing, plumbing and plastering. Because they concentrate on small scale work they tend to remain small businesses. On the whole, those businesses providing personal services tend to be owned by sole proprietors or partnerships where decisions can be made quickly.

D. LUXURY ITEMS

The size of the firm may be limited by the size of the market. Small firms may be able to fill the gaps in the market left by large firms. For instance, the large firm may be less interested in small production runs of high quality items and may, therefore, not compete in providing such products as custom-built cars or made-to-measure suits.

E. AMBITION

The owner of the business may have limited personal ambition. He or she may prefer a small family business so as to keep his or her independence.

F. LACK OF FINANCE

Small firms may be unable to obtain finance in order to expand. A small unknown firm may find difficulty in obtaining a loan as it might be considered a high risk by a bank.

   Of course the firm may be small simply because it is a new firm and will need time to develop. So, overall, there are two sets of forces which pull the firm in opposite directions. One suggesting the firm should grow in size, and the other that it should remain small, as seen in Fig. 6.8.

EXAMINATION QUESTIONS

QUESTION 1

A reduction in a firm's average costs resulting from an increase in the size of the firm is an _____

Specimen Question: London & East Anglian Group

QUESTION 2

Why do a firm's average costs fall as output rises? (3 lines provided)
Specimen Question: London & East Anglian Group.

QUESTION 3

A company manufacturing refrigerators has to consider a number of factors in choosing a suitable site in which to locate.

   Below is an advertisement which was used by the Warrington-Runcorn Development Corporation in 1986.

1. Of the factors listed what do you view as two important reasons for locating in that area?

    (i) _____ (1 mark)

    (ii) _____ (1 mark)

    What are the reasons for your choice in both cases.

    Reasons: (7 lines provided)   **(8 marks)**

2. Are there any factors which are not dealt with in the advertisement but which you feel are important in deciding where to locate a business.

    (7 lines provided)   **(5 marks)**

Which development area? Consider these questions.

OTHER DEVELOPMENT AREAS		WARRINGTON-RUNCORN

A successful business relies heavily upon its workforce. Ask yourself.
'Does the area have a skilled and dedicated workforce, one that's right for your business?'
'Does it have an enviable record of good labour relations?'
If so, move on.

Are government grants freely available to qualifying companies? Can you claim grants of up to 22%?
Are new premises available right now
(500–50,000 sq. ft.) from £0.98p sq. ft.?
Offices from £4.75 sq. ft.?

Modern communications? Has more than £300 million been spent in providing motorway access? Are rail links available? Is a major international airport within 20 minutes drive?

Location? Is it within easy reach of the whole of the UK and does it offer 15 million consumers within an hour's drive?
What's more, does it have beautiful Cheshire country side, superb leisure facilities and high quality housing?

Now ask yourself whether your company could benefit from the advice and professional guidance given to famous names like Guinness, Marks & Spencer, Sanyo, YKK, Digital and Data General.

If you've travelled this far, you've arrived at Warrington–Runcorn. You owe it to yourself and your business to find out more.

IT'S YOUR MOVE
Post this coupon to:
The Development Corporation,
P.O. Box 49, Warrington,
Cheshire, WA1 26F.

PLEASE TICK FOR FURTHER INFORMATION ON:
Offices☐ Factories☐ Warehouses☐

Name _____ Position _____

Company _____ Address _____

Telephone _____

OR RING EILEEN BILTON ON
☎ **WARRINGTON** 24 HOUR NUMBER
(0925) 33334

WARRINGTON-RUNCORN
The right move for growth and success

FN 01

Fig.6.9.

TUTOR'S   ANSWER   TO   QUESTION   3

1.   In answering this question you need to consider what type of business is considering moving to Warrington-Runcorn. Refrigerators are likely to be costly to transport, so that one answer could perhaps be:

(i)   the good transport communications network. If the business is relocating from another part of the country, then perhaps the second answer could be:

(ii)   the quality of the housing. You must try to *list* reasons that you could explain further in the next part of the question.

The reasons for your answer could be:

(a)   A good transport network is vital for a business in which the transport of the finished product is very costly. The area's closeness to major road, rail, air and sea links with a market of 15 million people close by, is an obvious benefit. The air and sea links will be particularly useful if the business sells the product abroad or uses imported raw materials.

(b)   Your reason for including the quality of housing might be that in moving from another area the company might wish some of its key staff to move. The staff are likely to be more positive about the move if they are told that good quality housing will be available.

2.   This is not an easy question because the advertisement has covered most of the important factors. You could, in fact, say that the advertisement has included many of the relevant features for locating in this area. However, perhaps something could have been included on the training establishments available, such as local colleges, which will be important in developing the particular engineering skills required. Or, again, perhaps the advertisement could have been more specific on what firms could qualify for a capital grant.

C   O   U   R   S   E   W   O   R   K

**ASSIGNMENT 1
LOCATION**

1.   Choose a local business. The choice can be made either because:
   (a)   someone in your family works in the business, or
   (b)   it is a business which interests you.

2.   Construct a questionnaire. You can either send this to the business or take it with you to use during an interview (if you can arrange one!).

The areas your questionnaire covers could include:
   (a)   What are the reasons which influenced the business in its choice of location?
   (b)   Has it been viewed as a good choice? If not why not?
   (c)   Has the business ever moved location? If so why?
   (d)   Are there other similar businesses in the area? If so do you know why they are here?

3.   Once you have collected all this information write it up in the form of a report to be presented to the board of directors. State whether you feel the present location is a satisfactory location or whether a better site is available in your area.

**ASSIGNMENT 2
SIZE**

1.   Choose a small corner shop and a large supermarket in your area. They could be the ones at which your family do their shopping.

2.   Large supermarkets are able to take advantage of economies of scale, whereas a small cornershop may not. Compare the two retailers in terms of:
   (a)   marketing economies
   (b)   financial economies
   (c)   technical economies
   (d)   management economies
   (e)   risk-bearing economies.

Some of the information can be obtained by simply visiting the two retailers, such as the variations in price. However, you may have to arrange a meeting with the owner or manager for more information.

3.   Why does the cornershop remain small? What are the advantages and disadvantages to the customer of each type of retailer?

4.   Once you have all this information, a report could be written and presented to the two retailers suggesting an area where you feel they could improve.

**ASSIGNMENT 3
GROWTH**

1.   Almost everyday in the newspapers there is a report of one company planning a merger with, or takeover of, another company.

You could monitor one such merger or takeover. Use the newspapers to follow the events, perhaps cutting the relevant bits out of your daily newspaper or taking notes from newspapers in the local library. The financial pages in particular may give details on the companies that are merging and sometimes carry adverts saying why the merger or takeover is a good thing. The information may be a little difficult in parts so you may only be able to note certain aspects of the merger or takeover.

2.   With the information you could build up a series of events.
   ▶ Who started the merger/takeover?
   ▶ Which were the companies involved?
   ▶ What was the reason put forward for the merger/takeover?
   ▶ Did the merger/takeover take place?
   ▶ Did the merger/takeover get referred to the Monopolies and Mergers Commission?
   ▶ If so, what happened?

You could also write to the companies involved asking for further information on their activities (e.g. their company reports).

STUDENT'S ANSWER – EXAMINER'S COMMENTS

The following is a student's answer to question 3, page 54.

3. 1. i) The skilled workforce available in the area.

ii) The communications network and the 15 million consumers in the area.

> **Two reasons given here instead of the one asked for.**

Reason for i). It will not be necessary to attract and move a skilled workforce to the area. Therefore the cost will be less, as people are already housed there, the company will not need to offer housing benefits and removal costs. The company will save time as staff will not need as much training, if they are already skilled.

> **You could make the point that the refrigerator manufacturer will be interested in *particular* skills.**

Reason for ii). The company can transport the refrigerators quickly and easily, not just relying on the type of transport. They can quickly obtain raw materials, even if it is necessary to import them, and especially as much of the U.K.'s industry is within an hours drive. There is the 15 million consumers in the area, which will hopefully be a good market for the refrigerators.

> " Very good. All the main points are included. "

2. Whether there is room for the company to expand if they wish to do so, with-out having to move plants.
Which type of manufacturers are already in the area. The refrigerator manufac-uring company may not wish to locate there if similar manufacturers are in the area already. It will affect their share of the market.
The necessary resources available eg. dumping facilities for waste, and the power supply. A firm manufacturing can not operate efficiently without these.

> " A very good answer, which shows that the student is thinking about the question set. It includes important points which the refrigerator company might be very interested in. "

CHAPTER

7

FINANCE
FOR
BUSINESS

HOW COMPANIES ARE
    FINANCED
INTERNAL SOURCES OF
    FINANCE
EXTERNAL SOURCES OF
    FINANCE
TYPES OF SHARE
ISSUING SHARES
WHY DO WE NEED MONEY
THE QUALITIES OF MONEY
THE ORIGINS OF THE
    BANKING SYSTEM
BANKING SERVICES TO
    BUSINESS
THE CITY
THE STOCK EXCHANGE

GETTING STARTED

As you can see from Fig. 7.1 on page 59, companies need money for all sorts of reasons and they can try to get it from a variety of sources. The banks and the Stock Exchange play a major part in this process. We consider the nature of *money* and the role of these institutions later in the chapter.

ESSENTIAL PRINCIPLES

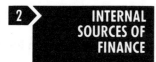

1 ▶ HOW COMPANIES FINANCE THEIR ACTIVITIES

Companies need money to:
▶ buy factories and machines;
▶ hire people;
▶ pay for other companies which they might want to take over;
▶ buy the materials they need to make their products.

Where this money comes from depends on whether the company is just starting out or whether it has been running for a number of years.

A small company just starting out might:
▶ use the savings of its owner;
▶ go to the bank and ask for a loan.

A larger, established company would be able to use the retained (or saved) profits of previous years. If it needs even more cash then it will have a number of possible sources of new finance, usually both *internal* and *external*.

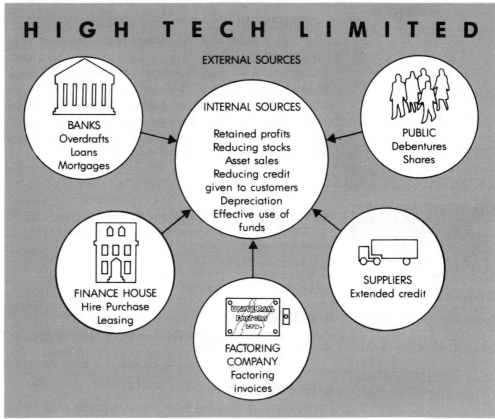

Fig.7.1. Sources of finance for business

2 ▶ INTERNAL SOURCES OF FINANCE

Using this method can save the firm quite a lot of trouble as well as save on interest charges. Companies can raise finance *internally* in a number of ways:
▶ retained profits
▶ funds obtained by reducing stocks
▶ funds obtained by selling under-used assets
▶ money made available by reducing the credit available to customers
▶ profits retained for depreciation
▶ money created by making sure that all funds are put to effective use (earning interest).

A. RETAINED PROFITS
This is money which has been earned as a profit in the past and then saved for the future.

B. STOCK REDUCTION

Stocks are the products of the firm that are kept ready for sale in warehouses or stockrooms. Most firms produce more than they need to supply current customers so that they will not be caught out if there is a sudden surge in demand. Stocks are money, however! They are valuable products and if a company builds up too many they can represent wasted money. A firm which reduces its stock levels is, in fact, releasing the equivalent amount of money for its own use.

C. ASSET SALES

Quite a few companies have buildings or land that they are not using and will not need in the future. If these 'assets' can be identified and sold then they will release large amounts of money for the company to use.

> **Although the assets are sold outside the business, the asset itself was held internally by the company *before* its sale. It is, therefore, an INTERNAL source of finance.**

D. LIMITING CREDIT TO CUSTOMERS

Cutting the total of outstanding invoices is a way of releasing cash for the firm's use.

E. DEPRECIATION

If we were sensible and had enough cash – but most of us do not – then we would make sure that, when our car got too old, there would be a fund in the bank ready to replace it. In other words we would set aside a certain amount every year in order to pay for a new car when it was needed. This may be difficult for individuals but it is ***absolutely vital*** for companies who need to replace machines, vehicles, and other articles at regular intervals. All companies keep back a part of their profits to allow for the depreciation of their assets due to factors such as age and usage. These profits may help the company to fund the future replacement of the assets.

 3 ▶ EXTERNAL SOURCES OF FINANCE

In order to raise finance ***externally*** the company can:

    Go to the bank. There they might be offered:
- ▶ an ***overdraft***
- ▶ a ***secured loan***, or
- ▶ a ***mortgage***

A. OVERDRAFT

In this case the bank manager has agreed to allow you to take more money out of your account than is actually in it – up to a certain limit, of course!

B. SECURED LOANS

Your bank may agree to lend you an amount of money but might want it ***secured***! In other words, they want some valuable possession of yours, legally signed over to them, just in case you are unable to pay off the debt.

C. MORTGAGES

These are a special form of ***secured loan*** – the bank will lend you money in return for the security of property that you own.

Finance can also be obtained from the general public or from financial institutions. A small business can often raise money by going to members of the family and asking for help. A larger company can get money from the general public in one of two ways:
- ▶ by borrowing from the general public or from financial institutions and promising to pay the loan back; or
- ▶ by inviting the general public or financial institutions to become shareholders.

In the first case the company gets the money in return for ***debentures***. In the second case it gets the money in return for ***shares***.

Remember: debenture holders are outsiders who have *loaned* the company money; shareholders are the *OWNERS* of the company.

D. DEBENTURES (LOAN CAPITAL)

Debentures are documents which are given to people or institutions who lend money to companies. The document will tell the lender *when* they can expect to be repaid and *how much* in interest they can expect to receive until then. If the interest is not paid in any one year then the holders of debentures can actually force the company to close down so that they can be repaid.

Debentures are very special forms of finance for business:
► holders of debentures *do not own* the company
► they do not have a vote
► they have no say in running the business
► but their interest *must* be paid every year
► and it is paid out *before* anything is paid to the holders of shares.

E. SHARES

A *limited* company – whether private or public – is one in which people can invest money (as owners) by buying *shares* in such a company. However, their financial risk is limited to the value of their investment. They cannot be held liable for any of the debts of that company beyond the value of their shareholding (see page 24).

F. OTHER METHODS OF OBTAINING FINANCE FROM OUTSIDE

There are several other ways in which companies might get money from outside sources.

(i) They might try to *hire* machines and equipment instead of buying them.
► This could be done by hire purchase – that is, paying for the machine in instalments – in the same way that we buy some of our household equipment (TVs, cars, etc). The company would go to a *Finance House* for this type of finance.
► Hiring equipment by *leasing*. When a company leases a piece of equipment it usually never intends to own it. It pays instalments, just as we do under a hire purchase agreement. However, unlike HP, the machine or the equipment is never actually owned.

Companies have good reasons for leasing machines and equipment rather than buying outright. They usually get repairs and maintenance either free or at very good rates and they can keep up with changes in technology much more easily. The most important reason why firms lease however, is money. Leasing involves putting down only a fraction of the cost of the machine and then making monthly payments. This enables firms to use the rest of the cash for other things. For companies, therefore, leasing means that they can:
► Keep up with new technology
► Have their equipment and machines maintained by other people
► Keep most of their money free for other uses.

(ii) Another way of getting money from outside to use in the business is to raise the finance by extending credit from suppliers. This is not the most pleasant way of raising finance but it is a technique used by many companies. Most firms who supply other firms with equipment, send in their bills (invoices) within a few days of supplying the goods. Most of these invoices allow a month for payment but some companies will take longer to pay.

(iii) A final method of getting money from outside the business is called *factoring*. This involves the somewhat strange process of selling the company's bills.

For example: a company may have a lot of people who owe money to it. The invoices it has sent out simply have not been paid – usually because the customers are trying to extend their *credit times* as described above. A company in this position can raise cash by selling the invoices to a special factoring company who will then take on the responsibility of getting payment on the invoices.

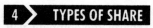

4 ▶ TYPES OF SHARE

There are a number of *types* of share that can be purchased:

A. ORDINARY SHARES

Most companies issue a number of Ordinary Shares (*equities*). Buying one of these shares makes you a part owner of the company with a right to a say in how it is run. This right is expressed at the regular shareholders' meeting. Ordinary shareholders also get the opportunity to share in any profits that are made. If any profit is left over after tax and interest has been paid, then the shareholders will get a share of this profit. It will be paid in the form of a **dividend**. However, the first claim on the profit will go to the preference shareholders. Only after they have been paid their dividend will any remaining amount be available for distribution to ordinary shareholders.

B. PREFERENCE SHARES

These are shares which carry a *fixed rate of dividend* – expressed as a percentage – which is paid out before the dividends to the ordinary shareholders. Preference shareholders often do not have the right to a vote.

C. CUMULATIVE PREFERENCE SHARES

A firm may not earn enough profit in one year to be able to pay a fixed rate of dividend on its preference shares. With a Cumulative Preference share any shortfall is carried forward to the next year.

D. PARTICIPATING PREFERENCE SHARES

These shares receive the usual fixed dividend but may also **participate** in further dividends if any money is left over after all dividends due on other shares have been paid.

Shares are not loans they are investments! If you lend £1,000 to a company in the form of a Debenture and the company runs into trouble and has to be closed down, you will be one of the first to be repaid if there is any money available. This is because you are a **creditor** of the company – someone who has simply lent it money. If, on the other hand, you had bought £1,000 worth of shares in the same company then you would be the very last to get any money back.

▶ Shares, therefore, tend to be risky but rewarding;
▶ Debentures tend to pay less but be very safe.

5 ▶ ISSUING SHARES

Only *public limited companies* (plc's) may issue shares to the general public (see Ch. 4) but they may do so in a variety of ways:

A. PUBLIC ISSUE

Shares can be advertised (bearing in mind certain rules and regulations) in the press and can be sold directly. This is usually done on the advice of a specialist company called an *issuing house*.

B. OFFER FOR SALE

The shares are sold to the *issuing house* which then sells them itself to institutions or stockbrokers.

C. PLACING

With this method the shares are sold in blocks of quite large numbers to institutions. This guarantees that all the shares will be sold but can usually only be done with relatively small numbers of shares. **Underwriters** are people or companies who agree to buy any shares from an issue which are not sold to the public or to institutions. In return they receive a fee whether they have to take any of the offer or not.

D. RIGHTS ISSUE

If a company is successful enough it can often go back to its own shareholders to sell them even more shares. In order to make sure that they buy the shares the company will usually offer the new shares at a cheaper price than the normal shares. The issue gives each present shareholder the *right* to buy, say, one new share for every three that they currently hold. In financial jargon this is a *one for three rights issue*.

MONEY AND BANKING – NATURE OF MONEY

What is money? It may seem a silly question because we all know what money is – it is the coins and notes which we have in our pockets! That is certainly true but the money you have in your pockets is not the only form of money:

▶ *money is anything which might be accepted in settlement of a debt or in exchange for goods and services.*

If you wanted to sell your car and someone offered to buy it but gave you a pile of 'ringetts' for it what would you do? The ringett is the unit of money used in Malaysia. It is 'money' but, because it is difficult for you to know the value of it and to change it into British pounds you probably would not accept the pile of cash for your car. Money can be almost anything but it must be acceptable.

Pacific Islanders have used shells, stones and even shark's teeth as money. In Europe, too, some very strange kinds of money have been accepted. In Italy in the late 1970s there was a shortage of small notes, so buses and railway stations used to give small amounts of change in sweets!

6 ▶ WHY DO WE NEED MONEY?

When people were farmers and lived in isolated communities there was rarely any need for money. People grew or made everything they needed for themselves. After a time, however, people began to specialise; that is they began to make or grow just one thing or one type of thing.

▶ some people chose to grow food
▶ some became hunters of meat and furs
▶ others became builders, carpenters, potters, spear-makers, etc.

When a spear-maker wanted some food he simply swapped a spear for some food. This process of swapping is called *barter*.

The problem with barter is that it needs two people to want to trade at the same time – and for each other's goods! It also runs into problems with the fact that some goods are very valuable and not easily divisible. A man who builds a house for a spear-maker has got to want a lot of spears! The answer is to find some *common* item which everyone will accept and which has a value known to everyone. This common item can then be used as *money*, i.e. the means of payment. Gold, silver and precious stones have all been used as money in the past and are still used as a store of wealth by some people.

Money has many uses but the most important ones are:

▶ *it is a medium of exchange* – it allows us to exchange different goods. A carpenter can make chairs, sell them to several different people and then buy a new hi-fi from someone totally different.

▶ *it is a unit of account* – it allows us to make comparisons between different goods. Without money the value of a donkey and a set of furniture is difficult to establish.

▶ *it is a store of value* – it provides a store of value for the future. In theory money remains valuable over a period of time but this does not take inflation into account.

▶ *it is a measure of debt* – it enables banks and individuals to keep a record of exchanges that have been made for settlement in the future. The technical term used for this function is to say that it is a *standard of deferred payment*.

7 ▶ THE QUALITIES OF MONEY

For money to be really useful it has to possess several qualities:

▶ *it has to be acceptable* – people must recognise that it is money and be prepared to accept it.

▶ *it has to be durable* – to be tough and to last a long time so that it can be passed from person to person, stored in a bank, and used in machines.

▶ *it has to be portable* – to be easy to carry around. Some Pacific Islanders used to use big stones as money (most were about a metre across!) They could not get many of those in their pockets!

▶ *it has to be scarce* – there must not be *too much* of it around. It might also, because it is scarce, have *intrinsic value* – that is, be valuable in itself and not just as money. Gold and silver both have intrinsic value. They can be saved and sold in the form of bars or of jewellery, and both have been used as money.

Today money is not just the coins and notes in our pockets, it is a wide variety of types of money. Some of it is in the form of actual cash while other types of money are *near cash* – that is, in a form which is easy to convert into cash:

▶ current accounts (cheque accounts)
▶ deposit account books
▶ building society savings books

As well as these forms of money there is yet another type which has become very important over the past few years, namely credit money.

The types of money and cash listed above are all 'real' in the sense that they have been earned or acquired in some way and have then been put into some form of bank account. *Credit money*, on the other hand, has not yet been earned – it does not yet exist but it can be spent.

8 ▶ ORIGIN OF THE BANKING SYSTEM

Banks in Britain have grown from the old *Goldsmiths* of the sixteenth and seventeenth centuries. There were about forty of them in London, offering banking services in the late seventeenth century. They kept people's money safe in strongrooms, gave loans, and even issued banknotes (until 1770). Gradually these goldsmith-bankers became known as *banks* and the number of banks in Britain grew until there were over 700 in the early 1800s. One of them was the original *Bank of England* which was then a private bank (formed in 1694). Since the early nineteenth century a series of mergers, takeovers and some failures have resulted in the number of individual banks falling until, today, there are just four very large banks:

▶ Barclays   ▶ Midland
▶ Lloyds   ▶ National Westminster

together with the TSB plc and several smaller ones.

9 ▶ BANKING SERVICES TO BUSINESS

Modern banks offer a very wide range of services to businesses – both large and small – including the following:

A. ACCOUNTS

Businesses need to be able to keep their money in a safe place and to be able to get to some of it quite quickly. Banks, therefore, offer businesses four main types of account:

(i) *Cheque Accounts*: which normally pay no interest on the money kept in them but which enable businesses to write cheques at any time (in other words, to be able to get to their money at any time). These are usually called *current accounts*.

(ii) *Deposit Accounts*: which pay interest on any money kept in them but make it less easy to get the money out. Usually there is no cheque book with this type of account (but some banks are now introducing interest-bearing cheque accounts).

(iii) *Foreign Currency Accounts*: companies which do a lot of business abroad and which, therefore, receive a lot of money in foreign currencies, can open bank accounts in which they can keep those foreign currencies. If they only had their British sterling (£) bank accounts the foreign currencies would have to be changed into sterling before they could be banked. Some companies keep these foreign currency accounts so that they can pay their own bills from abroad without constantly having to change British pounds into other currencies.

(iv) *Money Market Accounts*: these are special accounts which are really only for the largest companies which have very large amounts of money available for short periods of time. Various institutions – including the Government – need money for very short periods of time (often only overnight) and are prepared to pay for it. Banks can, therefore, arrange for companies' cash to be loaned overnight. This gives the company an income in the form of interest on money that it would normally have had to keep in a non-interest bearing cheque account.

B. ACCEPTANCES

Banks can help companies who get paid by what are called *Drafts* or *Bills of Exchange* (see p. 100) by arranging for them to be *accepted* – that is, converted into cash immediately.

> **Overdrafts occur when an account holder draws out more money than is actually in the account – they OVER-DRAW.**

C. LOANS

Companies can go to their banks for various types of *loan*:
► *Overdrafts*: short term loans (see p. 60)
► *Loans*: medium or long term loans, with or without security
► *Mortgages*: long term loans secured against property.

D. ACCOUNT SERVICES

Banks offer business a number of services to help them to run their current accounts more efficiently. Two of the most important are *standing orders* and *direct debits*:

Standing orders: if a company has to pay a fixed amount of money every month, say to the electricity board, it can ask the bank to pay it by standing order. The bank will make a note on its computer and the company's account will have the electricity payment taken out of it automatically each month.

Direct debits: these are similar to standing orders except that, instead of the bank being ordered to pay a specific amount each month, it is asked to pay whatever the electricity board asks for. This is useful if the amount to be paid varies each month.

E. BANKER'S DRAFTS

These are a way of making payments from your bank account which are *guaranteed* by the bank. Sometimes another person or company will not accept an ordinary cheque – cheques can 'bounce' (that is, fail to be honoured usually because there is not enough money in the account) or they can be 'stopped' (a person who writes a cheque and thinks better of it can, if quick, ask their bank to refuse to pay it when it is presented by the person to whom it was given).

Both of these problems are avoided by the use of banker's drafts. Once you have asked your bank to make a banker's draft out for you and have handed it over to the person you are buying something from, the draft cannot bounce or be stopped. The bank would not have issued the draft for you if there had not been enough money in the account, so that it must be honoured when it is presented for payment.

F. EXPORT SERVICES

Britain depends on its exports and British banks now give a number of different services to companies which export their products abroad. They will often provide finance for exports or will advise companies on the best way to set about selling their goods abroad.

G. OTHER SERVICES

These vary from providing insurance for business property and for business activities to providing computer services for companies which are too small to be able to afford their own computers. Computer services are often provided by banks for the weekly or monthly payroll of companies.

Banks also provide *night safes*, which are the safes you often see in the outside walls of banks. Customers of the bank who have paid for the arrangement, can deposit cash and valuables after the bank has closed. It would be dangerous for most retailers to keep the money from their tills in their own houses overnight – it might amount to many hundreds or even thousands of pounds – so most of them have an arrangement to use their bank's night safe.

H. ADVICE

Bank managers are highly trained and knowledgeable people who are able to offer business-people advice on many matters: setting up your own company, finding premises, working out cash flows and money requirements, and dealing with accountants and the Inland Revenue. Most banks are proud of their ability to give sound advice.

10   THE CITY

People often get confused because the City is both a real place and an idea.
► It is *real* because it is a unit of local government which dates from mediaeval times.
► It is an *idea* because it is the term given to the collection of financial institutions

upon which the wealth of the City of London (and a good deal of the wealth of the UK) is founded.

The City consists of:

- clearing banks
- merchant banks
- currency traders
- commodity traders
- stockbrokers
- market makers
- discount houses
- finance houses
- insurance companies
- unit trust managers

The City is a *money market* in that all of these institutions together form a market for money. The City is also centred around several other important markets:

- *The Stock Exchange* for stocks and shares.
- *Lloyds* for all types of insurance from ordinary household to insurance for oil tankers.
- *The Baltic Exchange* for shipping.
- *The London Metal Market* for metal commodities.

The City is also the world's largest international banking and insurance market and forms a major part of the UK's *finance sector*.

11 ▶ THE STOCK EXCHANGE

Originally people sold their shares by going to a particular coffee house in London and simply asking around until they found someone who wanted their shares. With thousands of companies and millions of shareholders on today's market that method would be impossible. So we have a **Stock Exchange** which is really a 'Stocks and Shares Exchange'. It is composed of about 4,000 members who are specialists in finding buyers for stocks and shares. From 1908 until 1986, the Stock Exchange was divided into two different types of member who did very different tasks:

- *Jobbers*. These were people who actually traded in stocks and shares. They were prepared to buy from, or sell to, people who either wanted to buy or sell shares.
- *Stockbrokers*. These were people who acted as middlemen between the public and the jobbers. They took orders from the public to either buy or sell shares and then found a jobber who was offering the right price for those shares. As a member of the public it was impossible to deal with a jobber direct – you had to go through a broker.

A. THE 'BIG BANG'

Since the election of the Conservative Government in 1979 there has been a series of important changes in the City and in the Stock Exchange. The changes to the Stock Exchange are known as the 'Big Bang'. Most of these changes occurred in 1986.

▶ From March 1986 outside firms (which were not members of the Stock Exchange) have been able to take over Stock Exchange firms. Before that date, member firms were protected against takeovers from outsiders.

▶ From October 1986 the distinction between jobbers and brokers ended. Both jobbers and brokers can now exist in the same firm. A single person can now perform both functions, although in practice the firms are still divided internally into the two types of staff. In addition, there are now *licensed dealers* who can trade in stocks and shares without being members of the Stock Exchange.

▶ From October 1986 stockbrokers (and the firms who employ them) have been able to charge any commission they like on share purchases and sales. Up to that date there were fixed scales for commission charges.

▶ From October 1986 all Stock Exchange firms have been able to offer their customers a full range of financial services.

B. THE UNLISTED SECURITIES MARKET

Yet another recent change has been the introduction of the *Unlisted Securities Market (USM)*. This is a sort of mini-Stock Exchange which has fewer regulations and is cheaper to join, and so has encouraged the shares of smaller companies to be traded.

C. WHY SHARE PRICES ARE IMPORTANT TO BUSINESS

The role of shares is to raise money for companies. We might think that, once the shares had been sold, the company would not really be interested in the price that they were fetching on the Stock Exchange. This is not, in fact, the case. Companies are interested in the share price because:

▶ shares are a form of ownership of a company; they represent votes and therefore control. Anyone who owns most of the shares or even a large percentage of them can influence what happens within the company.

▶ if the company's share price falls then it becomes easier for another person or firm to buy them and possibly to gain control of the company.

EXAMINATION QUESTIONS

QUESTION 1

Patrick McNab, who owns a manufacturing business, decides to acquire his own fleet of delivery vehicles instead of using independent road haulage contractors. He also decides to lease, rather than buy, the vehicles.

    (a)   Why do you think he chose to acquire his own fleet? **(6 marks)**

    (b)   How does leasing help to reduce the initial cost of the vehicles? **(3 marks)**

    (c)   What other advantages are there for Patrick in leasing rather than purchasing outright for cash? **(6 marks)**

TOTAL 15 MARKS

Specimen question: London & East Anglian Group

QUESTION 2

Examine the following newspaper clipping which appeared on Friday, 18 April 1986 and then answer the questions below:

FOOD, CATERING, ETC.

Argyll Grp	333	−5
AB Food	246	+5
Ass Dairies	140	
Ass Fish	100	
Bejam	179	−2
Brthwick	36	
Cadbry Sch	151	
Fitch Lovll	246	+1
Grand Met	351	−9
Kwik Save	224	−2
Nth Foods	272	−2
RHM	161	
Rowntree	395	−8
Sainsbury	346	−2
Tate Lyle	493	−7
Tesco	280	
TH Forte	139	−3
Unigate	206	
Utd Biscuit	186	−3

(a)   What is the name of the market where these prices arise?

_____ **(1 mark)**

(b)   What is being priced?

_____ **(1 mark)**

(c)   What was the price for Rowntree in pounds sterling on Thursday, 17 April 1986?

_____ **(3 marks)**

(d)   (i)   Which of the above is priced highest?

_____ **(1 mark)**

    (ii) Why do you think this is so?

_____ **(4 marks)**

(4 lines for answer.)

Specimen question: Northern Ireland Schools Examinations Council

TUTOR'S   ANSWER   TO   QUESTION   2

(a) The Stock Market.

(b) Shares.

(c) On Thursday 17 April, the price for Rowntree shares was £4.03. The reason for this is that on the following day the shares were priced at £3.95 having fallen £0.08.

(d) (i) Tate and Lyle are priced the highest at £4.93.

(ii) The reason for this could be that Tate and Lyle have announced a good dividend or have had a profitable period. Both these could have caused the price of their shares to increase as the demand for them increases. This increase in their share price is reflecting their success in the past. It could be, however, that they are likely to be successful in the future perhaps because they have developed a new product. This, too, could increase the price of their shares as buyers of the shares envisage larger profits and higher dividends in the future.

C   O   U   R   S   E   W   O   R   K

1 **SOURCES OF INFORMATION**

When you are doing your *coursework assignments* or looking for additional information on sections of this chapter the following hints may be useful:

GENERAL COMPANY FINANCE

You will find out a lot about how companies are financed by looking through any *Annual Reports and Accounts* that you can get hold of. The *Balance Sheet* and the *Profit & Loss account* contain lots of information about how the company uses its profits or, perhaps, how it finances its losses. You will also be able to see how the share capital is made up.

The *Notes to the Accounts* are particularly useful if you do not understand any of the headings. Another important source of information is the quality newspaper.

FACTORING

For more information on what services are available, how they are arranged, and how much they cost:

▶ see the *factoring section* in your local *Yellow Pages*

▶ or write to one of the large, national factors, such as

Griffin Factors Ltd; 87, Queen Street, London, EC4V 4AP

International Factors Ltd; 137–141, Regent Street, London, W1R 7LD.

LEASING

There will be several companies who specialise in leasing in your local copy of the *Yellow Pages* but you might also try:

Lombard North Central PLC; 31, Lombard Street, London, EC3V 9BD

BANKING & MONEY

The local branch of any of the *'Big Four' clearing banks* – Barclays, Lloyds, Midland, National Westminster – should be able to answer any question you have or, perhaps, branches of the TSB or the Cooperative Bank.

Also, the *National Girobank* can be reached by addressing letters to: The Public Relations Office, Bootle, Lancs.

The Banking Information Service at 10, Lombard Street, London, EC3V 9AT has a wealth of booklets and other material for students.

THE STOCK EXCHANGE

Information can be had direct from the Public Relations Office, The Stock Exchange, London, EC2N 1HP.

Do not forget, though, that your local stockbrokers might be able to tell you more and may even be prepared to come into schools to give short talks or to see small groups at their offices (by appointment only).

INSURANCE

The large insurance brokers in your local *Yellow Pages* will be able to give you a lot of information on what is available for business insurance and how much it costs.

It might also be possible to get some information from the local offices of the larger insurance companies such as:

Commercial Union	Cooperative Insurance
Eagle Star	Guardian Royal Exchange
Legal & General	Norwich Union
Provincial	Prudential
Royal Insurance	Sun Alliance

You will find their addresses and telephone numbers in the local telephone directory or the *Yellow Pages*.

2 ▶ FINANCE ASSIGNMENT

CAPITAL STRUCTURE OF FIVE COMPANIES

1. Get the **Annual Reports and Accounts** for five public limited companies (plc's) from different industrial sectors.

    You can write away for them, look them up in a local library, or, perhaps your school has a resource bank of them.

2. Use the **balance sheet** to identify each company's:

Loans	— under Liabilities (Long Term) and including Debentures (sometimes called 'Loan Stock').
Share capital	— Ordinary and Preference
Reserves	— money set aside out of profits each year to provide for a 'rainy day'

3. Use the **Profit and Loss Account** to identify each company's:

Profits	— distinguish between profits **before** tax and those **after** tax.
Retained profits	— compare them with last year's to see how well – or badly – the company is doing

4. For each company calculate:
    - ▶ the retained profits as a % of turnover (total sales)
    - ▶ the profits after tax as a % of turnover
    - ▶ dividends as a % of profits after tax
    - ▶ long term loans as a % of share capital plus reserves (this is called the **gearing** of the company.

5. Write a report for your school magazine which:
    - (a) Presents all this information clearly and usefully
    - (b) Explains all the important terms used
    - (c) Comments on the differences between the companies in:
        - (i) the way they have raised their capital between equities (shares) and loan capital
        - (ii) the proportion of profits paid out as dividends to shareholders, interest on long term capital and retained profits.

STUDENT'S ANSWER – EXAMINER'S COMMENTS

This is a student's answer to question 1, page 67.

1)   Patrick McNab.

a)   He may want his own fleet of vehicles because the haulage contractors are unreliable. His own fleet would always be ready whenever he wanted to use them. The haulage contractors may be too expensive over the long-term. Having his own fleet means that he can advertise his company on them.

> **Good. Another point is that the product will tend to be handled more carefully when it is his own fleet which is delivering; ie less damage.**

b)   Leasing helps to reduce the initial cost of the vehicles, because you lease over a long period of time, rather than pay all in one go at the beginning.

> **This is a good point.**

c)   Patrick can change the fleet of vehicles for something new/more up to date, rather than sell and buy new vehicles.

> **Another good point – but for 6 marks you need to mention other advantages. For instance, if your business is not doing well you can cancel the lease. The money you would have spent on buying a fleet of delivery vehicles (if you hadn't leased) can be used somewhere else in the company.**

PURCHASING AND PRODUCTION

PURCHASING
PRODUCTION
TYPES OF PRODUCTION
PRODUCTION
ENGINEERING
PRODUCTION
MANAGEMENT
CHANGE IN ENGINEERING
AND PRODUCTION

G E T T I N G   S T A R T E D

Production means actually making the goods or products and involves many stages in modern manufacturing.

Perhaps the easiest way to think of production is to see, in your mind's eye, the long car production lines which most of us have seen in films or on the television.

The basic bits and pieces (known as components) enter the factory at one end and are then put together, bit by bit, until the finished article leaves at the other end. This is known as line production and was one of the very earliest methods of *mass production*.

Before the Industrial Revolution, most goods were produced by individual craftsmen in their own homes or in small workshops. This was an early form of production which required the craftsman to be very organised about his work. A carpenter who was going to make a set of chairs would have to think about all the major production stages which we have today – except that he probably would not recognise them by the same terms.

1.   He would have to choose and buy the wood; making sure that it was of the right quality and that it was delivered to his workshop at the right time.

2.   He would have to make sure that all his tools were laid out in the right places in his workshop so that he could work easily. It would not help for him to leave his saws and planes at the other end of the workshop from the door at which the heavy timber arrived.

3.   He would have to do the work in the right order. Sawing and turning all the legs first; steaming and bending all the backs next; sanding and smoothing all the pieces; then gluing them all together and clamping them; and, finally giving them a final smooth before varnishing and polishing all the finished chairs.

The things which the old carpenter would have done by experience (because he had learned them all during his apprenticeship) have, today, become an extremely complex part of management.

ESSENTIAL PRINCIPLES

1 ▶ PURCHASING

The first stage in any business which is producing goods is the **buying** of the raw materials needed. Whether the firm is going to produce 'home-baked' cakes or machine tools it is going to need to buy the basic raw materials.

Purchasing is, therefore, an extremely important part of the activities of a firm. A good buyer can save the company substantial amounts by sensible buying policies, and lower costs can mean extra profit for the firm.

The role of the Buyer or Purchasing Officer is to know exactly where to go for a wide range of raw materials; how much to pay for them; what sort of contracts to enter into; and how to deal with suppliers who do not deliver on time or in the right quality or quantity.

The job can be summed up by *Double P; Double Q; Double T (P P Q Q T T)*:–

▶ Price
▶ Place
▶ Quality
▶ Quantity
▶ Times
▶ Terms

PRICE

The purchasing officer must know the prices at which the materials can be bought; what is too low a price (because, possibly, the quality will not be good enough) and what is too high a price.

PLACE

Components are of little use if they are delivered to the wrong location or, even, to the wrong unloading bay at your factory. The buyer must specify exactly where the materials are to be delivered.

QUALITY

❝❝ Buyers have to be experts, not only in the items to be bought but also in the product in which the items are to be used. ❞❞

It is vital that the quality of the components be exactly as required by the designers or production engineers. Obviously, the quality must not be poor because the finished goods will then be faulty, giving the company a bad name which will be very difficult to live down. It is not so obvious, but just as true, that the materials must not be of too **high** a quality. Goods are designed to last for a specific time. If they last too long then they get overtaken by newer designs. An article which has parts which are of too high a quality may last longer than the makers want it to last – in effect they will have paid for too much quality! The buyer must buy exactly the right quality of components.

QUANTITY

The purchasing officer must buy the right **amount** of the components. Enough must be bought to be able to take advantage of **discounts for large orders** but the buyer must not buy too much.

If a firm buys too much of a component then it will have to pay extra storage costs.

TIME

It is the duty of the purchasing officer to make sure that the components arrive at the right time. Too early and the firm will have to use up valuable storage space in storing them; too late and the whole production process might be held up.

TERMS

This means the agreement between the firm and its suppliers for a certain component and includes all the terms of the contract for the supply; how many are to be delivered; at what intervals; to what quality; and at what price. The buyer must make sure that his company pays only as much as it absolutely has to for the components.

For many years the Purchasing Department was very much underrated. Glamour has tended to be attached to the people in Sales and Marketing. However, the purchasing officers are vitally important to modern industry – they have to carry in their heads a mass of complex information about the materials which the firm needs; they must be good negotiators; and they must know a great deal about the law of contract.

2 ▶ PRODUCTION

In the discussion at the beginning of this chapter we talked about a carpenter needing to be well organised in order to produce chairs. It is also true that, if the carpenter is **not** well organised, he will produce the chairs very inefficiently; i.e. late or to a poor quality. In the same way, modern industry needs to be very well organised to produce its products efficiently. Any company which is not will find it very difficult to sell its goods and may well go out of business.

There are a number of ways of producing goods today. The easiest way to remember these types of production is by using the letters *JMB*, standing for *JOB*, *MASS*, *BATCH*.

3 ▶ TYPES OF PRODUCTION

A. JOB PRODUCTION
This type of production applies wherever a firm has to produce individual items to a special specification (set of requirements). High quality pottery, made-to-measure clothes, bridges, and ships are all made using *job production* techniques. With job production every item produced is different and the firm has to rearrange its production floor to meet the special requirements of each job. Because they are individually produced, job-production items usually require a large amount of human labour. The experts call this a *high labour to capital ratio*. This simply means that the production technique requires more labour than machines – the production is *labour intensive*.

B. MASS PRODUCTION
Most of us are familiar with the long production lines which produce everything from television sets to tinned peas and from cars to sweets. The idea of mass production is to make a very large number of identical products as cheaply as possible. It is often said that the idea was invented by Henry Ford in the USA. This is not so, although it is true that Ford was the first in *modern* times to put the principle into business practice. The *idea* was actually used to good effect by the Royal Navy during the Napoleonic Wars, a hundred years earlier, when they established a block-making factory at Portsmouth on mass production principles.

Anything which is needed in large numbers and in identical form can be produced using mass production, for example, light bulbs, soap, sweets, cars, vans, and hi-fis. The same techniques are used to produce large amounts of liquids and semi-liquids. The production process is then usually called *continuous-flow production* and is used to make: jam, petrol, glue, beer, chemicals and medicine.

There are two other things which need to be said about mass production techniques:
▶ they are almost always high in capital (machines) to labour ratio. Today some mass production lines are fully automated and require virtually no human operators at all;
▶ in order to be most efficient – i.e. to produce goods at the lowest cost – the production lines need to be kept going most of the time. Stopping and starting them costs more than continuous production. Therefore planning has to be good. Demand for your product has to be anticipated well in advance. If demand falls off for some reason, the lines are usually kept going for quite a while afterwards.

> You should note that it is very rare for firms to mix the various types of production in the same location.

C. BATCH PRODUCTION
This third production technique falls somewhere between the first two. Any product which needs to be made in reasonably large but limited numbers is usually made using batch production techniques. Many cargo ships these days are built in a series of identical units (perhaps three or four). They cannot be made using mass production

lines because there are not enough of them but they do require *some* of the same skills as mass production. Most modern furniture is not mass produced because the designs are only released in hundreds rather than the tens of thousands or millions to which mass production is suited. The designs are, therefore, made in batches. The same applies to things like high-quality motorcruisers; some clothes, etc.

Remember – JMB

4 ▶ PRODUCTION ENGINEERING

It is the job of the Production Engineer to make sure that the product is manufactured in the most efficient way.

A. SITE

The first thing to be done is to choose the right *site* for the factory. This has been discussed in some detail in Chapter 6 but it involves the correct choice of site with respect to:
▶ land
▶ labour
▶ raw materials
▶ climate
▶ transport
▶ social facilities

B. LAYOUT

It is extremely important that the factory is laid out properly so that work can progress easily from stage to stage. In the case of the carpenter (at the beginning of the chapter) all that was needed was for him to ensure that his tools were on the right side of his workshop. In a modern factory every machine, and its various tools, has to be in the correct place. Otherwise the product might have to be moved *back* down the factory, which would be inefficient and time consuming.

There are three basic types of factory layout:

1. *Process layout* – in this type of layout each part of the production of a product is separated out and placed in a different part of the factory. In the case of the motor-cruiser mentioned above the factory may well look like this:

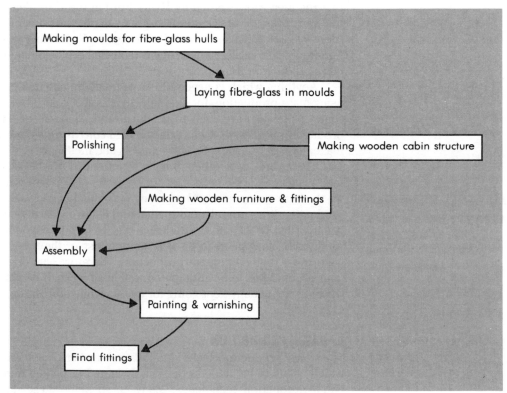

Fig.8.1. Process layout

> The difference between process and product layout is highlighted by the fact that "Process" layout can almost always make *many different types of product*. In contrast "Product" layout usually has to be radically altered before it can deal with a different product.

2. **Product layout** – here, the manufacture is done in stages along a single production line for each product. This is the type of production with which we are all familiar for things like cars and confectionary.

The manufacture of a chocolate bar might take place on one product line while a different type of sweet is produced on another line running alongside:

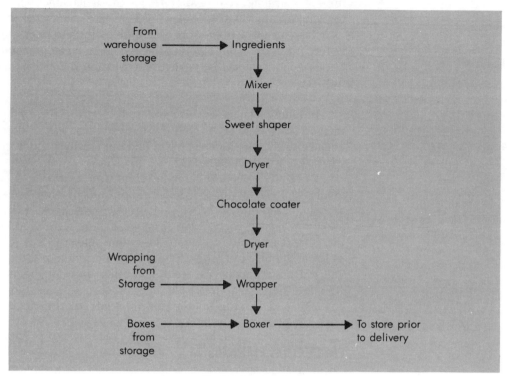

Fig.8.2. Product layout

3. **Group work** – in this type of layout the machines are all grouped together so that each member of a group of workers can take part in *every stage* of the production of the product. The object is to try to avoid the boredom which can result from production-line methods. On a production line each worker, in theory, only does one job – it could be checking sweets to make sure they all have wrappers on; or it could be adding a certain part to the wheels of a car. These jobs do not change very often and workers often get extremely bored.

The result of this boredom is often **absenteeism** – that is, the workers take time off work for any minor sickness which, in other circumstances, would not prevent them from working. It may also increase the staff turnover rate – the speed with which people leave the company and have to be replaced (the replacement and training of new staff being very expensive).

So, to try to avoid high rates of staff turnover, the idea of 'group work' was born. Each self-contained group is a factory in miniature making the **whole** product. The workers in the group have to decide their own methods of work and allocate the tasks amongst themselves. When this was tried by Philips, the electrical firm, for workers making electric light bulbs, they found that it had a remarkable effect – it stopped many workers becoming bored, it reduced staff absenteeism and it slowed down the rate of turnover.

There are undoubted benefits to the workforce from this method of manufacture but it can only be used in certain types of industry and it is sometimes not economic.

5 PRODUCTION MANAGEMENT

Production Management includes many aspects of production and each of them has its own experts. There are:

PRODUCTION ENGINEERS
These decide on the best way to actually make all the parts of the product. They decide
▶ how the product will be made;

▶ what machines will be needed;
▶ what the quality of the final product will need to be;
▶ what special *tools* or *jigs* will be needed.

Note: 'Tools' mean anything which has to be attached to a machine to allow it to do its job. Most machines these days are general purpose machines which do things like turning or drilling. To do a *specific* job those machines will need *special tools* attached to them; e.g. to drill exact holes or to create exact shapes.

'Jigs' means a framework which helps the engineers to build or make something. Before furniture is put together the engineers create a metal jig into which the bits can be slotted and glued. The jig gives them shape and keeps them together until the glue is fully set.

Production engineers also undertake *Method Study* and *Work Study*. The idea of method study is to try to find out the very best way of doing any particular task – the engineers will, for example, try to find out in which order the job needs to be done and what tools will be required.

Work study used to be called *time and motion study* and is still the subject of much suspicion by workers on the shop-floors of many firms. As many workers are paid a bonus based on how much they produce in a week, it is necessary for companies to know how much they would produce if they were working 'normally'. The work is, therefore, measured – a time-and-motion man will stand by the worker with a stop-watch and time exactly how long it takes for him to perform a certain task. After lots of adjustments are made the result is a *base time* for the job. From then on the worker who does better than this base time will earn a bonus. Work study today is often more sophisticated than this but the principles are still the same.

PRODUCTION PLANNERS

These, as their name suggests, are responsible for making sure that the production of an item is properly organised. They decide where and when to begin production; they make sure that the materials which are needed will be on hand and that there will be enough workers to do the work; and they plan which machines will be needed and for how long.

> Quality control is not simply a matter of trying to ensure that each product is of the correct quality. Today, most British firms are working towards a *complete structure*, or *system*, to ensure quality throughout every aspect of the firm's management and production system (the guidelines for this are laid down in a British Standard – 5750).

PRODUCTION CONTROLLERS

These are responsible for making sure that the plans made by the Production Planners are kept to. At one level they are called *progress chasers* and spend their time making sure that everything is following the original plan. As the work passes each machine, or each stage in the production process, the operators will hand in a slip to the Production Controller's office. By keeping an eye on these slips the progress chasers can see exactly where each job has got to and whether any delays are occurring.

INSPECTORS

These are people who are responsible for making sure that the materials which go into the product are of the right quality. They are usually, although not always part of a *quality control* system.

A. ROBOTS

Production lines have been partially automated for many years. All this means is that certain machines can automatically perform tasks which humans had previously to do by hand.

The first *semi-automatic* machines were probably watermills which carried on milling grain under water-power even when the miller was doing something else. During the nineteenth century most factories in Britain had semi-automatic machines which, using steam power, would happily stamp, drill or turn metal all day.

True automation, in which the machines do not need to be tended by a human being, did not arrive until the twentieth century. However, semi-automated production lines have been in operation for many years making all sorts of components or chemicals without people having to 'feed' them or reset them.

But none of these early attempts at automation were robots. A *robot* is an automatic machine which is able to do *more than one job*. The automatic machines of the past were only able to do one job; a machine for filling milk-bottles would need to be extensively changed if it was to be used to fill wine bottles; and a machine for drilling holes in a specific piece of metal would have to be almost completely changed if you varied the shape of the piece of metal or the number of holes to be drilled.

A robot, on the other hand, contains one or more computers and can be reprogrammed to do different tasks. A good example is the team of welding robots which Austin-Rover use to weld car bodies. This year the robots are programmed to put, say, twenty welds in twenty different places on the body of an Austin Montego. Next year, *without changing the robots themelves*, they could be reprogrammed to put 17 welds, in totally different places on a totally different car body – the Rover 200 series, for example.

The advantage of robots therefore, is that they can be re-programmed to do different jobs quite easily. They are also very accurate and, of course, do not get tired. A robot welding or painting shop can work twenty-four hours a day without breaks for tea or lunch. Although robots do break down every now and then, they are off work for less time than humans tend to be.

On the one hand, then, robots bring a great many benefits by allowing firms to achieve quite high levels of production with fewer human operators. On the other hand there are people who accuse robots of 'doing humans out of jobs'. The evidence from the countries which use robots the most, however – West Germany and Japan – is not so clear cut. Those countries have managed to employ very large numbers of robots while still keeping their rate of unemployment quite low (compared to the UK).

B. AUTOMATIC HANDLING SYSTEMS

These are simply highly computerised systems for handling all the various materials and products of the firm:

Automatic materials handling – uses a series of tubes, conveyor belts, and lifts to bring the material directly into the factory without human operators having to unload it.

Automatic warehousing – uses a similar set of conveyors to take finished goods straight off the production line and directly into the warehouse where they will be stored to await shipment to shops or customers.

Automatic transport between workstations – is a system of computerised trucks or trolleys which take the half-finished product from one work area to the next – again, without humans having to load and unload it. The best known example of such a system was the one seen in the TV advertisements for Fiat cars in which robot trolleys transported cars around without a human in sight.

C. COMPUTERISED DESIGN & MANUFACTURE

In many processes these days, especially in the high-tech industries of electronics, the whole production process from the design of the product through to its planning and production is aided by computers. The key ideas are those of:

▶ *CAD*
▶ *CAM*
▶ *CIM*

The letters CAD stand for *computer aided design* – by which designers can use the computer screen to help them design products. The computer allows the designers to draw the product, see it from many different angles, and experiment with different changes, without the need for the hundreds of detailed technical drawings which would have occupied the time of ten or twenty designers ten or fifteen years ago.

The letters CAM stand for *computer aided manufacturing* – in which parts of the production process are linked into one or more computers. These computers do many of the tasks which would have taken human beings many hours in the past. The computers can establish the production plan, timetable the machines needed, do the progress chasing and in some cases even keep an eye on quality.

The letters CIM stand for *computer integrated manufacturing* – in which the *whole* production process is overseen by a computer system. Such systems are only just being developed but offer significant improvements in efficiency because the computers can spot problems, communicate them to each other, and remedy them much faster than human operators and systems can.

EXAMINATION QUESTIONS

QUESTION 1
State three reasons why a manufacturing company might benefit from employing a purchasing department. (3 lines provided)   **(3 marks)**

QUESTION 2
Outline what is meant by 'job production' and 'batch production'.
(4 lines provided)   **(4 marks)**

QUESTION 3
Filby Wholefood Ltd are a company manufacturing biscuits. They are mass produced with part of the workforce involved in packaging the biscuits into boxes on an assembly line.
(a)   What is meant by the term 'mass production'? (2 lines provided)   **(2 marks)**
(b)   Give two reasons why Filby Wholefood Ltd might benefit from mass production.
(2 lines provided)   **(2 marks)**
(c)   Explain briefly what you view to be the disadvantages to the workforce of mass production. (4 lines provided)   **(3 marks)**
(d)   How might Filby Wholefood Ltd aim to overcome these disadvantages.
(4 lines provided)   **(3 marks)**

TUTOR'S   ANSWER   TO   QUESTION   3

(a)   Mass production means the production of a very large number of identical products as cheaply as possible, normally through components being assembled on a production line.
(b)   One reason for using mass production techniques might be to increase the output of labour. The employees of the company will be able to concentrate on one job, such as packing the biscuits into boxes. This, therefore, means that they can become expert and efficient in one particular area. A second reason could be to produce a more standard product for the market, so that the consumers would know exactly what they are getting.
(c)   One disadvantage to the workforce, of mass production is that by doing the same tasks the job may become boring. This boredom could lead to frustration and a low morale amongst the workforce. If the company has difficulty in selling its products then it may have to make some of its workforce redundant. Many of those made redundant may find it difficult to obtain further employment because they are specialised in a small area.
(d)   To relieve the boredom the company could rotate the workforce from one type of job to another every three months or so. This would ensure that the tasks they are engaged in do not become too repetitive. It would also allow the workforce to develop other skills.

C   O   U   R   S   E   W   O   R   K

ASSIGNMENT PRODUCTION

1.   Choose a product from the list below:
   ▶ Small wooden rowing boat
   ▶ Snow sled
   ▶ Summer dress for nurses
   ▶ Bird table for feeding and drinking – with shelter
   ▶ A special cake for young children

If you can think of anything else you would like to 'make' ask your teacher whether it would be a suitable subject for a project. The product you have chosen is to be your subject for 'production' (nothing actually needs to be produced, however).

2. You must **design** the product – and produce drawings which can be used by the people who will eventually have to make the bits and pieces and put them together.

3. You must produce a **production plan** which shows how the product will be made, in what stages, and how long you think it will take. You should also indicate what tools or machines will be needed.

4. The Production Plan should also list the **materials** which will be needed, how much they will cost, and where they should be bought.

5. Finally, try to estimate how long it will take to make each one of your products and whether there are any ways in which the job could be made more efficient. Could more machines be bought or could the job even be automated?

STUDENT'S ANSWER – EXAMINER'S COMMENTS

The following is a student's answer to question 3, page 78.

> This does not really answer the question. Mass production involves producing large numbers of an *identical* product (here a type of biscuit) on an assembly line.

3. a) many different types of biscuits are manufactured before being packed on an assembly line.

> Some good points. *Because* mass production techniques give high output per person employed, or per pound spent on capital equipment, the firm can produce more cheaply.

b) It is cheaper to buy the ingredients in bulk. You can produce cheaper, can sell cheaper and gain a large share of the market.

c) The work becomes boring very quickly, which makes it tedious for the workforce who may not produce as much, leading to poor efficiency within the company. The workforce are dependent on one another. If one group of the workforce is slow, this leads to a hold up in production. The workforce may not realise the role they play in the firm, as most will not see the final products.

> A good answer.

> Again a good answer which deals with the main point.

d) They could introduce job rotation so that the workforce perform a variety of jobs, which helps to reduce boredom. Attempt to improve communication between the management and sub-ordinates, so that sub-ordinates have greater participation within the company.

CHAPTER 9

MARKETING

MARKETS
TYPES OF MARKET
THE MARKETING MIX
PRODUCTS
PRODUCT POLICY
PRODUCT LIFE-CYCLE
PRODUCT
    DIFFERENTIATION
PRICING
COSTS
DEMAND
PROMOTION AND
    ADVERTISING
MARKET RESEARCH
DISTRIBUTION
TRANSPORT

GETTING STARTED

Most people think they know what 'marketing' is but very few are fully aware of the sheer scope of this management skill. It is often confused with sales or with advertising but it is these and much more. **Marketing** is a complete process within the business which includes:

▶ finding out what the customer wants – this is called **market research** and involves finding out what types of products are wanted (**product policy**) and what prices consumers are prepared to pay.

▶ helping to produce the **right product** at the **right price**.

▶ persuading customers to buy it – by means of **advertising** and **packaging.**

▶ getting the product to the customer in the most convenient and efficient way – **distribution**.

Within these broad areas there are many other aspects to marketing – some of which are looked at in greater depth in this chapter.

ESSENTIAL PRINCIPLES

1 ▶ MARKETS

We all have an idea of what a 'market' is, the most usual variety being the one which has many stalls set out in the town square on a specific weekday. Everyone knows this local market. At one time these markets were the only way in which goods were bought and sold. The open-air markets we are all familiar with are places where people with goods to sell can find people who want to buy them. Both types of person benefit because they know exactly where and when the market will be.

The markets which Marketing Managers are concerned with are just larger versions of the open-air market. All markets have:
▶ **sellers** who have goods or services to sell
▶ **buyers** who need the goods or services and have money to pay for them.

2 ▶ TYPES OF MARKET

> **Note that only the simplest of markets – the open air or enclosed ones – can be visited. The other types – consumer and industrial – are happening all around us, all the time.**

▶ **Open-air markets:** these are the simplest because all the buyers and sellers are together in one place at one time.
▶ **Consumer markets:** most goods and services, these days, are not sold in one place but across the entire country (or even the whole world). These 'consumer' markets are usually divided up into:
Single-use consumer goods – such as food, gas, newspapers
Consumer durables – such as televisions, freezers, refrigerators
Consumer services – such as post, photocopying, hairdressing, etc.
▶ **Industrial markets:** are for the goods and services bought by organisations such as companies, schools, local authorities, etc.
Industrial capital goods – machinery, buildings, etc.
Industrial services – parcel delivery, printing, cleaning, etc.

3 ▶ THE MARKETING MIX

The easiest way to remember what marketing is all about is to remember what the marketing people call the *marketing mix* – the four Ps:
▶ Product
▶ Price
▶ Promotion
▶ Place
Product: involves decisions about the product's quality, its style and design, the branding policy (what to call it and how to ensure that customers recognise the 'brand name'), how to package it, and what guarantees to offer.
Price: means the need to set not only the price itself but also any discounts which might be given and any allowances permitted (e.g. £50 for your old cooker when you buy a new one).
Promotion: marketing involves the choice of how the product is promoted – the advertising and the publicity it gets.
Place: how the product is distributed and through what types of shop or other organisations.

4 ▶ PRODUCTS

Consider the following two companies and the *products* – both toasters – which they want to sell:
▶ *Excello-Toaster Company Ltd*
This company has taken several years of technical development to design their 'Supa-toast, Mark 2' – it is very well made, of the highest quality materials and has many built-in additions. As well as toasting bread and rolls, it has a built-in clock, an adapter for browning cakes and pies, and an electric can opener. The company estimates that they can make a reasonable profit if they can sell the new toaster at £47 each.
▶ *Toast-Easi Ltd*
After a thorough period of market research, during which this company found out exactly *what* users of electric toasters want, this company has produced the 'Easi-Brek'; a basic toaster with no extras on which they can make a reasonable profit if they can sell it at a price of £17 each.

Which of these companies is more likely to be successful in the 'market' for electric toasters, and why?

The answers you have arrived at in response to the above example should already have told you a great deal about **product policy**. Most firms fall into one of two categories when it comes to product policy:

▶ they either invent new products and then try to sell them; or

▶ they find out what people want, find **better ways** of producing it and then sell it.

The first type of firm is called **product-oriented** while the second is **market-oriented**. With very few exceptions it is the second type of firm which does better in the real world.

5 ▶ PRODUCT POLICY

Product policy in marketing involves:

1. finding out what people want in a particular product and what they use it for: there is very little point in producing a radio for the mass market which has 12 different wavelengths on it if people only ever really use two or three.

2. deciding what the product should look like: this involves making sure that the design is not only up-to-date but that it is suitable for people to use (i.e. has no sharp edges, is easy to hold, etc).

3. making sure that the price is right for the people who the company thinks will be likely to buy the product.

4. getting the 'slot' in the market right with regard to other factors such as status.

6 ▶ PRODUCT LIFE-CYCLE

Almost all products have a lifetime during which they are used. During this lifetime the product will first be very new to the market and only a few people will know about it. After a while the product will become widely known and, its producers hope, popular. Then towards the end of a product's life it will become less popular and will be replaced by other newer products.

Different products have different life cycles – both in length and shape, but every life-cycle goes through a series of common stages:

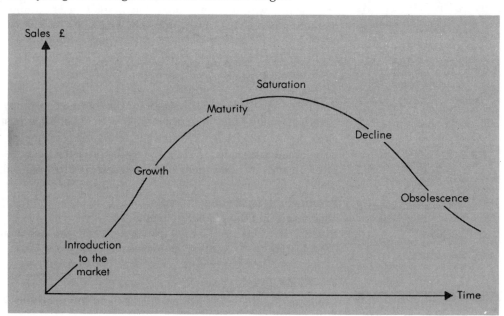

Fig.9.1. Product life-cycle

> **Although it is possible to consider the life cycle of a complete product – e.g. the television – the length of time involved is extremely long. It is more usual and useful to consider the life cycle of *individual products within the broad group* – e.g. the 'Supercol 3400 TV'.**

The **length** of the life-cycle will differ for different types of product – a television may have a very long life-cycle, whereas an item of fashion-wear may have a relatively short one. The length of a product life-cycle can be extended by improving the product or by changing the way it is marketed (eg. the way in which it is advertised, packaged, or presented to the customer).

This is just a rather technical way of saying 'making the product different'. It would be difficult to sell a new light bulb on today's market for light bulbs unless you could convince consumers that it was, somehow, different to all the others on the market. In terms of shape, light output, technology and life expectancy your light bulb would probably be the same as those of the other companies. In order to sell it you would have to **differentiate** it. This could be done by attractive packaging, competitive pricing, incentive offers (free coffee mugs with 10 labels returned, etc.) or by creative advertising (see below).

8 ▷ PRICING

Before a product can be priced you have to find out how much it is going to **cost** you to produce and how much **profit** you require from it.

9 ▷ COSTS

> ❝ Direct Costs
> + Indirect Costs
> = Total Costs
> Variable Costs
> + Fixed Costs
> = Total Costs ❞

The cost of a product may be worked out from two separate calculations:
▶ How much does it cost to make the product? This is the **Direct Cost** including such things as raw materials, pay and energy (these can also be called **Variable Costs**).
▶ What does it cost to provide the firm in which the product is to be made or, simply, for the firm to remain in existence. These are called **Indirect Costs** (or sometimes **Fixed Costs** or **Overheads**) and consist of rent for offices and factories, management salaries, and administrative costs (all of which have to be paid whether or not a product is made).

Indirect Costs are usually the same however many units of the product are made, whereas the direct costs increase as the number of units produced increases.

Companies need to know at what point in the production of a product they will begin to make a profit. This is called **break-even analysis**. The **indirect costs** are fixed and will be represented on a graph by a horizontal line = Total Fixed Costs (TFC). The **direct costs** increase as the amount produced increases and their line will be an upward sloping one = Total Variable Costs (TVC). Both sets of figures added together will give a line representing Total Costs (TC).

If one then plots on the graph a line representing the money which would come in from sales at a specific price one can see the effect of selling the product at various prices.

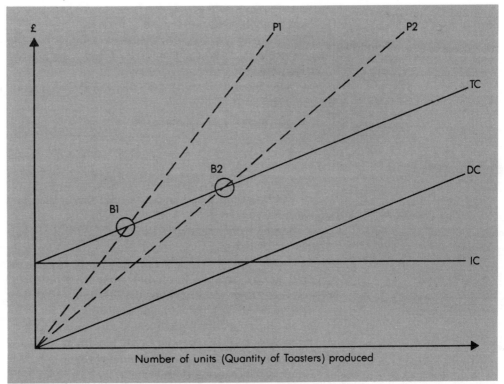

Fig.9.2. Calculating the Break-even Point

Figure 9.2 shows:
    Indirect Costs
    Direct Costs

Total Costs   line TC (TC = TFC + TVC)

The income from pricing the product at one price   line (P1)

The income from pricing the product at another price   line (P2)

In each case there is a break-even point (B1 and B2) which shows that P1 will result in the firm making profits earlier than P2.

Try to do the following example yourself:

The Sick Parrot Record Company has decided to release cheap LPs of the group **Over the Moon, Brian**. They have several people working for the group on a full time basis and have had to take on an office from which the LPs can be marketed. The first LP will have to be produced (using an expensive recording studio and several very expensive sound engineers and producers) and then manufactured (by another company). The final product will then have to be sold to the record trade, advertised to the general public and promoted to the TV and radio companies for 'air-time'. Even without producing a single record the company will have to bear weekly costs of £500 in rent, salaries and administration. Once production begins, the figures will look like this:

Production (per week)	Direct costs (variable) £	Indirect costs (fixed) £	Total costs £
0	0	500	500
100	200	500	700
200	400	500	900
300	600	500	1100
400	800	500	1300
500	1000	500	1500

Table 9.1 Pricing of Sick Parrot LP

BREAK-EVEN ANALYSIS

The company will now want to know at what point they will begin to make a profit.

Draw a graph of the three lines for direct, indirect and total costs using the figures from Table 9.1.

Now work out what sales revenue would be if Sick Parrot were to charge:

(a)   £3 for their LPs.

(b)   £4 for their LPs.

Which price would you advise them to charge?

How many LPs per week would they have to sell to break even?

This process of **break-even analysis** shows the company at what point they can begin to make a profit at a given price but it does not tell them what prices to charge. What would happen to the Sick Parrot Record Company for example if the price you have advised them to charge is one that the record buying public is not prepared to pay for a new and untried group?

10 ▷ DEMAND

It is important for a company to know what the demand for its product will be at a whole series of prices. In the case of the record company they will conduct a survey to find out. People will be asked whether they would buy a Sick Parrot LP at a variety of prices ranging from, say, £6 to £2.

It should be obvious that Sick Parrot fans will be quite prepared to pay as much as £6 while many other people would not buy their LPs unless they were quite cheap, say £2. You would almost certainly find that the higher the price, the less people would be prepared to buy, and the lower the price the more people would buy. This could be presented as a **demand curve** for the LPs on a weekly basis:

The survey of Sick Parrot might show that:
- ▶ at £5 per LP, 300 people would buy them
- ▶ at £4 per LP, 400 people would buy them, and
- ▶ at £3 per LP, 500 people would buy them.

Converted into a **graph** this would look like that in Fig 9.3.

Should the company aim to produce 300 albums a week because they can get £5 each for them, or should they aim to produce 500 albums a week at £3 each? The only way this question can be answered is to find out what the size of the profit is at each level of demand.

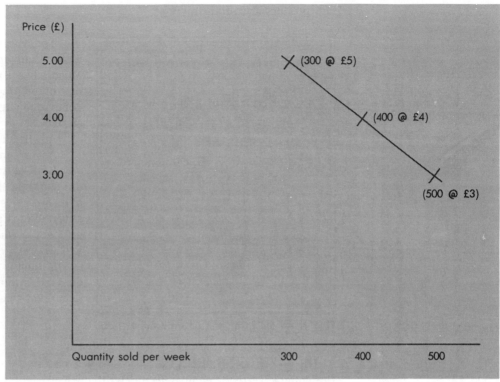

Fig.9.3. Demand curve for Sick Parrot Records (weekly)

Using all the figures you now have for the Sick Parrot Record Company Limited, fill in the gaps on the chart below:

Selling price £	Number sold per week	total sales revenue £	Total cost £	Profit £
5.00	300	1500	1100	
4.00	400			
3.00	500			

Table 9.2 **The Sick Parrot Record Company Ltd – Profit Statement**

What would be the most profitable production figure for this company and how much profit would they make per week? Remember that Total Profit = Total Revenue – Total Cost. (The answers to this question are given at the end of the Tutor's Answer section in this chapter).

You should note that changing the price or the amount of production will not necessarily make a firm more profitable.

LOSS LEADING

Sometimes a firm will deliberately ignore the pricing techniques described above and will sell a product at a very attractive, low price on which the firm actually makes a loss. The idea is usually to get people interested in the product and to attract their attention to other products in the range. It is called 'loss leading' and is most common in supermarkets.

Customers are attracted by a very low price for one product – say, sugar or potatoes – and once in the store tend to buy other things. The supermarket hopes to make up on all the other purchases what it loses on the sugar or potatoes.

Some products do not need to be advertised, as such. If they are very specialised products made in small numbers, the customers can simply be informed by letter that a new or different product is available. Most products, however, are designed for the mass market and people need to be informed that a new product is available. That was the way advertising began – simply as a way of informing a large number of people that a new product was on the market:

> **Mr Jeremiah Postlethwaite**
> begs leave to inform his many
> esteemed clients that he has,
> *AT GREAT EXPENSE,*
> developed a new
> and completely efficacious cure
> for the common cold
> and other diverse ailments.
> ———●———
> The patented *Postlethwaite Curative*
> may be purchased from Mr Postlethwaite's
> elegant new premises in the High
> Street for the sum of just
> *one shilling and sevenpence halfpenny*
> per large bottle.

Fig.9.4. An old fashioned advertisement (1870)

Today, advertising is about much more than merely giving information. Most advertising also performs at least one other function – the promotion of a company image – and, of course, persuasion.

Advertising . . . . . . ***informs,***
Advertising . . . . . . ***persuades***.

Both of these objectives can apply to the same product but at different stages of its life-cycle. When a product is new the advertising is mainly concerned with telling people what it is, how much it costs and where it can be bought. Later, when the product is mature, advertising may be directed towards increasing or defending its market share.

A. THE ADVERTISING AGENCY

Designing advertising campaigns and writing advertisements is something which should be left to the skills of ***advertising agencies***. Within an agency there are people such as copywriters (who actually write the text of the advert), artists (who draw any illustrations or who draw a series of frames to represent different stages of a TV advert), and designers (who design the overall look of the advert).

The agency is responsible, therefore, for two main functions:

1. The ***Message*** – the design and wording of the actual advertisement or the same functions for a TV or radio advertisement, and,
2. The ***Medium*** – the way in which the message is transmitted to the people who are supposed to receive it.

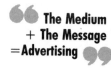
The Medium + The Message = Advertising

The ***medium*** used can be any one of (or a combination of) the following:

▶ Posters
▶ Cinema
▶ Newspapers (National Dailies and Sundays; Regional and Local)
▶ Free Newspapers (often called 'free-sheets')
▶ Magazines
▶ Leaflet 'Drops' (circulation of leaflets, through special organisations, direct into the home or business)
▶ Television
▶ Teletext
▶ Radio
▶ Direct Mail (by leaflets posted direct into the home or business)

Within each category the actual medium chosen will depend upon requirements.

B. POSTERS

Poster sites will have differing values for advertisers depending upon where they are and who will see them: hoardings outside airports are ideal for advertising airlines; those in railway stations are good for advertising snacks or magazines.

Poster sites are actually graded by a score known as the 'OTS Score' (that is the Opportunity-To-See Score) and potential advertisers can choose their poster site depending on how much they have to spend, how many people they want to see the poster and how quickly. Buses, trains and tube trains are forms of 'mobile' poster sites. The outside posters on buses are often seen by a great many people and can be very effective advertising.

C. CINEMA

Cinema advertising reaches a fairly limited audience these days and the adverts have to be tailored to the audience which attends the cinema most – the young (that is, the under 24 age group) and the unmarried. Most cinema adverts are for those products which are bought most by this age group – motorcycles, clothes, soft-drinks, etc. Cinema advertisements are expensive to make and, therefore, tend to be screened for long periods. The screening of a cinema advertisement can cost anything from £500 to £14,000 for a sixty-second advertisement, depending on where in the country it is shown.

D. NEWSPAPERS

Newspapers are very varied – from the quality national press to small specialised local papers. The type of advertisement has to be chosen very carefully according to what is being sold.

The *daily nationals* can be divided into:

1.   The *tabloids* – those popular newspapers which have a small size and generally have a high proportion of photographs to text. The tabloids rely on high circulation and the advertising which this draws to make them profitable. At the moment there are a large number of national tabloids, including:

> The Sun
> The Daily Mirror
> The Daily Mail
> The Daily Express
> The Star
> Today

2.   The *quality dailies* which are usually much larger in size and contain much more writing than pictures. The amount of detail is greater and the people who buy them are usually interested in knowing a lot about what is happening. Five papers fall into this category:

> The Times
> The Guardian
> The Financial Times
> The Independent
> The Daily Telegraph

There are also the *Sunday nationals* – those papers which are only printed for the special Sunday newspaper-reading audience. The readers are special to advertisers because Sunday newspapers tend to be read for longer and by more people in the household than the daily papers. Sunday newspapers, too, fall into 'quality' and 'mass circulation' groups:

> ► *Mass Circulation*
> The News of the World
> The Sunday Express
> The Mail on Sunday
> The Sunday Mirror
> Sunday Today

> ► *Quality*
> The Sunday Telegraph
> The Observer
> The Sunday Times
> The Independent on Sunday

66 **You can work out 'value for money' so far as newspaper ads are concerned by finding out** *how many copies the paper sells* **and** *what its average readership is.* **Both figures are available through the Audit Bureau of Circulation (ABC). Then divide the cost of the ad by each of these figures to get, respectively, the 'COST PER COPY' and the 'COST PER READER'.** 99

Advertising in national newspapers can be very expensive. The cost, like all newspaper advertising, depends on how much space you take, where it is in the newspaper (on the front page or tucked away at the bottom of an inside page, for example), and whether it is a *classified* advertisement (which means that it is all words and placed together with lots of other advertisements in a 'classified column', under a particular heading or classification such as 'Holidays in France' or 'Houses for Sale') or a *display* advertisement (one which takes up more space, is specially laid out, and usually has pictures or photographs).

In the national dailies and Sunday newspapers one insertion of a full-page advertisement can cost between £28,000 and £36,000. Smaller ads cost less, of course, but even a very small ad such as one single centimetre in one column of the classified section usually costs between £80 and £120 for a single insertion.

Against these national costs the local newspapers seem very cheap. In most local papers you could have a full-page advertisement for between £800 and £2,000, and a single column centimetre (what the papers call an SCC) in the classified section would usually cost between £5 and £10. It must be remembered, however, that it is not the total cost which really matters but the 'cost per issue' or 'cost per reader'.

E. 'FREE' NEWSPAPERS AND MAGAZINES

The traditional national, regional and local newspapers depend for their income on a combination of advertising revenue and what they call the 'cover price' (what the customer pays for the newspaper in the shop). The newspaper gets only a small proportion of the cover price because there are distribution costs to pay and the newsagents need to take a small amount for their trouble in selling the papers.

Free newspapers – which began in the United States in the 1960s and were called 'Free-sheets' – tackle the problem in a totally different way. Instead of relying on people to buy their paper in the shops they deliver it directly into people's homes. Their revenue comes entirely from the advertising which they sell in their pages.

F. MAGAZINES

Magazines also vary a great deal in the markets they are aimed at. One has only to look at the magazine display in a good newspaper store to see that it is possible to direct advertising very carefully to almost exactly the group of people for which your product is designed – from fishermen to footballers and from computer buffs to collectors of stamps.

Magazines are not only better able to direct advertising at specific groups of people, they also tend to be read by more people, and for longer, than newspapers. Newspapers are usually read for a very short time and only rarely for more than one day. Magazines, on the other hand are kept by their readers for weeks and months (depending on what type of magazine it is). A good example of this is the radio and TV magazines: *The TV Times* and *The Radio Times*, both of these magazines are kept in the homes of their readers for at least one week, and are usually looked at each day. Research has shown that they both have a 'reading life' of about 8 or 9 days. Both of these magazines have circulations of over 3 million copies every week and a full page advertisement can cost anything from £12,000 to £45,000.

There are also such things as free circulation magazines which are distributed to their readers free of charge and which, like free newspapers, survive on their advertising revenue.

G. TELEVISION

Television – specifically the commercial channels which come under the control of the IBA (the Independent Broadcasting Authority) – is one of the most powerful advertising media. The advertisement costs a great deal to make and must be prepared by experts. Once made, however, it can be shown to an audience which will be very close to the one the product is designed for.

Television companies divide the advertising day up into special *time-zones* which are priced according to the numbers of people who will be watching at the time. In addition, they can provide detailed information on the composition of the television audience at any particular time of the day (see Social Groups, below).

There are now a wide variety of TV advertising opportunities:
1. The independent stations including Yorkshire, Granada, Anglia, Borders, Thames, Grampian, Ulster and HTV (Wales).
2. Channel 4
3. Breakfast TV
4. Cable TV (In 1987 there were four cable TV networks in Britain.)
5. Satellite TV

TV advertising, as was explained above, is priced on the basis of when the advert is to be screened and how long it is. A 30 second advert on Thames TV at peak viewing times would cost around £35,000; at off-peak times the same slot would cost about £21,000.

H. TELETEXT

The *Oracle* service sells pages of ads for between £200 and £500 per week and is becoming more popular with advertisers as the number of TV sets with the ability to receive *Oracle* increases. The more sophisticated **Prestel** service also sells advertising space.

I. RADIO

Modern commercial radio provides the same sort of advertising as television and requires similar specialisms from the advertising agencies. There are now well over 50 commercial radio stations selling advertising time for varying rates. On some small stations a twenty-second slot can cost between £2 and £40. Capital Radio in London would charge between £20 and £830 for the same length of time. 1992 saw the introduction of the UK's first national commercial radio station, Classic FM.

In addition to the normal radio stations it is also possible to advertise on taped radio in hotels.

J. DIRECT MAIL

Direct Mail is now becoming a very popular form of advertising. A company can buy or rent very detailed mailing lists from specialised agencies and can, therefore, be sure of getting details of their products direct into the homes of the sort of people who will be interested in them. Most direct mail shots, these days, include some sort of 'sweetener' to attract the buyer. The most common is for the order form for the goods to double as an entry form to a competition which offers attractive prizes.

Registrar General's List	National Readership Survey List	Occupations
I	A	Higher managerial; administrative & professional
II	B	Intermediate managerial, administrative & professional
IIIn	C1	Supervisory, clerical & junior managerial
IIIm	C2	Skilled manual
IV	D	Semi-skilled & unskilled manual
V	E	State pensioners, casual earners, low-grade earners, widows, etc.

Table 9.3 Social divisions for advertising and marketing

Newspapers, television and radio all divide their readers up into the categories shown in Table 9.3 in order to assist advertisers in choosing the medium which will reach almost exactly the sort of people who are likely to want to buy their product. *The Times*, for example, is read mostly by people in the AB range, whereas *The Daily Telegraph* has a wider spread of readers from A to C1.

12 ▶ MARKET RESEARCH

Before any product can be properly marketed its producers or sellers must know a great deal about:
- ▶ the market it is to be sold into;
- ▶ the demand for the product itself;
- ▶ the needs of the buyers for design, quality, colour, etc.;
- ▶ the best media to advertise the product in;
- ▶ the best way of getting it to the buyer;
- ▶ the price which people are prepared to pay for it.

Most of this information is obtained by specialist marketing people who arrange for two types of research to be carried out:

1. **Desk Research** – which involves finding out what has been written already about the product and the market for it; and,

2. **Field Research** – which is the testing of the product idea by asking people what they think of it and by looking at the competition (how good are competitive products and how much is being charged for them).

Desk Research is highly-skilled work and requires patience and the ability to know which facts are useful and which are not. **Field research**, on the other hand, requires skill in writing questionnaires and in arranging samples of the public to try out the product.

13 ▶ PLACE

For most people, *distribution* means two things;
▶ it means how the goods are actually *transported* to the point at which the customer will be able to buy them, and
▶ it means the *type* of organisation which will actually sell the goods to the customer.
In marketing these are usually kept quite separate by calling the first *transport* and the second *distribution*. For example, a company which manufactures clothes will first want to decide what type of organisation it will use to distribute its clothes, and then it will decide how it will transport them to the final destination. We will deal with these two aspects below.

14 ▶ DISTRIBUTION

Fig.9.5. Simple distribution

The clothes manufacturer mentioned above is in the business of making clothes. As long as it decides not to get into the business of selling clothes then the avenues of distribution might look like Fig. 9.5.

The advantage of this type of distribution is that large amounts of clothes can be transported at once to only a few wholesalers in separate regions. Then the wholesalers can break down the clothes into smaller collections which the wholesalers own transport can deliver to the many clothes shops.

Fig.9.6. Complex distribution

Another possible avenue of distribution would be for the manufacturer to sell its products to one or more *mail-order catalogues* which would then sell them direct to the public. The manufacturer might even decide to sell direct to *large retail stores* but to keep several wholesalers as well to supply the smaller clothes stores.

It may even decide to sell direct to the public by *direct mail* – a method of distribution which is growing in popularity because it gives the manufacturer control over the whole process, from actually making the clothes to seeing them into people's homes. It can also be more profitable.

The avenues of distribution are many, therefore, and it will depend on the needs of the manufacturer as to exactly which ones are chosen.

15 ▶ TRANSPORT

Transport of goods can be broken down into a number of categories:
▶ Road Haulage
▶ Railway Freight
▶ Canal and River
▶ Air Freight
▶ Sea Freight
These methods are well known to most people but the major revolution in transport over the past twenty or thirty years is less well known: the use of containers.

A. CONTAINERS

These standard shaped boxes which carry cargo have made transporting goods much quicker and easier. Because the containers are all a *standard shape* and have special hooks at each corner they can simply be lifted by crane from one form of transport to another without the cargo itself being unloaded.

For example, once sugar was transported in 'hundredweight' bags – about 50 kilos – and a ship load of, say, 5,000 tonnes of sugar would actually be carried in 100,000 bags, each of which would have to be separately loaded and unloaded. Today, the same amount of sugar would be carried in about 200 containers and these would be loaded and unloaded by special crane. Containers are used on almost every type of transport – lorries, railways, ships and aircraft.

B. PIPELINES

Although they are not seen, because they are buried under the earth, pipelines carry a large amount of cargo these days. Most of it is oil and gas but, in some places, liquified coal is transported in this way.

C. CANALS

British canals are narrow, very slow, and shallow. This means that they are unsuitable for much cargo. In fact, except for certain river-linked modern canals like that for the River Severn, the cargo-carrying days of British canals are virtually over. On the continent of Europe, however, this is not the case. European canals are much wider and deeper than the British ones and so carry a great deal of cargo – especially where they link up with the great river systems of the Rhine and the Rhône.

EXAMINATION QUESTIONS

QUESTION 1

The life expectancy of a branded article is known as a product life-cycle and generally it has five phases:

(a) Introduction   (b) _____   (c) Maturity

(d) _____   (e) _____

Specimen question: London & East Anglia Group

QUESTION 2

Name three reasons why a manufacturer might carry out market research.

(i) _____ (2 marks)

(ii) _____ (2 marks)

(iii) _____ (2 marks)

Specimen question: Northern Ireland Schools Examinations Council

QUESTION 3

Franco's is a small firm making ice cream in a variety of flavours. The ice cream is sold from vans in nearby seaside resorts. Their sales vary a lot throughout the year. This means that they have a number of production and financial problems which they would like to reduce. The most they have sold in any one month is 20,000 litres.

(a) (i)   Draw a graph to show how their sales might vary from January to December.
    (ii)   Explain your reasons for drawing the graph in the way that you have.

(b) Explain what 'production and financial problems' the firm might suffer from because 'their sales vary a lot throughout the year'.

At the moment Franco's only sells ice cream. The sales have not been increasing as much as they would like. They want to expand the business but are not sure of the best way to do it. These are the choices they are considering.

1. Sell ice cream in containers to shops and supermarkets.
2. Make and sell iced lollies as well as ice cream.

3. Buy in and sell soft drinks as well as ice cream.

(c) Consider these three options and advise the firm on the choice they should make. Give reasons why this choice of action would be best.

(d) How useful do you think market research would be in helping this firm?

(e) What factors must the firm take into account before launching an advertising campaign to sell their new line?

Specimen question: Northern Examining Association

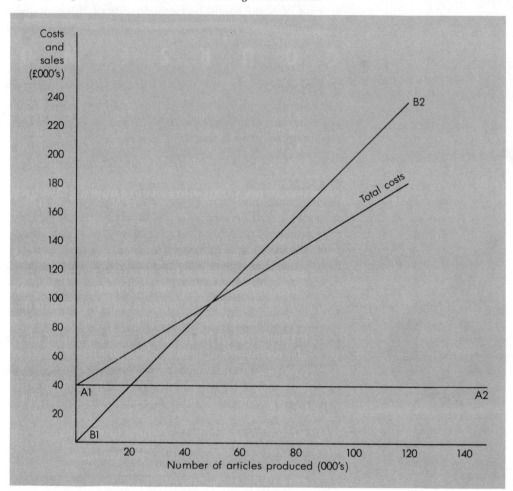

Fig.9.7.

QUESTION 4

The graph (Fig. 9.7) was prepared for the marketing manager of Mammoth Enterprises Ltd. It is used as part of a test given to applicants for a job vacancy in the marketing department. Complete the test as best you can.

(a) What do the following lines on the graph represent?

    (i) A1 to A2 _____ **(1 mark)**

    (ii) B1 to B2 _____ **(1 mark)**

(b) What is the level of output at the break-even point?

_____ **(1 mark)**

(c) What is the income from sales at the break-even point?

_____ **(1 mark)**

(d) Use the graph to find

    (i) the profit and loss if 100,000 articles are sold.

_____ **(1 mark)**

    (ii) the total revenue if 80,000 articles are sold.

_____ **(1 mark)**

    (iii) the output if total costs are £88,000.

_____ **(1 mark)**

(e) What is the selling price of an article produced by Mammoth Enterprises?

_____ **(1 mark)**

(f) Explain why total costs increase as production increases.
(4 lines for answer)   **(2 marks)**

Specimen question: London & East Anglian Group

TUTOR'S ANSWER TO QUESTION 4

(a) (i) Fixed costs   (ii) Sales Revenue
(b) 50,000 articles produced. The break-even point is where total costs equal sales revenue (total revenue).
(c) £100,000.
(d) (i) If 100,000 articles are sold the total costs are £160,000 whilst the income from sales is £200,000. The difference between the two gives a profit of £40,000.
(ii) If 80,000 articles are sold then the total revenue is £160,000.
(iii) If total costs are £88,000 then the output level is 40,000.
(e) To find out the selling price of an article you have to divide the total revenue from sales by the total production, i.e.

$$Price = \frac{Total\ Revenue}{Total\ Production}$$

So, referring to the graph, if you take any level of production the price will be the same, e.g. for a total production of 100,000 articles there is total revenue of £200,000, so the price is £2.
(f) The total costs of Mammoth Enterprises Ltd will consist of both fixed costs and variable costs. If the business produces nothing then it will still have the fixed costs to pay. These costs will include the rent and rates on the premises and interest on any loans they have obtained from a bank and as the graph shows they are fixed at £40,000. Variable costs on the other hand vary with how much is produced and include such things as raw materials, lighting and heating and the wages of labour. Total costs will therefore increase because variable costs increase as production increases.

Answers to the Profit statement (Table 9.2) for Sick Parrot Records.

Sales price	No. sold	Total revenue	Total cost	Profit
£5.00	300	1500	1100	400
£4.00	400	1600	1300	300
£3.00	500	1500	1500	0

C O U R S E W O R K

ASSIGNMENT 1 – PRODUCT POLICY

Most companies conduct regular surveys to find out how their products are faring in the marketplace and to see whether any changes will have to be made. Choose an everyday product from the range of consumer products on the market today – toasters, washing machines, microwave ovens, cars, motor-cycles, computers, TV's, stereos, etc. Make up a questionnaire in order to find out what people around you – your family, neighbours, friends, teachers, etc – feel about this product. The questionnaire should cover at least the following points (but you will be able to think of more):
1. What is the main use of the product; are there any other uses to which it is put?
2. Where is it used and at what times of day; how often is it used?
3. What do people think about the design of the product – is it awkward to use or dangerous?
4. Is the price right or is it too high or too low?
5. What do people think of its colour, packaging, etc?
6. What improvements would people want to make to it?
When you have finished the questionnaire and have surveyed a reasonable number of people, put all the results into a chart or written report so that they will be of use to 'Product Planners'. Add to that chart your own detailed recommendations for the development of the product.

ASSIGNMENT 2 –
ADVERTISING

Choose a particular type of product which has a number of competing brands on the market. It can be any product which is on sale in your area – from cars to perfume, from food to washing machines – as long as there is more than one brand. If you were to choose washing machines, for example, you would find that there are many competing brands, such as Hoover, Hotpoint, Servis, Zanussi, and Bendix.

How is this product advertised? Make a list, with examples where possible, of all the types of advertising of this particular product. Do the sellers use papers, radio, TV, posters, etc? What sort of brochures do they produce? Which brand of the product do you think has the most effective advertising and why?

When you have completed the necessary research, write up your findings, with illustrations and samples, into a report on the advertising of your product and its effectiveness. Make some recommendations of your own as to how the advertising could be improved.

STUDENT'S ANSWER – EXAMINER'S COMMENTS

This is a student answer to question 4, page 92.

4. a) i) Fixed costs of producing the articles.

      ii) Sales Revenue line.

b)   50,000 articles.

c)   £100,000

" Good idea to present the formula. "

d) i) Revenue - Costs = Profit.

      200   - 160   = £40,000 profit.

                     Loss = 0.

" Try not to confuse the Total Revenue and Total Cost lines on the graph. The answer is 40,000. If the output _was_ 44,000 then Total Cost would be £92,000. "

      ii) £160,000

      iii) 44,000

e)   £2

" A good final part and a good answer overall. "

f) Because the costs include fixed costs, eg. rent, and variable costs, eg. electricity, manpower. These variable costs increase as output increases ∴ Total Cost increases.

10

INTERNATIONAL
TRADE

G E T T I N G   S T A R T E D

You may have seen articles like those shown in Fig. 10.1 in the newspapers or on the TV news and most of us assume that these exports are good for Britain. Likewise, most people seem to believe that imported goods are somehow bad. In the past, governments have spent a great deal of money trying to get people to '**Buy British**' and even today, the Government spends many hours negotiating limits on the number of Japanese cars which may be imported.

If exports are good because they earn us lots of money from other countries, can imports be bad? After all, every export is someone else's import!

Most economists today agree that trade is almost always good for the whole world because everyone benefits from it in the long run. The simplest reason for trade is that countries sell goods to each other because they produce goods which other countries want at a price which is cheaper than they can make them themselves.

The case of Japanese cars illustrated this point. Although cars are made in the UK, the Japanese manufacturers are very efficient and can make them cheaper and then, in theory, sell them cheaper in Britain. If a British consumer can choose between having a British car for £7,000 or a Japanese car of the same quality for £6,500 then it is likely that he or she will choose the car from Japan. In doing so, a saving of £500 is made which can be spent on something else. Trade allows these sorts of savings to be made all over the world and, if each country specialises in making those goods which it can make cheapest and best, brings benefits to everyone.

INDIA
£¹/₂m contracts for Tungstone

Tungstone Batteries Ltd
Lathkill Street
Market Harborough
Leicestershire LE16 9EZ

Contracts worth more than £¹/₂m to supply batteries and equipment for a major new 3000 megawatt thermal power station currently under construction at Rihand in Uttar Pradesh, India, for the National Thermal Power Corporation have been won by industrial standby power specialist Tungstone Batteries Ltd, a Hawker Siddeley company.

The order, from main contractor NEI, gives Tungstone responsibility for the engineering and supply of all the battery, charger and distribution board installations. The standby systems, which include 24 separate batteries totalling 1750 planté cells, will provide power for the UPS, telecoms, pumping, lighting and switchgear tripping and closing systems in the main plant and sub-stations of this new station Mirzapur district, which in its first phase will have two thermal units each generating 500 megawatts.

Rihand power station is the sixth major order won by Tungstone in the past three years, including contracts for Hong Kong, Saudi Arabia, Chile and Korea.

CANADA
£2m order for British computers

Immediate Business Systems plc
3 Clarenden Drive
Wymbush
Milton Keynes

British portable computer specialist, Immediate Business Systems (IBS) of Milton Keynes, has been given a £2m order to supply 550 portable computers, support equipment and software to Hydro-Quebec of Canada, the largest utility company in North America.

The hand-held computers will be used for in-field reading of electricity meters. As well as providing software for the operation of individual computers, IBS is also supplying a system to link 69 field offices spread throughout Quebec with Hydro-Quebec's central computer facility in Montreal.

Source: *Overseas Trade* (the magazine of the British Overseas Trade Board) Nov. 1986.

Fig.10.1. Export Orders

ESSENTIAL PRINCIPLES

1 > UNITED KINGDOM TRADE

Note that a thousand millions is ONE BILLION while a million millions is ONE TRILLION. Although these differ from the old-fashioned British versions they are now the internationally recognised definitions of the terms 'billion' and 'trillion'.

The size of British trade is staggering: Britain is one of the countries in the world which relies on trade for a large proportion of its economic activity. Almost 30% of everything we earn comes from trade. In value it amounts to well over £100,000,000,000 (£100 billion) every year. Almost two-thirds of British exports go to Europe – some 68% – and half of our exports go to other members of the European Community (the EC). Of the rest, about 11% of UK exports go to the USA and 2% to Japan.

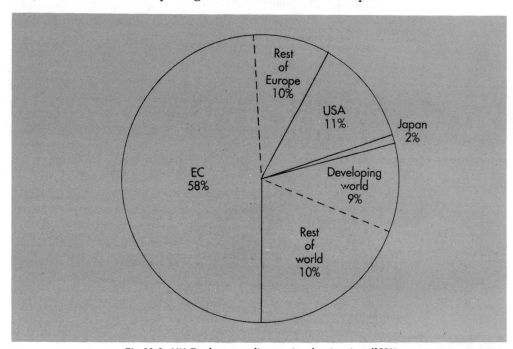

Fig.10.2. UK Trade according to its destination (1991)

Since 1960 there has been a substantial change in the countries with which Britain trades most (see Table 10.1). In 1960 only 21% of British trade was with the EC; today it is 58%. In 1960 over 30% of British trade was with the 'developing world' (the countries of Africa, South America and the Middle and Far East). Today, the proportion of trade taken by these countries is only 9%. Britain did not really begin to make its Empire independent until the 1960s and, during that decade, was still trading a great deal with the colonies and with the new members of the 'Commonwealth'. By the mid 1970s, Britain had joined the EC and had made most of its former colonies independent. Trade to and from Britain has, therefore, changed from being mainly worldwide to being mainly European.

	1960	1991
Western Europe	32	68
(of which EC Countries)	(21)	(58)
USA	10	11
Japan	1	2
Developing Countries	31	9

Table 10.1 The changing nature of British trade: (% of total UK trade)

THE GEOGRAPHY OF UK TRADE 1960 TO 1991

Most of the exports leaving Britain used to be manufactured goods; such as cars, machines, clothes, and washing machines. Today, that has changed. With the discovery of large amounts of oil in the North Sea in the late 1960s, oil has become one of Britain's most important exports. In 1960 oil and fuel used to account for just 4% of British exports; by 1991 it accounted for almost 10%. Similarly, whereas manufactured goods used to make up half of our exports in 1960, they accounted for only 34% in 1991. Unfortunately, Britain has been losing her place as a major trading nation. In the late nineteenth century, half of all world exports came from the United Kingdom. In 1960 our share had dropped to just 17% and by 1991 it was only 7%. In 1991 the world's greatest trader was Japan, closely followed by the United States and Germany.

The reasons for this decline are many, but the following would appear to be the main ones:

1. Other countries throughout the world have become industrialised and have competed against Britain in the world markets.
2. Many of these new competitors have had an initial advantage of having relatively cheap labour costs (compared to wages in the UK).
3. Britain's industry has been very slow to compete in world markets.
4. The quality and the design of goods made in Britain has been poor for many years.
5. There is some reason to believe that Britain has had too few qualified managers – especially in the field of marketing.
6. Most British managers do not speak foreign languages.
7. There is also reason to believe that the value of the pound may have been 'too high' for most of the 1950s and 1960s. The result of this would have been that British exports would have been very expensive for people in other countries to buy.

1990	£m
Visible exports	102,038
Visible imports	120,713
Balance of trade (Visible balance) =	– 18,675
Invisible exports	117,350
Invisible imports	113,055
Invisible balance =	+ 4,295
Balance of payments on current account =	– 14,380

Table 10.2 The balance of trade and the balance of payments on current account

2 ▶ THE BALANCE OF TRADE

There are two types of exports and imports: *visible* and *invisible*.

Visible trade – consists of all those goods which can be seen and touched such as machines, televisions, motorcycles, refrigerators, food and, of course, the raw materials which Britain exports, mainly oil.

Invisible trade – refers to all those items which we export, which cannot be seen or touched, such as sales of insurance, banking services, airline seats, or sea cargo space. One of Britain's fastest growing invisible exports is *tourism*. Every year millions of visitors come to visit Britain. Unfortunately, British tourists abroad spend more money than do foreign tourists in Britain, so we have a *deficit* in our tourist trade.

 Tourism is an **EXPORT** even though the money is spent in this country. We are really selling £'s abroad – exporting our currency in return for other currencies – in exactly the same way as we sell clothes abroad in return for other currencies.

The balance of trade is obtained by taking all visible imports away from visible exports. If the result is a minus value (negative) then it is said that there is a *deficit* in the balance of trade. If the answer is positive, then there is a *surplus*. In 1991, Britain exported more oil than we imported. The result was a *surplus* of £1,518 millions on our oil trade. In 1990, Britain imported more manufactured goods than we exported. The result was a *deficit* on manufactured trade of £8,750 millions. The *balance of trade* for 1990 ended up in deficit at minus £14,380 millions.

3 ▶ BALANCE OF PAYMENTS ON CURRENT ACCOUNT

The balance of payments is similar to the balance of trade, but takes more information into account.

CURRENT ACCOUNT

Whereas the balance of trade takes only *visible* exports and imports into account, the *Current Account* includes the balance of trade *plus* any invisible transactions which have been undertaken between Britain and other countries during the year.

4 ▶ EXPORTING AND IMPORTING

Selling a new car within the UK is a relatively straightforward affair – one simply transports the car to the garage and the garage sells to the customer. The only taxes to pay are Motor Tax and VAT to the British Government.

Selling the same car in a foreign country is a different prospect entirely. The foreign government will have to be assured that the car is fit for use on the roads (and they may have different laws on lights, indicators, seat belts, exhaust emissions, etc.). They may also charge a tax before you can take the car into the country to sell it. This tax, payable at the border is called a *tariff* (or customs duty). Such tariffs are called a *barrier to trade*, since they increase the price you will have to charge for your new car in the foreign garage and make it easier for the native manufacturers to sell their cars instead.

5 ▶ EXPORTING

A. EXPORT PROCEDURES AND DOCUMENTS

The process of exporting can be extremely complex. The goods have to be transported to the docks or airport, passed through British customs, cleared through another set of customs on arrival and eventually presented to the correct customer. In addition, if the goods are dangerous or are composed of chemicals or drugs, or are perishable foodstuffs, then certificates will be needed to show that various health or safety checks have been made. For certain countries, a licence may be needed before a particular product can be sold to the customer.

Here are just some of the forms and documents which might be needed:

1 Bill of Lading
Containing details of the goods being shipped, their destination and which ship they will be travelling on, etc.

2 Export invoice
The 'bill' to the customer, requiring payment once he has received the goods.

3 Certificate of origin
To prove that the goods have come from the UK and are not being imported under false pretences from a different country whose goods might be prohibited from entry.

4 Certificate of value
To prove the goods are worth what the invoice says they are worth – usually, so that the correct duty can be levied.

5 HM Customs declaration
A signed statement of what the parcels, packages or crates contain.

6 Declaration of dangerous goods
Required by international law for certain classes of goods such as explosives or volatile chemicals.

7 Certificate of insurance
Needed by the shipping company, or airline, or by your customer, so that they can be assured that the value of the goods is covered should an accident happen.

8 Health certificate
Needed for drugs and similar products and for transport of animals.

9 Import licence
Permission to import your goods. Needed for certain countries and products. In some cases, for example high technology goods, an *export* licence might be needed.

B. PAYING FOR EXPORTS
Obtaining payment for goods has always been an uncertain process. Even in the UK domestic market, a great deal of trade goes unpaid for and producers often have to engage in lengthy and expensive court cases to get their money. When sending goods

> 66 All imports also have to be paid for. But because foreign businesses don't want £'s (they cannot spend them in their own countries) we have to *SELL* £'s to *BUY* foreign currencies. 99

abroad, the dangers of non-payment are even worse because it is much more difficult to 'chase' non-payers through foreign courts. Consequently, it is vital to be extremely careful about payment when sending goods overseas.

There are various ways of getting paid. Some are more reliable than others:

1 Open account

This can only be used where you know the buyers very well and trust them to pay. It involves you simply sending the goods, and then sending an invoice by post (in exactly the same way as with a UK customer). The buyer is then expected to pay after, say, one month. If they do not then it can be almost impossible to get them to pay and will certainly cost a great deal of money – often more than the value of the shipment!

2 Payment with order

This is the way that all exporters would like to be paid. However, few buyers will send money for a product they have not yet seen, so it is not used for any but the smallest items.

3 Draft

This is the modern name for a **bill of exchange** and there are two basic types of draft: sight drafts and term drafts.

▶ **Sight draft**: the seller draws up a document saying that the buyer agrees to pay as soon as the goods are delivered and the documents handed over.

▶ **Term draft**: this is the same except that the buyer does not need to pay until 30, 60 or 90 days after the documents have been handed over.

4 Letter of credit

This is a more modern way than the draft system. Letters of credit are arranged through a buyer's bank and the seller's bank and are normally made **irrevocable** – that is, they cannot be cancelled once signed, and the seller is guaranteed payment.

C. THE EFFECT OF THE EC

The European Community (EC) is a group of twelve countries, as follows:

United Kingdom	France	Spain	Greece
Netherlands	Luxembourg	Italy	Germany
Portugal	Eire	Belgium	Denmark

The EC is described in more detail in Ch. 18. Apart from many other agreements, these countries have agreed to do away with all Tariff Barriers between themselves. The object of this is to make international trade between the members of the EC much easier. Instead of each country of the EC having its own separate tariffs for goods coming into Europe from the rest of the world, they have all agreed to have one common tariff called the **Common External Tariff** (CET). Regardless of where goods enter the EC, the same tariff has to be paid.

6 ▶ IMPORTING

BARRIERS TO TRADE

There are a number of ways in which countries seek to discourage imports.

1 Tariffs

These make trade between countries more difficult. Tariffs are taxes on goods coming into the country.

2 Quotas

These are a way of preventing too many imports from coming into any country. A quota on a product simply means that only a certain number can be imported in that year. In recent years, many EC countries have put quotas on the number of Japanese cars allowed to be imported, so as to protect their own car industries against the Japanese imports.

3   Subsidies

These are amounts of money given by governments to certain industries to help them to stay in business or to protect jobs. Because they make it easier for those companies to stay in business, the subsidies also make it easier for them to compete *against* imported products. In the last few years, American steel firms have complained that they find it difficult to export steel to Europe because of the subsidies given by European governments to their own steel firms.

4   Other barriers to trade

Firms which export have to face a great many additional barriers such as:
▶ the fact that they are usually exporting to a country with a different language and currency.
▶ possible exchange controls – limit on the amount of money which a firm can take out as profits.
▶ import regulations – involving lots of complex forms.
▶ different technical standards for certain goods in foreign countries.

A good example of how standards can become barriers to trade occurred between Britain and France in the early 1980s. The French would not allow British lamb to be sold in France because, they argued, it had too many preservatives in it and did not, therefore, meet the French health regulations. Britain, on the other hand, refused to allow French UHT milk into the country on the grounds that it was not sterilised to a sufficiently high standard.

Summary of barriers to trade:
▶ Tariffs
▶ Quotas
▶ Subsidies
▶ Language
▶ Exchange Controls
▶ Money/Currency
▶ Import regulations
▶ Standards

> ❝ Note that, until 1987, it was difficult to export beer to Germany. The West German government had a very strict law which said that no beer sold in that country could contain any artificial additives or chemicals. ❞

---

7 ▶ ORGANISATIONS IN INTERNATIONAL TRADE

There are a great many organisations involved in international trade today. Some come under the control of the *United Nations* in New York, while others have been set up by groups of countries. Among the organisations which come under the United Nations are:

A. THE INTERNATIONAL MONETARY FUND (IMF)

This organisation was set up in 1947 to try to ensure that the world's currencies were kept at reasonably stable rates against each other. The IMF had a system of what were called *Fixed Exchange Rates* so that, no matter how long the duration of a contract, a firm anywhere in the world would know exactly how much they would get for selling their product. Unfortunately, this system broke down in the early 1970s and since then we have had a system of *Floating Exchange Rates*. This means that the value of any currency can change at any time in terms of another currency. For example:

If you sell a car to an American, he may well want to see the car when it arrives in the US before actually paying for it. You want £5,000 for the car, and the current exchange rate is $2=£1. A simple calculation tells you, therefore that you will have to charge the American $10,000 (5,000×2=10,000), and that is the agreed price. You then put the car on a ship and wait for it to arrive in the USA. Two months later, the car arrives, and is examined by the American, who is very satisfied with it. He immediately sends you a cheque for $10,000.

Unfortunately, the exchange rate has changed during the period, and is now $2.50=£1. Another simple calculation, $10,000÷2.50 reveals that you will only receive £4,000 for the car, even though the American paid the full $10,000 as agreed.

If you multiply this situation many times then you can see why business people worry about the way in which the exchange rate is moving.

Try the same example, but this time assume that the £/$ exchange rate weakens to $1.75=£1. How much will you receive for your car?

B. THE UNITED NATIONS CONFERENCE ON TRADE AND DEVELOPMENT (UNCTAD)

Set up in the mid-1960s, UNCTAD has interests in many areas regarding international trade. It is concerned with:

▶ transport by sea and the charges which shipping companies levy.

▶ the activities of *multi-national companies*; those giant companies which have factories making products in many different countries (eg. Ford, General Motors, IBM, British Petroleum).

▶ how barriers to trade work and, especially, how they work to the disadvantage of the poorer countries of the world.

▶ setting up systems to protect the prices of certain commodities (copper, tin, tea, sugar, etc.) which are particularly important to the economies of the world's poorer countries.

C. THE GENERAL AGREEMENT ON TARIFFS AND TRADE (GATT)

GATT was established after World War II with the object of reducing the average levels of tariffs on manufactured goods throughout the world. In this it has been very successful. In 1945 it was not unusual to find tariffs of 80%, 100% or even 150% on certain types of goods. Today, the average levels of tariffs on manufactured goods is just 7%. GATT operates through a series of discussions between member countries. These discussions can take many years to arrive at a conclusion and they are called 'rounds of negotiations'. The most recent 'rounds' were the 'Kennedy Round' (1961–63), the 'Tokyo Round' (1972–75), and the 'Uruguay Round' (1986–92).

There are two other organisations which must be mentioned. Neither is a United Nations organisation: both were set up by European countries to solve their own trade problems.

D. THE EUROPEAN FREE TRADE ASSOCIATION (EFTA)

EFTA's main member, when it was set up in 1959, was the UK. The object of EFTA was to reduce tariffs to zero between the member countries, so that trade could increase. The members were: UK, Portugal, Switzerland, Austria, Sweden, Norway, Ireland and Iceland. Since several of these members have since joined the EEC, EFTA is now a very small organisation mainly comprised of the four non-EEC countries of Norway, Sweden, Austria and Switzerland.

E. THE EUROPEAN COMMUNITY (EC)

The EC began with very similar aims to those of EFTA but was formed earlier. The original six members, West Germany, France, Italy, Belgium, Netherlands and Luxembourg, formed the EC in 1957. Unlike EFTA, the aims of the EC were much wider than simply reducing tariff barriers. The members wanted to co-operate on a wide variety of issues, from agriculture to energy and from industry to education. The Treaty of Rome, under which the EC is governed, says that the eventual aim of the Community is unity for the people of Europe. The EC affects trade in a large number of ways, but the following are the main ones:

▶ by subsidising farming through the Common Agricultural Policy (CAP), the EC helps European farmers to avoid competition from farmers in other parts of the world.

▶ similar subsidies apply to certain industries like steel.

▶ the 'Competition Policy' has been set up to make sure that very large companies, or groups of companies, do not use their power to make the public pay too much for their goods.

▶ the 'Social Policy' gives money for training and, thereby, hopes to make European firms more able to compete against overseas firms such as those from Japan.

8 ▶ MARKETING ABROAD

British firms which decide to try to sell their products *abroad* can get a great deal of help from various institutions:

A. THE BRITISH OVERSEAS TRADE BOARD (BOTB)

The BOTB is a very large organisation whose main aim is to help British companies to sell their products and services overseas. They can give advice on all of the things which business people might be concerned about, including:

▶ what the regulations are in the countries they are exporting to.

▶ who they can use to help market their product in that country (for example an agent or distributor).

▶ how they can try to make sure that their overseas customer actually pays the bill.

▶ how to guard against losing money because of currency movements.

▶ the chance to go on trade missions to other countries to see whether there are any customers who might wish to buy their products.

B. TRADE ORGANISATIONS

Almost every type of business has its trade association, which gives its members help and advice on exporting matters.

C. BANKS

Banks will, of course, help exporters with loans to tide them over while they are waiting for payment for exported goods, but they also do much more. Many banks will give advice to small exporters about how they should set about the task of exporting. Bank managers will arrange finance and will suggest all sorts of other experts who might be able to help.

D. THE EXPORT CREDITS GUARANTEE DEPARTMENT (ECGD)

The ECGD is a Government organisation whose job is to help British firms bear the risks of exporting. Just as with sales within the UK, bad debts might arise from overseas customers not paying for their goods. The ECGD offers a special 'insurance' scheme, known as the Export Credit Guarantee Scheme, whereby in return for a premium, the Government will pay most of any bad debts which occur, subject to approval of the customer's status and any particular risks associated with certain countries.

E. OTHER TRADE ASSISTANCE

In recent years commercial firms have also set up schemes by which they help exporters; they now offer a wide range of services including:

▶ lending money to the exporter to cover the period while they are waiting to be paid,

▶ help to collect payment from the customer,

▶ help with the necessary sales documentation and record-keeping,

▶ checking on customers credit rating i.e. whether they will pay their bills,

▶ arranging credit insurance similar to that offered by the ECGD.

EXAMINATION QUESTIONS

QUESTION 1

Name a government organisation which offers insurance against many of the risks involved in exporting.

_____

Specimen question: London & East Anglian Group.

QUESTION 2

What is meant by

    (i)   visible trade?_____

                                                      (1 mark)

    (ii) invisible trade?_____

                                                      (1 mark)

Specimen question: Northern Ireland Schools Examinations Council.

QUESTION 3

The information given is the trading figures for Rurilanda in 1993.

	£m
Visible Exports	55,000
Invisible Exports	50,000
Visible Imports	70,000
Invisible Imports	30,000

(a) Using the figures calculate
    '(i) the Balance of Trade   **(2 marks)**
    (ii) the Balance of Payments on Current Account   **(2 marks)**
(b) Name three items of invisible trade. (1 line provided)   **(3 marks)**
(c) Outline three ways in which British businesses benefit from international trade.
    (3 lines provided)   **(6 marks)**
(d) Why might the UK government urge the UK consumers to 'Buy British'?
    (2 lines provided)   **(2 marks)**

TUTOR'S ANSWER TO QUESTION 3

(a) (i) Visible Exports (£55,000m) minus Visible Imports (£70,000m) equals the Balance of Trade (−£15,000m)
(ii) Balance of Trade (−£15,000m) plus Invisible Exports (£50,000m) minus Invisible Imports (£30,000m) equals the Balance of Payments on current account (£5,000m)
(b) Insurance, banking and tourism.
(c) (i) The British business may obtain a number of its raw material requirements from abroad (visible imports).
(ii) The British business may sell a large proportion of its finished products abroad (visible exports).
(iii) The British business may wish to hire specialist services from abroad. One way in which it could achieve this is by a consultancy arrangement with a foreign firm (invisible import).
(d) The UK government may urge the UK consumer to 'Buy British' because it wants to protect jobs in UK industries and improve the Balance of Payments on current account.

C O U R S E W O R K

**ASSIGNMENT
ADVERTISING
TOURISM**

Tourism is a growing contribution to Britain's trade and, wherever you live, you will undoubtedly be close to a tourist area.
▶ Try to get hold of a copy of the local tourist guide book. Every area in the British Isles produces a booklet which tells visitors what attractions there are in the region.
▶ Make a list of the attractions which you think would be of most interest to American tourists in your region and make up an advertisement which might be placed in an American travel magazine and which would attract them to your area.
▶ What sort of businesses benefit from tourism in your region and why?
▶ Are there any parts of the region which you think tourists would not want to see? Is there any way that these 'unattractive' areas could be made more interesting and attractive?
▶ Make a list, with explanations, of the ways you would improve your region for tourists.

STUDENT'S ANSWER – EXAMINER'S COMMENTS

This is a student's answer to question 3, page 104.

3) 'Trading figures for Ruritanda.'

> **Imports and exports the wrong way round! Answer should be – £15,000(m).**

1) i)   Balance of trade
         Imports less Exports
         70,000   –   55,000 = £ 15,000 (m)

ii)   Balance of payments on current
                                    Account.

         Visible Imports + Invisible Imports =
                                    70, 000
                                    30, 000
                                    £ 100,000 (m)

less

> **Again, the wrong way round. The answer should be +£5,000(m). The usual *method* is to take the Balance of Trade and *add* that to the Invisible Balance.**

         Visible Exports + Invisible exports =
                                    55, 000
                                    50, 000
                                    £ 105,000 (m)

                         £ –£5,000 (m) deficit

> **Good. Should strictly say British Government expenditure on armed forces and embassies overseas.**

2) 3 items of invisible trade are – the British Governments' expenditure on armed forces; the British Governments' expenditure on embassies; and British Tourists' expenditure overseas.

> **Good, though language a bit clumsy.**

3) Three ways in which British businesses benefit from International trade:– what raw materials the U.K. is lacking from can be obtained from other countries – this is very important for home businesses; foodstuffs which

> **The last two ways are about *consumers* benefit, but the question is about *business* benefit.**

Britain can't supply must be imported eg. cereals, sugar, tea coffee. U.K. producers can't meet the total home demand, so they have to import many finished goods to satisfy the demand.

" A good answer. "

4) The U.K. Government may urge U.K. Consumers to 'Buy British' to boost the production of home companies and so reduce unemployment. Also to reduce the threat of unfair competition from other countries whose labour is very cheap and can steal our market with their cheaper products.

BUSINESS ACCOUNTS

G E T T I N G   S T A R T E D

If you should start your own business you would usually begin in a relatively simple fashion; there will be products or services which you make or provide, you will sell these to the public, and, with luck, there will be profits.

Let us imagine that Julie decides to start up in the clothing trade under the name of Julie's Fashions. She has an assistant (Sally) who is good at selling, whilst Julie is good at designing and making clothes. Julie's first task will be to design the clothes, after which she will make up a set for demonstration and try to sell these and further copies. The very first thing which needs to be done is to try to see what the demands of the business will be for cash.

CASH FLOW
BOOKKEEPING
DOUBLE ENTRY
THE TRIAL BALANCE
PROFIT
THE BALANCE SHEET
ANALYSIS OF ACCOUNTS:
  BUSINESS RATIOS

ESSENTIAL PRINCIPLES

All firms need to make payments for wages, rent, goods purchased, electricity, etc., but these payments are not all going to be made at the same rate throughout the year. Julie's first task therefore, is to try and calculate what payments will have to be made month by month and what cash will be coming in during these same months. The chart she might use would be similar to Table 11.1.

(£) Month	Jan	Feb	Mar	Apr	May	Jun
Bank balance on 1st of month	0	3,500	3,400	2,900	(600)	250
Sales	0	5,000	6,000	5,000	8,000	9,000
Owner's capital	10,000	–	–	–	–	–
Total Receipts (A)	10,000	8,500	9,400	7,900	7,400	9,250
Outgoings:						
Purchases	5,000	3,000	5,000	6,000	4,000	3,000
Wages	1,000	1,000	1,000	2,000	2,000	2,000
Rent	500	500	500	500	500	500
Electricity	–	600	–	–	650	–
Total Payments (B)	6,500	5,100	6,500	8,500	7,150	5,500
Bank at month end (A-B)	3,500	3,400	2,900	(600)	250	3,750
( ) = overdrawn						

Table 11.1 Cash flow forecast

The chart shows a ***cash flow forecast*** for a business which has begun with £10,000 of capital from its owner. The owner has calculated how much cash is likely to come in over the first six months, from his ***capital*** plus cash from sales. It represents an estimate of what the firm will be 'earning' on a month by month basis. Beneath these are all the ***outgoings*** of the firm, including wages, purchases of materials, and electricity.

The chart looks complicated, but it is a very useful way of planning what the cash needs of a business will be. For example, the owner now knows he might have to seek an overdraft of £600 in April.

In the case of Julie's Fashions, we are assuming that Julie has not calculated her ***cash flow*** requirements but has merely begun business. This is a very common way for businesses to start, but it is inadvisable. Proper planning at the start can help to avoid many problems. Indeed, if the business is going to need to borrow money from the bank to help it get started, the bank manager will insist on seeing a full cash-flow forecast before he will consider lending any money.

Assuming that Julie's Fashions has begun business, the minimum that Julie has to do is keep some financial records. Keeping accounts does not come easily to many business people, and few have had any formal training.

At the end of the first month of trading, let us assume that Julie's Fashions has had the following transactions:

Day		£
1	from Julie to start business	1000
2	bought material	150
5	bought new sewing machine	360
6	paid Sally wages	30
9	sale for cash to 'Young Fashions'	400
11	bought materials	600
17	Julie took for herself	100
20	sale for cash to 'Jim's Market Stall'	300
23	paid rent and electricity for new workroom and office	150
25	sold on credit to 'Stephanie's Boutique'	50
28	sold on credit to 'Maison Roger'	1000

At the end of the month, Julie is likely to wonder whether her business has made a profit, and also whether she is running the business efficiently. To answer such questions, one needs to keep 'books', and it is not enough simply to keep lists of amounts spent and amounts received.

3 ▷ DOUBLE-ENTRY

Bookkeeping methods have remained largely unchanged for hundreds of years, but nowadays, computers are likely to be used by many businesses to speed up the process. Double-entry bookkeeping sounds very difficult but it simply means that two separate records are made for each transaction. This sounds like a great way of making extra work for accountants, but it is also very good sense.

Every transaction of a firm has two effects; for example, when Julie bought the sewing machine, *two* things happened; firstly, Julie had to take £360 out of the business's cash, and secondly, she was able to bring in a new sewing machine as an *asset* for the business.

To record this in the books, she needs two entries:
▶ firstly taking £360 out of the Bank Account
▶ secondly adding a machine worth £360 to the Machinery Account.

We can take some of the other transactions and see how the double-entry works. For example, the sale of clothes to Young Fashions for £400 can be split into an addition to the Bank account of £400, but also an entry is made in the Sales account to show that £400 of goods (at selling prices) have left the business. A second example could be when Stephanie's Boutiques bought some clothes *on credit*. This means that Julie has sold the goods but has not yet received the cash for them. The book entries would be £50 in the Sales account, this is shown on the *credit side* (right-hand side) of the account; the other entry is in a *debtors* account for Stephanie's Boutiques, entered on the *debit side* (left-hand side), showing the amount of money which Julie is owed by Stephanie's Boutiques. *No money* has yet been received, so we cannot make an entry in the Bank account!

4 ▷ THE TRIAL BALANCE

Before we are able to say whether the business made a profit or loss, a check must be made that all the bookkeeping entries are correct. We can check the arithmetic is correct by producing a Trial Balance, which is simply a list of all the accounts, showing whether they have a debit balance or a credit balance. Because all the transactions are entered in two accounts (a debit entry matched by a credit entry), the *total* of all the debits should equal all the credits. For Julie's Fashions, the Trial Balance at the end of the first month would look like this:

> ❝ The amount in the Bank Account of Julie's Fashions is a DEBIT total not a CREDIT one. ❞

	DEBIT £	CREDIT £
Bank Account	310	
Capital Account		1000
Debtor (Stephanie's Boutique)	50	
Debtor (Maison Roger)	1000	
Drawings (i.e. cash for Julie)	100	
Materials purchased	750	
Machinery	360	
Wages	30	
Rent and electricity	150	
Sales		1750
	2750	2750

As both totals are equal, we can be sure that the arithmetic is correct. Unfortunately, it is not a perfect check, as certain types of error (e.g. wages might be entered on both sides incorrectly as £300) will not be disclosed.

5 ▷ PROFIT

One of the most important questions that business people will ask is, 'Am I making a profit?'. The word *profit* can mean various things:
▶ it is the reward to the owner for the risks taken in setting up and running the business

▶ it is the surplus which provides the money for future investment in the business or in other projects

▶ it is the difference between *income* and *expenses*.

Profit is calculated by setting out whatever sales have been made by the business (regardless of whether the customers have all paid the money for those sales), and taking away from this total the amount of the expenses of the business. One expense is *depreciation*, which is the loss in value of the *fixed assets* (see p. 111) such as cars, computers, sewing machines, caused by these assets being used in the business. In Julie's Fashions, we can make an estimate that her sewing machine will last 3 years, and so the depreciation to be shown as an expense in her first month of trading will be:

$$£360 \div 36 \text{ months} = £10 \text{ per month}$$

To show the profit for the first month, we can draw up a simple *trading and profit and loss account*, as follows:

Julie's Fashions Trading and Profit and Loss Account for Month 1	£	£
Total sales		1,750
(including those on credit)		
Less materials used for making the dresses		750
GROSS PROFIT		1,000
Less expenses		
Wages	30	
Rent and electricity	150	
Depreciation of sewing machine	10	190
NET PROFIT		810

NOTE: Gross Profit is the difference between the sales revenue and the cost of the products sold, but before overheads such as rent have been deducted.

Net Profit is the Gross Profit less all the overheads.

In our simple example, we have followed a number of accounting *concepts*, including *depreciation, accrual and realisation*. The reason for depreciation has already been explained, but the reasons for the other two are as follows;

The accrual concept simply means that the expense of the period should be matched with the period in which the relevant income occurs, regardless of when money is actually paid or received. For example, if Julie still had £300 of materials in stock at the end of the month, the 'materials used' total would have been only £450, and the Gross Profit shown as £1,300, i.e.

	£	£
Total Sales		1,750
(including those on credit)		
Less materials used for making the dresses	750	
Less closing stock	300	450
GROSS PROFIT		1,300
Less (total) Expenses		190
NET PROFIT		1,110

The realisation concept stops a business person 'counting chickens before they are hatched'. For example, if the boss of 'Maison Roger' had only said that he *might* make an order worth £1,000, then Julie would not have been able to include this in her sales total. It is only when the customer has committed himself to the order (e.g. by accepting the goods), that the sale becomes real.

6 > THE BALANCE SHEET

Having found out what the profit has been in the first month of trading, it is now necessary to construct a balance sheet to show all the **assets and liabilities** of the business on the last day of the month. For Julie's Fashions, the balance sheet will look like this:

Julie's Fashions
Balance Sheet as at end of Month 1

	£	£
FIXED ASSETS: Sewing machine at cost	360	
Less Depreciation	10	350
CURRENT ASSETS: Stock and work-in-progress	–	
Debtors (Stephanie and Roger)	1,050	
Cash at Bank	310	
	1,360	
Less CURRENT LIABILITIES: Creditors (amounts owing to suppliers)	–	1,360
TOTAL ASSETS LESS LIABILITIES		1,710
Represented by:		
Julie's Capital Account:		
Cash introduced by Julie	1,000	
Add Net Profit	810	
	1,810	
Less Julie's Drawings	100	
TOTAL CAPITAL EMPLOYED		1,710

The various headings in the balance sheet have the following meanings:

A. FIXED ASSETS
These are assets which the firm buys which are of relatively high value and are going to be used for earning profits for several years. In most cases, they are subject to depreciation.

B. CURRENT ASSETS
These are the things which belong to the business, just like fixed assets, but they are not as permanent. They include stock, work-in-progress (i.e. partly finished goods), debtors (such as the money owed by Stephanie) and cash.

C. CURRENT LIABILITIES
These are amounts which the business owes to suppliers. Although Julie did not owe anything at the end of the month, if for example she had not yet paid the rent and electricity bill of £150, then this would have appeared under this heading. There would have been no change to Profit, but the Cash at Bank would have been £150 greater. The middle section of the balance sheet would then be:

	£	
CURRENT ASSETS: Stock and work-in-progress	–	
Debtors (Stephanie and Roger)	1,050	
Cash at Bank	460	
	1,510	
Less CURRENT LIABILITIES: Creditors (amounts owing to suppliers)	150	1,360

The difference between the current assets and current liabilities (£1,360) is known as the company's *working capital*.

Note that some businesses also have Long Term Liabilities, such as loans from banks which are repayable over a number of years.

D. CAPITAL

This is the amount which the owner is owed by the business as a result of the money lent to the business by the owner and the profits which the business makes. In Julie's balance sheet, the capital owed to her is £1,710, which is the same total as the assets less liabilities of the business.

7 ANALYSIS OF ACCOUNTS BUSINESS RATIOS

In a small business like Julie's Fashions, there will be relatively few people who are interested in the accounts; these include Julie herself, her bank manager and the taxman. For larger businesses, particularly public limited companies, there are many more interested parties such as employees, trade unions, managers, shareholders and creditors. To tell them how the business is going, *ratios* might well be used to analyse the figures in three main areas:

1. *Profitability* – how profitable the business is.
2. *Liquidity* – whether it has enough money to stay in business.
4. *Asset usage* – how efficiently it is being run.

The main ratios under each heading are:

A. PROFITABILITY

(i) Gross Profit Margin

$$\frac{\text{Gross Profit}}{\text{Sales}} \times \frac{100}{1}$$

This shows the overall gross profit percentage on sales. For example, a company which makes £1,000 gross profit on sales of £10,000 has a gross profit margin of 10%.

(ii) Net Profit Margin

$$\frac{\text{Net Profit}}{\text{Sales}} \times \frac{100}{1}$$

This shows the net profit as a percentage of sales.

(iii) Return on Capital employed

$$\frac{\text{Net Profit}}{\text{Capital employed}} \times \frac{100}{1}$$

This shows how profitable the business is in relation to the amount of money 'tied up' in the business.

B. LIQUIDITY

(i) The working capital ratio (also known as the *current* ratio) is

CURRENT ASSETS: CURRENT LIABILITIES

This shows the proportion by which the current assets exceed the current liabilities.

(ii) A variation on this is the *acid test* ratio, which is

CURRENT ASSETS LESS STOCK: CURRENT LIABILITIES

This shows how likely the business is to survive a crisis where most of the current liabilities have to be repaid quickly.

C. PERFORMANCE

(i) Stock Turnover

$$\frac{\text{Turnover (total sales)}}{\text{Stock}}$$

This is not a ratio, but the number of times on average that the stock is sold each year. In theory, if the rate at which stock turns over can be increased, then the profit made by the business will increase.

(ii) Debtor Turnover

$$\frac{\text{Turnover}}{\text{Debtors}} \times 12$$

This shows how many months the firm takes to collect its debts from those who owe it money.

EXAMINATION QUESTIONS

QUESTION 1

Study the balance sheet of XYZ Ltd and answer the questions printed below.

Balance Sheet
as at 31 December 1992

Authorised Capital	£		£
30,000 £1 Ordinary Shares	30,000	Premises	22,000
		Machinery	12,000
Issued Capital		Stock	8,000
25,000 £1 Ordinary Shares	25,000	Debtors	5,000
10% debentures	4,000	Cash	1,000
Reserves	8,000		
Creditors	4,000		
Overdraft	7,000		
	48,000		48,000

(a)   Give ONE example of a fixed asset owned by XYZ   **(1 mark)**

(b)   Give ONE example of a current liability owed by the company.   **(1 mark)**

(c)   How much does the company pay each half year to debenture holders?   **(1 mark)**

(d)   Calculate the working capital of XYZ.   **(2 marks)**

(e)   What indicators are there that XYZ is a private company? (4 lines for answer)
                                     (2 marks)

(f)   Why do you think that XYZ Ltd may wish to remain a private company?
     (6 lines for answer).   **(3 marks)**
Specimen Question: London & East Anglian Group.

QUESTION 2

The balance sheet of a business shows the value of the _____ (items owned)
and the extent of the _____ (items owed).
Specimen question: London & East Anglian Group.

TUTOR'S ANSWER TO QUESTION 1

1. (a)   Premises (or machinery)
    (b)   Creditors (or overdrafts).
    (c)   The company pays each half year to the debenture holders an amount of £200.
    This is obtained by taking 10% of £4000 which is £400 and halving this to take
    account of it being half yearly, ie the £200.
    (d)   The working capital of XYZ is £3000. This is obtained by taking the current
    assets minus the current liabilities.

Current Assets	£	Current Liabilities	£
Stock	8,000	Creditors	4,000
Debtors	5,000	Overdraft	7,000
Cash	1,000		
	14,000		11,000

So the working capital is 14,000 − 11,000 = 3,000.
(e)   The indications that XYZ is a private company are the word 'limited' in the title

of the company, i.e. XYZ Ltd, and the fact that the company has less than the £50,000 issued capital necessary to become a Public Limited Company.

(f) XYZ Ltd may wish to remain a private company because as such it will be able to keep more control over its own affairs. It may be a family business which, if it went public, would be accountable to a greater number of shareholders.

C O U R S E W O R K

**ASSIGNMENT 1
ANALYSIS OF
COMPANY
ACCOUNTS**

For this project you need to write to at least three large public companies in the same business, for example, all food companies, or all oil companies. Ask them if they could please send you a copy of their latest Annual Report and Accounts. When you receive them, read through them carefully. Do not worry if you do not understand all the figures and the technical terms, but just get an idea of what the companies are doing, how they see the future, and how successful they are.

The Chairman's Report is perhaps the most interesting part of the document, as it gives a review of what has happened and a forecast of future developments. You could also try and apply some of the *ratios* which were explained in the text.

You should write a report to a potential investor in these companies which explains the companies' financial performance, the problems they have faced and the things which have affected their businesses. Advise whether the investment should be made.

**ASSIGNMENT 2
LOCAL
ACCOUNTING
SYSTEM**

Most businesses are too small to employ their own accountant. Instead they use independent firms of accountants.

Look through the *Yellow Pages* for your area, and choose four accountancy firms. Find out what sort of services they offer and an idea of the costs. Do they produce any informative brochures for their clients? Do they have any links with local banks or solicitors?

Write a report for the owner of a new business explaining how a firm of accountants might be able to help, the range of services available, and give an idea of the likely costs involved.

BUSINESS DOCUMENTS

GETTING STARTED

All businesses must have formal documents. They need letterheadings – headed notepaper – in order to write to their customers, suppliers and staff. They also need lots of other documents to carry on business efficiently, so as to *record* all important events and transactions, and to provide *proof* if needed, perhaps to settle a legal dispute.

Documents are very important, and need to be kept safely. Some of the largest companies use computers to issue and store these documents; others use the older system of typing the documents, but then have them all *microfilmed* for easier storage.

NON-FINANCIAL DOCUMENTS
TRANSACTION DOCUMENTS

E S S E N T I A L   P R I N C I P L E S

There are two main *types* of document; firstly, *non-financial documents*:

▶ Letterheads   ▶ Compliment Slips   ▶ Business Cards

and secondly, *transaction documents* which record transactions of money, goods and services:

▶ Letter of Enquiry	▶ Quotation	▶ Order Form
▶ Invoice	▶ Pro-forma Invoice	▶ Advice Note
▶ Delivery Note	▶ Consignment Note	▶ Credit Note
▶ Debit Note	▶ Statements	

1 ▶ NON-FINANCIAL DOCUMENTS

The essential *non-financial* business documents required by all businesses are as follows:

A. LETTERHEADS

These are printed with the firm's name, address, telephone, telex and fax numbers, plus any legal information required for a limited company, such as the registered number, registered office and directors' names. People often gain their first impression of a business from the letterheading, so it is important that it should be well designed and printed.

B. COMPLIMENT SLIPS

These are small slips of paper, with the words *'with compliments'* on them. They are usually sent with brochures, price lists, and samples, so that the recipient knows which company sent them. They are also cheaper than using a full letterhead.

C. BUSINESS CARDS

These are small cards carried by senior personnel to give to business contacts. They contain their name, position, business name and address and telephone number.

AARDVARK ENGINEERS LIMITED

Peter J. Aardvark
Production Director

The Mill, Bolton
Telephone 87967
Telex 87623

---

2 ▶ TRANSACTION DOCUMENTS

The main *transaction* documents are:

A. LETTER OF ENQUIRY

A detailed letter, sent to a company, which asks for information on one or more of their products. It usually asks for *price* and *delivery* details and gives full information – called a *specification* – of what the buyer requires.

B. QUOTATION

In return, the seller will send a quotation. This sets out exactly what the terms of sale will be (including any discounts available), how much delivery and postage might cost, and the estimated completion or delivery time.

C. ORDER FORM

If customers wish to order goods after receiving the quotation (or after seeing the goods in a catalogue or price list), they will use an order form. It is often pre-numbered for ease of reference and contains details such as date, name and address of both supplier and customer, exact details of the goods being ordered and the agreed price and delivery date, if relevant. It will be signed by one of the buying firm's senior officials, usually one of their purchasing officers. If an order is made by telephone, it is usually confirmed in writing on an official order form immediately afterwards.

D. INVOICE

The invoice is the bill for the goods or services supplied. It is usually numbered and gives details of:
▶ the names and addresses of buyer and seller,
▶ an order number, if any, and the date of the order,
▶ details of the goods and services supplied,
▶ cost of the goods and VAT details.

Details of any discounts will be noted at the foot of the invoice (e.g. 2½% for payment within one month), together with the letters 'E & O.E.', which stands for 'Errors and Omissions Excepted'. This protects the seller against any mistakes on the invoice and allows them to be corrected at a later date (see Debit and Credit notes below).

E. PRO-FORMA INVOICE

Although invoices are used in most cases to allow customers to pay after they have received the goods or services, on some occasions, the seller might not be prepared to use this system, particularly if the customer is new or the goods are very expensive. In such cases, a pro-forma invoice is used, which is sent and must be paid before the goods are despatched.

F. ADVICE NOTE

This is a form sent either immediately before the goods are despatched, or sent with the goods. It gives details of the goods being sent, enabling the customer to check that the correct items have been delivered.

G. DELIVERY NOTE

This is sent with the goods, signed by the customer, and brought back by the lorry driver as proof that the customer has received them. Because this is a form of *receipt*, the person signing the delivery note must be authorised by the customer to do so.

H. CONSIGNMENT NOTE

If the firm is not using its own transport to deliver the goods, they will send them with a consignment note to the haulage firm which has been hired to make the delivery. It asks the haulage firm to accept the goods and gives them instructions as to where they should be delivered.

I. DEBIT AND CREDIT NOTES

Once an invoice has been drawn up it must not be changed. Crossing out and writing over invoices can cause confusion in the accounts department. If errors occur on the invoice, or if the customer cancels part of the order before delivery, the amendment is made by using one of the following forms:

Debit Notes

These *add* amounts to invoices. For example, if the original invoice charged the customer £50 instead of £500, then a debit note will be made out for £450.

Credit Notes

These *deduct* amounts from invoices. For example, if the invoice charged the customer £340 when the correct total was £300, a credit note for £40 will be issued. Credit notes are also issued if goods are returned after delivery (if they are unsuitable or faulty for instance).

J. STATEMENT

This is a copy of the customer's ledger account in the seller's ledger, usually covering a period of one month. It shows the opening balance at the start of the month, the invoices sent to the customer, and any cheques received. The final balance will be the amount owed at the end of the month and which is due for payment.

EXAMINATION QUESTIONS

QUESTION 1

A document used to notify the buyer of the amount due is an

Specimen question: London & East Anglian Group.

QUESTION 2

HIT & MISS SPORT LTD.				
Ellis Road		**Tele: 0227 2543**		
Newbridge		**Invoice No: 2883**		
Carsmere		**VAT Reg No: 232-2254-62**		
CA2 2DF		**Date: 11 December 1992**		
Godfrey Sportswear High Street, Broxford BR1 1PT			**Order No:** 1237.	
Quantity	**Description & Product Code**	**Price per unit**	**Total**	
100	Tennis racquets XJ5	30.00	3,000	
50	Rugby balls SPS7	10.00	500	
10	Snooker cues SQ15	15.00	150	
200	Squash balls SB20	1.50	300	
20	Footballs FB10	25.00	500	
	Discount	10%	4,450 445	
	+ VAT	17.5%	4,005 700.87	
		TOTAL DUE	4,705.87	
Terms: 2½% 14 days. **E&OE.**				

(a) What is meant by an invoice? (2 lines provided)   **(2 marks)**

(b) Why should Hit and Miss Sport Ltd offer Godfrey Sportswear a 10% discount? (2 lines provided)   **(2 marks)**

(c) On an invoice, 'Terms' and 'E & O.E.' will normally be found. What do these signify? (4 lines provided)   **(4 marks)**

(d) What do you view to be the advantages of using an invoice? (3 lines provided)

                                                                                                      (2 marks)

TUTOR'S ANSWER TO QUESTION 2

(a) An invoice is a bill sent by the supplier, here Hit & Miss Sport Ltd, to the customer, here Godfrey Sportswear. The invoice gives details of the goods, the price per unit, the total cost including VAT and the discount offered (if any).

(b) Godfrey Sportswear may purchase a large amount of its stock from Hit & Miss Sport Ltd and because it buys in bulk be allowed a discount of 10%. It is, perhaps, easier for Hit & Miss Sport Ltd to process bulk orders and so it is worth giving a discount for such orders.

(c) 'Terms': This signifies that if the account is settled within a particular period of time then the customer will be allowed a discount. In the above invoice the period in which Godfrey Sportswear has to pay, to obtain the discount of 2½%, is 14 days. The reason for this is to encourage prompt payment.

'E & O.E.': This means Errors and Omissions Excepted and it protects the supplier against any errors or omissions on the invoice.

(d) The advantages of using an invoice are that it acts as a record or proof for the buyer and seller. It helps avoid confusion, as it makes both parties fully aware of their dealings with each other.

CHAPTER

13

POPULATION

GETTING STARTED

Population may seem a strange subject for a business studies book but it is less strange when you realise how vital people are to business: they are one of its most important *factors of production* – without people most goods could not be made; they are also the ***customers*** for all types of firms. Numbers and types of people, their income and wealth are, therefore, very important to business.

Almost all firms are interested in how many people there are in their market area, what age or sex they are, how much money they have, how much free time they have, how many children they might have, and so on. Each of these pieces of information can help a company to plan how many of its goods it is going to be able to sell.

For example, a firm producing disposable nappies may decide to build a new factory. How large should the new factory be and how many nappies should it produce a year? The answers are going to depend on approximately how many babies are going to be born in the next few years and how many of those babies will be using disposable nappies.

These may sound like impossible predictions to make but, using fertility rates and market surveys, the company can make a pretty accurate guess.

ESSENTIAL PRINCIPLES

1 ▶ WORLD POPULATION

> The FERTILITY RATE shows the number of babies born to every thousand women of child-bearing age.

Before we go any further it might be useful to see how the population of the whole world has been growing recently. Table 13.1 shows how the population of the world has grown from just 2.5 thousand million people in 1950 to over 5 thousand million in 1992.

1950	2.5 billions
1985	4.9 billions
2000	6.3 billions
2025	8.5 billions

Note 1 billion = 1 thousand million = 1,000,000,000.
Source: Population Trends, Spring 1991.

Table 13.1 World population (United Nations figures)

The world's population was growing so fast in the 1960s that experts believed that it would reach over 10 billion by the year 2000. However, in the past ten years the rate of growth has slowed down and the prediction for total world population by that date is now just over 6 billion.

The experts at the United Nations now believe that the world's population may reach a state of balance (that is, of very little growth) by the year 2100 (just 108 years from 1992).

Even so, it is surprising how fast the world's population has grown. In the year 1900 it was estimated at only 1.25 billion (and it had taken several million years to reach that figure). It then took 50 years for the figure to double to 2.5 billion and only another 37 years for it to double again. It is to be hoped that the really fast rate of growth is now over – for, in just 100 years the world's population will have grown by 5 times!

2 ▶ POPULATION OF THE UK

> The fastest population growth appears to occur *as countries change* from being mainly agricultural to being mainly industrialised. Then, as the standard of living further increases, the birth rate appears to slow down.

GROWTH OF POPULATION

Like the world's population, the number of people in the UK has been growing, but much more slowly. The fastest rate of population growth for the UK was during the nineteenth century, just after the industrial revolution. Since 1900 the UK's population will have grown from about 38 million to 59 million by the year 2000 (see Table 13.2). In the nineteenth century it was fairly common to find families with anything between 8 and 10 children, whereas today the most common size is 2, with even 4 children being regarded as a large family.

Year	0–4	5–14	15–29	30–44	45–59	60–64	65–74	75–84	85+	Total
1901	4.4	8.0	10.8	7.5	4.6	1.1	1.3	0.5		38.2
1951	4.3	7.1	10.2	11.2	9.6	2.5	3.7	1.8		50.3
1985	3.6	7.3	13.4	11.3	9.3	3.1	4.9	2.9	0.7	56.6
2001	12.0		10.8	13.2	11.1	7.6		4.4		59.0

Source: *Social Trends* (17) 1987

Table 13.2 Age structure of the UK (millions)

3 ▶ CHANGING STRUCTURE OF POPULATION

A. AGE STRUCTURE

Although the rate of growth has slowed down quite a lot, the actual make-up of the population has been changing quite rapidly. Table 13.2 shows the way in which the *age structure* has been changing.

Between 1900 and 1986 the number of children under 14 decreased but people in the 15 to 29 year old category increased. Each of the over 30 age groups has increased in size since 1900, but the major growth has been in those over 60. In 1900 there were just 2.9 million people who were over 60 years of age. In 1986 that figure had reached 11.8 million. In other words, there are now almost four times as many elderly people as there were at the turn of the century. Important reasons for this are the improvement in medical care and in both standards of living and conditions of work.

Business can use the figures showing changes in the age structure of the population to predict demand for a wide variety of goods and products. The increase in the numbers of 30–44-year-olds between 1986 and 2001 will mean increased demand for the goods which are bought by this age group – including cars, houses, household goods, and insurance.

Population can change in size and structure in a number of different ways:
► more people can die
► more people can be born
► people can leave the country (emigrate)
► people can enter the country (immigrate)

Average change per year in thousands				
Year	Birth	Deaths	Migration	Annual change
1901–11	1,091	624	–82	385
1931–51	785	598	+25	213
1961–71	963	639	–32	312
1971–81	736	666	–44	42
1981–89	749	655	+14	111
1990	782	664	+47	174
Projected:				
1991-96	810	639	0	170

Source: *Social Trends* (22), 1992.

Table 13.3 **Population change**

B. THE DEATH RATE

Table 13.3 shows how the UK population has changed since the year 1901. It is important to note that, although the **numbers** of deaths from 1901–11 were **less** than they were from 1989-90, the **death rate** was much **higher** from 1901-11. This is because it is wrong to compare the numbers of deaths when the total populations at the two periods were different (only around 38 million in 1901 and about 56 million in 1990). In 1901 about 16 people died every year **per thousand population** whereas the death rate had dropped to around 11 people **per thousand population** in 1990. Table 13.4 shows the death rates since 1961. Due to better living and working conditions and improved medical facilities people are living longer. As the Table also shows, women have a lower death rate than men.

> Population can increase just as fast because the *death rate is dropping* as because the birth rate is increasing. In fact, decreasing death rates is one of the most important reasons for rapidly growing populations.

	Male	Female
1961	12.6	11.4
1971	12.1	11.0
1981	12.0	11.4
1986	11.8	11.5
1990	11.2	11.1

Source: *Social Trends* (22), 1992

Table 13.4 **Death rates (per thousand population)**

The comparison of how long men and women can expect to live shows that this is not just so for the UK. Table 13.5 demonstrates that only in the poorest of countries do males live longer, on average, than females. Why do you think this is?

C. THE BIRTH RATE

Another influence on population change is the rate at which children are born. Table 13.6 shows how this is also falling. In 1901 there were roughly 29 births per thousand population. By 1990 this had fallen to under 14. Part of this fall in the **birth rate** can be explained because families need to have less children to make sure that some will survive into adulthood: the death rate among children during the nineteenth century was

(1986)	Males	Females	% of Population aged 60 or over
United Kingdom	71.4	77.2	21
W. Germany	70.2	76.8	20
France	70.4	78.5	18
USSR	64.0	74.0	13
Portugal	65.1	72.9	15
India	46.4	44.7	6
Japan	74.2	79.7	14
USA	70.5	78.2	16

Source: *Social Trends* (17) 1987

Table 13.5 **Expectation of life at birth (in years)**

very high. Children died of a great many diseases and of industrial and domestic accidents. Today, far fewer children die from these causes, so that many parents feel that they need to have fewer children.

One interesting feature of Table 13.6 is the fact that the average age at which mothers had their first child has dropped slightly since 1950. Why do you think this has happened?

	Crude Birth Rate	Mean* Age of Mothers (at first birth)
1951	15.9	28.4
1961	17.9	27.7
1971	16.1	26.2
1981	13.0	26.8
1986	13.3	27.0
1990	13.9	27.5

*Mean = average

Source: *Social Trends* (22), 1992.

Table 13.6 **Crude birth rate (total births per thousand population)**

D. MIGRATION

Migration consists of people leaving the country (Emigration) and people coming to live here (Immigration). NET MIGRATION is the difference between the two.

The later years of the nineteenth century and the early years of this century were those of large scale *emigration* from the UK. People went mainly to the countries of the 'Old Commonwealth' – to Canada, Australia and New Zealand – but also to the United States and to South Africa. Part of this emigration is shown by the fact that an average of around 82,000 more people were leaving the UK than were coming in during the period 1901–11 (see Table 13.3). From the 1930s, however, that trend reversed to one of *immigration*, as more people began to enter the UK than to leave it.

There was another period of net immigration during the early 1960s but, since then, the numbers of people leaving the UK have generally exceeded those entering it. The explanation for this is, almost certainly, that the numbers leaving the UK had dropped to a very small number while those entering the UK were increased by quite large numbers of people returning to the UK from Zimbabwe and South Africa.

4   OCCUPATIONAL STRUCTURE OF THE UK

There are three main ways to consider the *occupational structure* of the UK. One is to look at the balance of the working population as it is split between the various *sectors* – primary, secondary and tertiary. A second is to look at the *status* of employment – such as whether employee, self employed, or in the armed forces. A third is to look at the *sex* of the employed.

A. SECTOR OF EMPLOYMENT

Primary Sector: this is to do with the extraction of raw materials (coal, oil, tin, etc.) or with the production of food (agriculture). The primary sector accounts for only about 3% of the UK working population.

Secondary Sector: this means industries involved in actually making things – manufacturing, construction, etc.

Tertiary Sector: this includes what are usually called the service industries, namely transport, communications, insurance, banking, education, tourism, etc. The tertiary sector now accounts for over 60% of the UK labour force.

It is one of the trends of modern industrial society that, as western industrialised countries become richer, the numbers of people working in industry and manufacturing become a much smaller proportion of the total workforce. In the UK the balance between the various sectors has changed a great deal even since 1961 (see Table 13.7).

	Primary	Secondary	Tertiary
1961	6.5	46.8	46.7
1971	3.7	43.8	46.7
1981	3.2	37.4	59.4
1987	3.0	35.5	61.5
1990	3.0	29.7	67.3

Table 13.7 **The changing balance between the sectors (% of total employment)**

B. STATUS OF EMPLOYMENT

The second way of looking at the occupational structure is to list the status of the people employed in the economy: such as whether they are employed by someone else, self-employed, or working in the armed forces.

Table 13.8 lists the working population by this method. It is important to note that the term 'working population' includes those who are unemployed. This is because, officially, the unemployed are looking for work and are part of the total number of people who are able to work.

Employed Workforce	11,607 males
	10,650 females
	22,257
Self-employed	3,143
	25,400
Members of HM Forces	297
	25,697
Work related Government training	352
	26,049
Unemployed	2,241
Total working population	28,290

Source: *Monthly Digest of Statistics* (May 1992)

Table 13.8 **United Kingdom working population (June 1991) (thousands)**

C. SEX AND EMPLOYMENT

Another trend which has to be noted is the growth of the female labour force and the decline in the employment of men (see Table 13.9).

The reasons behind this trend are extremely complex but it appears to have a great deal to do with:

1.   The decline of the older, heavier engineering industries. This has tended to put men out of work rather than women.

2.   The relative growth of newer industries in the electronics sector. Women tend to be preferred over men in certain electronics industries because, on the whole, they tend to have better manipulative skills (their hands are smaller and they are able to perform the extremely delicate operations necessary when assembling electronic components).

3.   The growth of the service sector. Banks, shops, and insurance companies all employ a large proportion of women in their labour force. This is partly because women have, traditionally, done the sorts of jobs required by these companies (counter work, secretarial duties, clerical work). It is also because the service sector uses a large number of part-time workers and women tend to be more willing to work part-time usually because of family obligations.

4. The increasing numbers of 'working wives'. In 1951 only 21% of all women had jobs. Today that figure is well over 55% and is expected to reach well over 60% by the year 2000. The later years of the twentieth century have increased the opportunities for women to work.

▶ Smaller families mean that women are tied to the home for shorter periods.

▶ There has been a change in social attitudes which has given women greater status and equality with men.

▶ Most household chores, such as washing, are now almost fully automated, and shopping – which took hours every day at the turn of this century – now takes only a couple of hours each week (on average).

▶ Single parent families: there has been a higher rate of marriage breakdown and of illegitimate births in recent years and this has meant that more women have to go out to work to keep their families.

	Males	Females
1970	14,009	8,470
1975	13,536	9,174
1980	13,110	9,401
1986	11,890	9,638
1990	12,057	10,807

Table 13.9 Employment by sex (thousands)

5 ▷ UNEMPLOYMENT

Table 13.8 shows how the numbers of *unemployed* people have grown since the early 1960s. In the decades of the 1950s and 1960s the unemployment rate was so low – with only about 300,000 unemployed at any one time – that jobs were easy to find. The UK actually had to encourage immigration in order to make sure that all the jobs were filled.

During the 1970s unemployment began to grow, and had reached 1.3 million by 1980. Then came a period of explosive growth in the numbers of people unemployed. Between 1980 and 1983 unemployment climbed from 1.3 million to 3.1 million.

There are several reasons which may explain unemployment:

A. FRICTIONAL UNEMPLOYMENT
This occurs when people change jobs and spend some time looking for a new one; or when people lose their jobs and have difficulty – due, perhaps, to a lack of information – in finding a new one (even though there are new jobs to be had).

B. CASUAL UNEMPLOYMENT
Many people work in casual jobs: for example in catering, construction, printing, hotels, seaside resorts. Some unemployment results when these staff are laid off and have to find more work. It is really a slightly different form of frictional unemployment.

C. SEASONAL UNEMPLOYMENT
This occurs when people who work in 'seasonal' occupations such as the tourist industry or farming, are laid off.

D. STRUCTURAL UNEMPLOYMENT
This happens when the demand for certain products falls – perhaps because they have gone out of fashion or been replaced by better products. It usually happens to whole industrial sectors at a time. In Britain the shipbuilding, heavy engineering and textile industries have suffered massive decline during the period since 1945. The unemployment resulting from this decline is known as structural because it is caused by a change in the actual industrial structure of the country.

E. CYCLICAL UNEMPLOYMENT
This is sometimes called *Demand Deficient* unemployment and is the result of a lack of demand throughout the whole economy for goods and services.

6 ▷ REGIONAL UNEMPLOYMENT

One of the most important problems about unemployment in Britain today is the way in which it seems to be concentrated in the North. Because the North of England was the centre of the first industrial revolution, its industries were the first to be affected by the structural decline of the older heavy industries, such as shipbuilding. Similarly, when the competition faced by industries of the second industrial revolution – manufacturers of cars, motor cycles, radios, etc. – increased from the rest of the world, the Midlands suffered structural decline.

Today, unemployment rates in certain areas of the north can be as high as 25% of the labour force and in certain towns and villages over 50% are unemployed. In the South, where the newer industries have grown up since 1945 (in electronics, light engineering, computers, etc.) unemployment rates are much lower (averaging just 8%).

7 ▷ CHANGING SKILL REQUIREMENTS

The population of the late twentieth century in the United Kingdom will have to be particularly flexible with regard to the skills which they are able to offer. In the nineteenth century a young person would leave school, undertake an apprenticeship for a trade, and would then work in that trade for the rest of his working life. The speed of technological advance was slow and the person would probably not have needed to learn how to use many new machines. Besides, the differences between one machine and the next were usually so small that the operator could learn how to use the new machine in a morning.

Unfortunately for today's workforce this is no longer so. The speed with which machines and techniques change means that workers have to be almost constantly retrained to use the next generation of machines.

Young girls who left school in the 1960s after learning shorthand and typing expected to be able to use the same skills throughout their working lives. The typewriters might change from manual to electric but the skills required would be exactly the same. Unfortunately for them the electronic revolution has changed their jobs almost out of recognition. Shorthand has largely given way to audio-typing (and, in the next generation of typewriters possibly to direct speech input) and typewriters have given way to wordprocessors. For the secretary this revolution has meant continual retraining, as wordprocessors have become more and more powerful. Each new development which occurs often means a completely new word-processing system to learn.

In industry the speed of change has been just as fast and has left many old skills high and dry. In the printing trade the old skills of 'hot metal' composing (setting the newspaper stories in molten lead in order to print the paper) have given way to highly computerised word-processing systems which link up with photographic printing processes. In engineering, many of the older skills such as turning (using a lathe), fitting (making fine adjustments to a metal component after it has been produced), have been replaced by computer controlled machines.

8 ▷ RETRAINING

Briefly, the population of the twenty-first century will have to be:
- ▶ prepared to retrain at quite short intervals in new skills.
- ▶ perhaps prepared to change their jobs entirely as new techniques replace the old ones.
- ▶ prepared to move quite long distances away from their first jobs in order to find new ones.

EXAMINATION QUESTIONS

QUESTION 1
Give three reasons why less than half the total United Kingdom population is included in the working population.

(i) _____ **(2 marks)**

(ii) _____ **(2 marks)**

(iii) _____ **(2 marks)**

Specimen question: Northern Ireland Schools Examinations Council

QUESTION 2

Study the following data and answer the questions printed below.

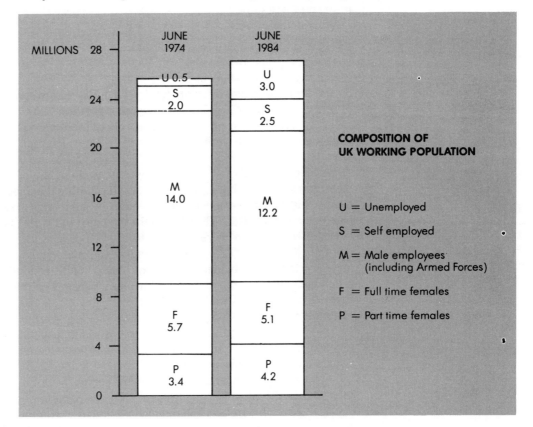

COMPOSITION OF
UK WORKING POPULATION

U = Unemployed

S = Self employed

M = Male employees
(including Armed Forces)

F = Full time females

P = Part time females

(a) By how much has the working population risen between 1974 and 1984? Label the categories in your calculations. **(4 marks)**

(b) By how much has the employed population fallen between 1974 and 1984? Label the categories in your calculations. **(4 marks)**

(c) Which section of the employed population has suffered most in the period between 1974 and 1984 and suggest reasons? **(6 marks)**

(d) Suggest reasons why the number in the self-employed category has risen.
(6 marks)

(e) Why do you think the number of female part-time workers has risen in the ten years under review? **(4 marks)**

(f) Why do you think that Northern Ireland has the highest unemployment rate of any region in the United Kingdom? **(4 marks)**

Specimen Question: Northern Ireland Schools Examination Council

TUTOR'S ANSWER TO QUESTION 2

(a)	1974 (millions)	1984
unemployed	0.5	3.0
self employed	2.0	2.5
male employees	14.0	12.2
full-time female	5.7	5.1
part-time female	3.4	4.2
	25.6	27.0

So the working population has risen by 1.4 million. When answering this type of question you must remember that the **unemployed** are **included** in the **working population** figure.

(b)   1974   (million)   1984
self employed   2.0   2.5
male employees   14.0   12.2
full-time female   5.7   5.1
part-time female   3.4   4.2
                     25.1   24.0

So the **employed population** fell by 1.1 million between 1974 and 1984. The unemployed are **excluded** from the employed population.

(c)   The section of the employed population which has suffered the most is the male population with a fall from 14.0m to 12.2m which represents a fall of approximately 13%.

Reasons for this fall could be the structural decline of basic industries such as the steel industry, coalmining, shipbuilding and traditional industries like engineering. Males have a higher proportion of employment in such industries than compared to, say, banking and education. This decline in the basic industries is the result of a number of reasons. The world-wide recession and overseas competition being important.

(d)   One reason for the increase in the number of self-employed might be the increase in unemployment. Some of those made redundant may have used their redundancy pay to start their own businesses instead of becoming employees of other firms. There have also been a range of measures by successive governments to encourage people to start their own businesses e.g. grants, reducing paperwork etc.

(e)   The number of female part-time workers may have risen partly because of the increase in the number of male unemployed. It has become even more important for the female members of the household to bring some income into the home. Also the period 1974 to 1984 has seen a rapid growth in the service sector of the economy. Many of these jobs are usually taken by females and many are part-time.

(f)   Northern Ireland has the highest rate of unemployment of any region in the UK for a number of reasons. Northern Ireland suffers from being some distance from the main areas of growth in the UK such as the South-East. Being at a distance from the large markets within the UK means higher costs for transporting finished products to these markets. Northern Ireland also lacks natural resources and finds it harder to attract businesses because of the current political unrest.

C   O   U   R   S   E   W   O   R   K

ASSIGNMENT 1 – A CASE STUDY OF INDUSTRIAL AND POPULATION CHANGE

Produce an illustrated report on the way in which your town or area has changed in recent years. Do not make the period too long because you will find it more difficult to get information. The period since 1970 would be the most interesting for most areas of the country.

How to set about it:

1.   Go to the local central library and ask for information on the town or area. You will find that they will have an entire section of books and reports on your area and will be able to recommend reports you should look at.

2.   Collect information on:

▶ The way in which population has changed – how has it grown and in what areas of the town?

▶ What new facilities, if any, have been needed to cope with the new population – new schools, housing estates, roads, hospitals?

▶ What new industries have come to the area and which old ones have disappeared? Your parents, family, friends, and teachers may be able to help you best here.

3.   When you write up the report pay particular attention to the growth of population and how it is related to the changes in the areas industry and commerce.

4.   Include a section on what you believe the future holds for the area.

**ASSIGNMENT 2 –
A HISTORICAL STUDY OF
POPULATION CHANGES**

How has your town or area developed over the past hundred years or so? Has it grown, shrunk, or have roughly the same number of people living in it? What jobs did people in the area do a hundred years ago? How did they live and what were their working conditions like?

How to set about it:

1. Use the local central library as your main source of information. You will find that they have a great deal of information about local history and may well be able to put you in touch with Local History groups who have already looked at this area of study.

2. You should be looking for information on:

    ▶ What the population of the area was and how it has grown; use local history books and the census information (the librarians will show you where to look for this).

    ▶ How they lived; what were their houses like? Where did they get food? What did they do for entertainment?

    ▶ Where and how they worked – did they work on the land or in factories? What hours did they work and what were they paid? Was it dangerous? What were the names of the main companies and what did they make?

    ▶ What were the transport facilities like? When did the railways come to the area? When did stagecoach services stop operating?

3. Try to find old pictures (usually available in the older books or reproduced in newer, local history books) which show what the town was like, what the factories or farms looked like and what people's homes looked like. Include photocopies of these in your study.

C H A P T E R

14

RECRUITMENT, SELECTION AND TRAINING

RECRUITMENT
SELECTION
CONTRACT OF
    EMPLOYMENT
INDUCTION
TRAINING
REDUNDANCY,
    RETIREMENT AND
DISMISSAL

G E T T I N G   S T A R T E D

All businesses whatever their size may need to take on extra staff. This could be because the business is growing and there is a need for new posts to be created, or because *existing posts* become vacant as:

1. The employee may have obtained a job elsewhere,
2. The employee may have obtained promotion within the company,
3. The employee may be retiring,
4. The employee may have been dismissed.

Recruitment is the first stage of filling a vacancy in the business. The recruitment process will involve a careful study of the vacancy, so that the *activities* expected of the new employee can be clearly defined in a job description. A decision must then be made on *how to advertise* the vacancy (what to say, and which newspapers and job agencies to use), and *what questions* should appear on the application form. Once the recruitment process has been undertaken, there then needs to be careful *selection*, first of the candidates to be interviewed, and then on which candidate to offer the job to.

The firm's responsibility does not end there. Once a person is employed, the firm has an interest in ensuring that its new member of staff is fully equipped to perform present and future activities. This brings us on to training. *Training* involves the sharpening of *existing* skills and the development of *new* skills and knowledge, so that best use can be made of the staff employed.

This chapter will deal with the recruitment, selection and training of a Junior Clerk/Receptionist, although the GCSE examination could ask about any kind of job. There is also a brief section on Redundancy, Retirement and Dismissal.

ESSENTIAL PRINCIPLES

1 ▷ ° RECRUITMENT

> ❝ You may be called upon to plan out a job description in the exam. It will help if you practice writing out job descriptions for different jobs you see advertised in the newspaper. ❞

A. JOB DESCRIPTION

The job description sets out in broad terms the duties and responsibilities of a particular job. It gives information such as:

1. Job title
2. The job location
3. What the job entails
4. Who the employee will be responsible to
5. Whether the employee is responsible for the work of any other members of staff.

It is the responsibility of the personnel department to produce job descriptions and this can be undertaken in a number of ways:

▶ The present job holder can be asked to write their own job description.
▶ The job holder can be interviewed in order to find out what the job entails.
▶ The job holder can be observed actually doing the job.

A *job description* for the post of Junior Clerk/Receptionist would include information like:

> *Job Title:* Junior Clerk/Receptionist
> *Job Location:* Personnel Department
> *Duties:* Answering the telephone
> Office filing
> Typing
> Welcoming customers
> General office duties
> *Reports To:* Assistant Personnel Manager

The job description would also include a more detailed description of the day-to-day duties of the Junior Clerk/Receptionist.

B. PREPARING A JOB ADVERTISEMENT

Figure 14.1 shows a typical job advertisement which might appear in a local newspaper. It advertises the post of Junior Clerk/Receptionist and invites candidates to apply within a certain time.

A great deal of time and effort is taken in designing *job advertisements* because it is important that the right candidates apply for the post. The advertisement has included certain information.

▶ job title
▶ the type of work involved
▶ where the office/factory is located
▶ qualifications/experience required (if any)
▶ salary/working conditions
▶ training given (if any)
▶ age of candidate required
▶ how the candidate should apply, e.g. application form, CV or by telephone.

As the job advertisement is being prepared, the Personnel Department at Edwards Foods Ltd will need to bear in mind its cost and destination. If a *budget* has been placed on the amount spent on the job advertisement it may be necessary to reduce its size. If this is the case then some of the less important information may have to be omitted. The *destination* of the advertisement may determine the way in which it is written. For example the

---

JUNIOR CLERK/ RECEPTIONIST

EDWARDS FOODS LTD, a leading food manufacturer require a Junior Clerk/ Receptionist at their new offices in Cambridge.

Applicants, ideally school leavers, should have a minimum of four GSCE's including Mathematics and English, an outgoing personality and be able to communicate with customers both on the telephone and in person.

This is an interesting and varied job requiring enthusiasm and commitment for which full training will be given.

Salary will be in the range £4,000 to £5,000 per annum, 23 days holiday a year and a subsidised canteen is available.

The closing date for application forms is 9th December.

Send for an application form and further details to:

Mrs P Parke
Personnel Department
Edwards Foods Ltd
East Road
Cambridge

Fig.14.1. Typical job advertisement

wording may be different if it is to be placed in a Job Centre, a newspaper or a school careers department. The personnel department will also need to take account of the law relating to recruitment when planning the job advertisement. Relevant Acts are:

1. The Disabled Persons (Employment) Acts 1944 & 1958
2. The Childrens and Young Persons Acts 1933 & 1969
3. The Sex Discrimination Acts 1975 and 1987
4. The Race Relations Act 1976.

Further information on the law relating to employment can be found in Ch. 18.

C. ADVERTISING THE POST

Internal

The post may be advertised in the staff magazine or on the staff noticeboard and be filled by a member of the *existing* staff. The advantages of this are that the company will be aware of the employee's capabilities and it will be a cheaper and quicker method of recruitment. If, however, there is no suitable internal candidate then there will be a need to advertise the post *externally*.

External

There are various places which could be used to advertise the post, such as:

▶ The Job Centre   ▶ Factory Gate
▶ Private Agency   ▶ Newspapers: Local and National

1.   Job Centre. You will find one of these in your local town or city; they are self-service centres. Jobs are displayed on boards and are mainly for manual, clerical and unskilled work. In larger cities Professional and Executive Recruitment centres can also be found which cater for professional people who are looking for employment. Both the Job Centre and Professional and Executive Recruitment are organised by the Department of Employment.

2.   Private Agency. There are a number of nationally organised private agencies such as Alfred Marks who deal with secretarial, office and retailing vacancies. The agencies advertise in newspapers and in their shop windows. If the agency fills a vacancy, the employer usually pays a fee calculated as a percentage of the starting salary.

3.   Factory Gate. Certain jobs may be advertised on noticeboards near to the factory gate. Now, of course, the term 'factory-gate advertising' is more likely to refer to noticeboards near to an office or administrative centre.

3.   Newspapers/Journals. Many jobs are advertised in local and national newspapers. *Local Newspapers* are normally used for *clerical* and for *manual* (skilled and unskilled) employment. They are often used to recruit school-leavers such as the advertisement in Fig. 14.1. Have a look in your local newspaper. The job vacancies will normally be advertised on a particular night each week. *National Newspapers* are normally used for *professional* employment opportunities to attract applicants from different areas of the country, many of whom would have a degree or professional qualification.

The appropriate *method* of advertising depends upon various factors:

1.   The type of post. If it is to be filled by a school-leaver then local newspapers may be the most effective form of advertising. If the vacant post is for a secretary then the more successful way of advertising could be to register the vacancy with a private employment agency.

2.   The time scale. If it is important to fill the post quickly then it may be worth advertising the post internally.

3.   The budget. If there is a limit to the amount of money that can be spent on advertising then this may rule out national newspapers which are very expensive. National newspapers may only be used for vacancies which the company believes require skills or qualifications which are in short supply locally. The cheapest way would be to advertise in Job Centres and at the factory gate.

4.   The type of person you want to apply for the vacant post. If you want to attract specialist staff then you may advertise with a specialist employment agency such as Professional and Executive Recruitment or a specialist journal such as *Computing World*. For this type of appointment you may also advertise in a national newspaper.

<table>
<tr><td>2 >   SELECTION</td></tr>
</table>

A. DESIGNING A JOB APPLICATION FORM

When a post is advertised it will normally state that the person interested should send for further details and an application form. The personnel department will then send out a standard printed form as in Fig. 14.2. The candidates fill this in, giving information to support their application for the post in question. The application form shown here refers to the post of Junior Clerk/Receptionist.

The *advantages* of the application form to the business are:

1. It gives a precise picture of the individual applying for the post.
2. It outlines the candidate's suitability for the post.
3. It will also serve as a personnel record and be of legal importance in the employment contract.

Businesses lay out their application forms in different ways but the information they require will, in most cases, be the same as in Fig. 14.2. The information given on the form will be helpful in assessing the candidate's suitability for the post, in comparing that candidate with other applicants and, therefore, in selecting certain candidates for

❝Address to which all correspondence should be sent. Is it local?❞

❝Is the applicant old enough/too old for the post?❞

❝Has the applicant obtained the relevant qualifications?❞

❝Has the applicant undertaken any work which may be useful for the post. Is it relevant experience?❞

❝Has the applicant been given any positions of trust?❞

❝Asked so that further information can be obtained as to the applicant's suitability for the post.❞

EDWARDS FOODS LTD
Application form for the post of:

JUNIOR CLERK/RECEPTIONIST

Please fill in the application form and return it to us as soon as possible

1) FULL NAME:
2) FULL ADDRESS:

3) TELEPHONE NUMBER (IF ANY):
4) DATE OF BIRTH:
5) MARRIED OR SINGLE:

6) EDUCATION: Secondary School(s), Address(es)	DATE	
	From	To

7) QUALIFICATIONS	DATE TAKEN & GRADES	

8) WORK EXPERIENCE	DATE	
	From	To

9) POSITIONS OF RESPONSIBILITY

10) LEISURE ACTIVITIES

11) NAME AND ADDRESS OF TWO REFEREES

12) I certify that to the best of my knowledge all the entries on this form are correct.

Signed.. Date...............................

Fig.14.2. Job Application Form

interview. In figure 14.2 information is given at the side as to why the firm is asking certain questions.

From the candidate's point of view the application form is the first impression the firm will obtain of him or her and will form the basis of the firm's short list for interview. It is, therefore, important that the candidate completes the form clearly and carefully.

B. PROVIDING A CURRICULUM VITAE

> **It would be useful for you to produce your own CV.**

The advertisement for the post of Junior Clerk/Receptionist asked that anyone interested should send for an application form and further details. Instead of this the firm could have asked the applicant to send a curriculum vitae (CV). The CV should contain brief, relevant information on the applicant such as schools attended, qualifications, interests and activities and the name and address of two referees (see Fig. 14.3).

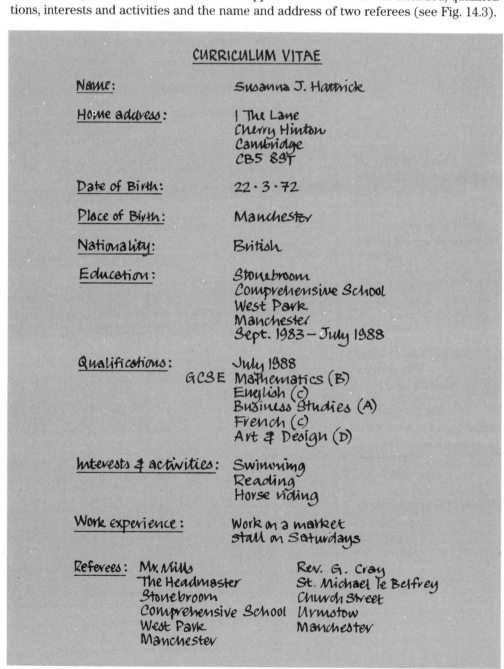

Fig.14.3.

C. REFERENCES

Many application forms will require the name and address of at least two individuals who can act as referees (i.e. provide references). The referees may be contacted and asked whether or not they consider the applicant suitable for the post. Normally the firm will ask for the names of present and former employers or supervisors. In the case of the Junior Clerk/Receptionist, where the applicants are likely to be school-leavers, then the name and address of the Head Master or Mistress and the school attended are more likely to be requested. The candidate may also have to name one other person to act as referee, such as a vicar, a doctor, an old family friend or an employer who has employed them for part-time work.

D. CHOOSING SUITABLE CANDIDATES FOR INTERVIEW

Once the company has obtained all the completed application forms the next step is to compare them. This can be a lengthy process, trying to match the attributes of the applicants to the needs of the post. Some application forms will be discounted straight away because, for example:

▶ they are badly written (perhaps they have poor spelling and are untidy);
▶ the applicant's qualifications may be inadequate for the post;
▶ the applicant may be too old.

These applicants will be sent a letter informing them that they were unsuccessful in their application. In choosing applicants for interview the company needs to observe the Sex Discrimination Acts and the Race Relations Act, which make it illegal to discriminate on the grounds of sex and race (see Ch. 18). Of the application forms remaining, a 'short list' will be drawn up. This is a list of the applicants seen as best suited for the post. A letter will be sent to those listed inviting them for interview on a certain date. At the same time the company will usually send for references (as dealt with in the previous section).

E. THE INTERVIEW

This is the major way companies assess whether a candidate is suitable for a particular post. It allows the company to make a judgement on:

▶ the candidate's personality (will they fit into the company and get on with the other staff?)
▶ the ability of the candidate to communicate;
▶ whether the information on the application form is correct.

It also gives the candidate the chance to find out more about the company, such as the working conditions, hours of work, pay, and training. It is important that the interview is planned carefully. With this in mind, the *interviewers* should make sure that:

1. They are not interrupted whilst the interview is taking place.
2. The application form has been read carefully so that they can decide which are the relevant questions to ask.
3. The interview does not have to be rushed because of a lack of time.
4. The interviewee is put at ease, perhaps by asking a few simple questions at the beginning such as, how did the candidate travel to the interview.
5. The questions are phrased in such a way that they encourage the candidate to talk and to give his or her own views and opinions. Questions should be avoided which call for one word answers such as, 'I can see you are interested in horseriding'.
6. The candidate can understand the questions asked. The wording and type of question the interviewer would ask a candidate for a management post would be different to those asked of an applicant for the post of Junior Clerk/Receptionist.

F. MAKING A SELECTION

Once all the candidates have been interviewed then the interviewer must compare the information obtained from each candidate and decide on the most suitable person for the post. The candidate may have been interviewed by more than one person, perhaps someone from the personnel department and a staff member from whichever department the post was advertised for. The two interviewers would then compare notes before deciding which candidate to appoint.

In arriving at a final choice, the candidates may have been given a test. Here the candidates *potential* to perform the necessary activities is being tested. The aptitude test will cover areas such as:

▶ *mental abilities* (e.g. powers of reasoning)
▶ *physical qualities* (e.g. coordination)
▶ *arithmetical abilities* (e.g. addition and multiplication)

An *intelligence test* may be used to find out the candidate's *general* powers of reasoning. The test will normally be a written one, made up of numerical, diagrammatical and verbal questions, such as identifying one or more shapes which have common features, writing down the next number in a series, or comparing a series of words to see which have similar meanings. Once the test is completed, it is marked and a score obtained.

Medical checks. The company may insist on a medical examination before the job offer is confirmed. This will give a clear indication as to whether the applicant is physically suitable for the post. For example, if the applicant for the Junior Clerk/ Receptionist post is hard of hearing, then answering the telephone will be a problem. The firm will also be interested in knowing whether there is likely to be a high degree of absenteeism through sickness.

3 CONTRACT OF EMPLOYMENT

Once an applicant has accepted a post they will be sent a letter confirming the appointment. In the same letter the *conditions of service* will often be included. This sets out the employee's statutory legal rights and obligations as covered by the Employment Protection (Consolidation) Act 1978. The conditions will cover areas such as the:

▶ name and address of the employer and employee
▶ date employment begins
▶ job title and job description
▶ level of pay and whether it will be received weekly or monthly
▶ holiday entitlement
▶ hours of work
▶ conditions relating to sickness pay
▶ conditions relating to the pension scheme
▶ amount of notice the employee has to give the firm if he/she is leaving
▶ notice of any grievance or disciplinary procedure used by the company.

4 INDUCTION

Any new employee needs to be introduced to his or her new working environment, in much the same way that first year students are taken round the school at the beginning of term, so that they can become familiar with their new surroundings.
New employees may:
▶ be introduced to their new colleagues
▶ be told how the firm is organised (see Ch.5)
▶ be given talks by relevant departmental managers
▶ be taken on a tour of the office/factory to see where fire exits, lavatories, canteens etc., are located.
This *induction programme* may last for a day or a week depending on the level of the post, and often takes place *before* the job actually starts.

5 TRAINING

Once appointed, staff may need *training* in their particular post. Such training can be either *internal* (within the company) or *external* (taking place outside the place of work). The aim is to improve the employee's ability to do the job.

A. INTERNAL TRAINING
1. 'On the job' training may be undertaken. Here the employee learns to do the job during the normal working day. In the case of the Junior Clerk/Receptionist post, this could involve being taught to use the telephone switchboard. The advantages of internal training are that it is usually less costly to the company, and that it is undertaken in the environment the employee will actually be working in.
2. The company may organise short courses which the employees attend on the company's premises. Organised by the training department, they are an important form of 'off the job' training.

B. EXTERNAL TRAINING
1. 'Day release' courses at local colleges are an important type of external training. For example the banking profession sends staff on day release to undertake Chartered

Institute of Bankers (CIB) courses.

2.   It is possible that courses, like the one above, could be undertaken by correspondence course. Here the employee would enrol with a correspondence college, which would send study-books and exercises for the employee to work through. The exercises would then be sent to the college for marking and comment. The advantage to the company of correspondence courses is that the staff do not require time off work.

C. YOUTH TRAINING (YT)

The aim of YT is to provide young people with the broad based skills necessary for a flexible and self-reliant work-force, and with training leading to National Vocational Qualifications. YT is guaranteed to all those between the age of 16 and 17 years who are not in full-time education or training.

A. REDUNDANCY

An employee may be made redundant if his or her job is no longer required by the firm. It may be that the firm is closing down or is reorganising its operations. The employee may be eligible for redundancy pay and this will be calculated on the basis of how long the employee has worked for the company, also on age and salary.

B. RETIREMENT

Retirement is at sixty-five for men and sixty for women, although women now have the option of working until they are sixty-five if they wish. The employee may have paid into the employer's pension scheme and this will mean that the individual will obtain a pension on retirement based on the number of years of service.

C. DISMISSAL

On page 136 we dealt with the contract of employment. This can be terminated by employers if they are dissatisfied with the work or conduct of the employee. Normally, notice of dismissal will be given to the employee. This could be for failure to obey an instruction, stealing from work, violence towards other staff, or excessive absence. Notice of dismissal usually follows a number of verbal and written warnings. Dismissed employees may feel they have been unfairly dismissed. If so they have certain rights, as granted by the Employment Protection (Consolidation) Act 1978. This allows the employee to take his or her grievance to an industrial tribunal which will review the case of unfair dismissal.

EXAMINATION QUESTIONS

QUESTION 1

A _____ is an agreement under which an employee offers service in return for wages.

Specimen question: London & East Anglian Group.

QUESTION 2

The _____ department of a business is responsible for the recruitment of employees.

Specimen question: London & East Anglian Group.

QUESTION 3

Read the information alongside which has been taken from a local newspaper and then answer the questions which follow.

(a) Why is the firm advertising for staff?
_____ **(1 mark)**

(b) In which of the jobs is experience essential?
_____ **(1 mark)**

(c) Give two benefits, apart from salary, which successful applicants might receive.
(2 marks)
(i) _____
(ii) _____

(d) What other information would you want to know before applying for any of the jobs: **(2 marks)**
_____
_____

(e) Put yourself in the place of the Personnel Officer of Phillips Motor Group and design a job application form suitable for the jobs advertised. **(10 marks)**
Specimen question: Northern Ireland Schools Examinations Council.

Due to the impending launch of a new Peugeot Talbot outlet at York Road, Belfast, The Phillips Motor Group urgently require the following staff:

SALES PERSONNEL

Experience in all aspects of New and Used Car Sales is essential. The successful candidates must have the enthusiasm and determination to make substantial contributions to the success of this new outlet.

AFTERSALES SUPERVISORS

Vacancies exist for both Parts and Service Supervisors. Experience of Peugeot/Talbot procedures preferred, but not essential.

SERVICE PERSONNEL

Experienced Mechanics plus Third and Fourth Year Apprentices required.

The above posts offer an exceptional opportunity to participate in the success of this new outlet from inception. The rewards for suitable applicants will be attractive and will include the numerous benefits associated with a large expanding company.

Applications in writing only to:

F. S. A. HEWITT

Phillips Motor Group
226 YORK STREET, BELFAST

Fig.14.4.

TUTOR'S ANSWER TO QUESTION 3

(a)   The firm is advertising for staff because it is launching a new outlet.

(b)   Experience is essential in the Service Personnel job.

(c)   The two benefits which successful applicants might receive could be a subsidised canteen and membership of a private medical insurance scheme.

(d)   Before applying for the jobs you may wish to obtain information on (1) salary (2) number of week's holiday per year (3) pension scheme (4) the length of the working week (i.e. hours worked per week).

(e)

THE PHILLIPS MOTOR GROUP

Application for the post of _____

Full Name _____

Address _____

_____

_____

Date of Birth _____

Education: Schools and Colleges attended plus dates.

_____

_____

_____

Qualifications: Grades, plus dates taken.

_____

_____

_____

_____

Work Experience: with dates

_____

_____

Other information

_____

_____

Name and addresses of TWO referees

_____

Signature _____   Date _____

C O U R S E W O R K

ASSIGNMENT – JOB ADVERTISEMENTS AND APPLICATION FORMS

1.   Choose the type of job you would like to do on leaving school.

2.   Choose *three* ways in which the job is likely to be advertised. It may be in (a) the local job centre, (b) the local newspaper (c) the school careers office.

3.   Obtain information on the chosen job from all three sources. You will have to visit the local Job Centre and, perhaps, buy the local evening newspaper a number of times before the type of job you want appears.

4.   Compare the three ways of advertising a job vacancy. Do they differ? Is there any important information they have omitted? Could you suggest ways the advertisements could be improved? Once you have obtained the information and made your decisions, your findings will need writing up in a presentable form.

5.   Send for the application forms and further details (if they are sending out printed forms). Compare the forms. What are the differences, if any? Have you got the right

experience/qualifications for the job? Could you suggest ways in which the forms could be improved? Again write up your findings in a presentable form.

6. Having obtained the advertisement and application forms and presented your findings, did you find:
    (a) That the advertisements were misleading?
    (b) The application forms were difficult to understand and complete? If so why?
    (c) That you would stand a good chance of obtaining one of the jobs you chose? If not why not?

(Item 6 could also be written up as part of the assignment.)

STUDENT'S ANSWER – EXAMINER'S COMMENTS

The following is a student's answer to question 3, page 138.

Do read the question carefully. the firm is launching a new *outlet*, not a new car.

3. (a) The firm is launching a new Peugot Talbot.

Experience is 'required'; *essential* is a stronger term.

b) Experience is essential with a sales personnel and a (service personnel.)

It doesn't actually say that the company is a PLC.

c) i) a share in the company.
    ii) company car.

Fine. You may also want to know the number of weeks of holiday per year.

d) Before applying for any of the jobs I would want to know the salary/wages, work hours, age and sex of the person required.

At the top of the application form you might put: Application for the post of . . . .

e)

Surname :	Mr. / Miss / Mrs.
Christion name (s) :	Date of birth.
Address :	Tel. no :

Driving licence   Yes / No.   (Vehicle?)
Previous Employers: References?

Qualifications: **Is this necessary?**

Quite a good application form. Perhaps a bit 'squashed'! also need space for signature and date at the bottom.

Why do you want this job?

Why do you consider yourself suitable?

Hobbies?

CHAPTER

15

MOTIVATION

WAGES
SALARIES
EARNINGS
WAGE DIFFERENTIALS
TYPES OF PAYMENT
THE WAGE SLIP
GROSS AND NET PAY
DEDUCTIONS FROM PAY
ALLOWANCES AND
    OUTGOINGS
TAX CODES
FRINGE BENEFITS
JOB SATISFACTION
MANAGEMENT AND JOB
    SATISFACTION

G E T T I N G   S T A R T E D

Throughout the UK there are a great number of different occupations, in which individuals contribute to the production of goods and services. There are three broad categories of productive activity (often called stages or sectors) in which the working population is involved, namely:
1. Primary, 'extractive' stage workers (e.g. farmers and miners).
2. Secondary, 'manufacturing' stage workers (e.g. steel workers and car workers on a production line).
3. Tertiary, 'service' stage workers (e.g. bankers and advertisers).
The various stages are part of the 'chain of production' and are dealt with in more detail in Ch.3. You can perhaps think of many reasons why people go to work, but I am sure without too much thought you would put 'to obtain an income' at the top of your list.

'Motivation' means the reason why people act or behave in a particular manner. Two extremes of motivation, low and high, can be seen if one compares a student's willingness to get up for school on a Monday morning with the willingness to get up to go out with friends on a Saturday morning. Motivation is an important area for any company because if the workforce is not motivated then the company will not be achieving its full potential.

There are a number of factors which could influence a worker's motivation:
1. Wage level.
2. Attractive working environment.
3. Fringe Benefits.
4. Effective management team.
5. Satisfaction in the work.
It may be possible for you to memorise the above factors by the mnemonic WAFES (W = wage level, A = attractive working environment, F = fringe benefits, E = effective management team, S = satisfaction in the work.)

Many managers would go along with the 'carrot and stick' theory of motivation: the 'carrot' being the reward you offer an employee, usually money, so that he or she will work harder; the 'stick' being that if they do **not** work harder they will lose money or even their job. This chapter deals with the factors which influence motivation, concentrating mainly on the financial incentives.

ESSENTIAL PRINCIPLES

1 ► ○ WAGES

(i)   This is money which is paid weekly, often in the form of a pay packet including notes and coins. Many companies, however, are now insisting that their employees are paid in the form of a direct transfer into their bank account. This involves less administration for the company and is therefore less costly. As it avoids the need to transport large amounts of cash, it is also more secure.

(ii)   Waged employees are usually manual workers.

(iii)   The wage is, in most cases, expressed as a rate per hour and the employee is paid extra for any overtime worked, beyond their basic working week. This overtime is usually paid at 'time' (i.e. the basic rate per hour) plus a 'quarter' or 'time plus a half'. Overtime beyond a certain number of hours or at an unsocial time (e.g. Sunday morning) is usually paid at 'double time'.

2 ► SALARIES

(i)   These are paid monthly, normally directly into a bank account.

(ii)   Salaried staff are usually 'white collar' workers and are given greater notice of dismissal than waged employees. Weekly paid workers are normally on one week's notice while salaried staff usually get, and have to give, a month's notice.

(iii)   The salary will in most cases be expressed as an annual amount which will not normally be based on hours worked. Salaried staff are not usually paid overtime.

3 ► EARNINGS

The wage rate can be seen as the 'basic rate', which is the wage an individual would receive for working a normal working week. ***Earnings*** include the wage rate ***and*** payments for such things as overtime and bonuses (which may be for increased productivity). Earnings will therefore tend to be much greater than the wage rate.

4 ► WAGE DIFFERENTIALS

Wage differentials are the differences in wages earned by employees in different jobs. Workers will view their level of pay as being very important since it determines their standard of living and may also determine their status within the firm and, perhaps, also within society at large. For these reasons they will be interested in how their pay compares to other groups of workers. Wage differentials may also affect individual or group motivation at work and can lead to industrial disputes, as one group of workers may feel their differentials are inadequate compared to another group.

5 ► TYPES OF PAYMENT

There are a number of ways that the employer can calculate the employee's wage:

> **Make sure you understand the differences between time rate, piece rate and standard rate.**

A. TIME RATE

With a time rate of payment all employees doing a similar job (maybe working on a production line) are paid a certain amount per hour. For example they may be paid £3.00 per hour (the basic rate) for a normal 40 hour week thus giving them a ***gross*** weekly wage of £120. Any hours worked over 40 hours may be paid at an overtime rate, perhaps one and a quarter times the basic rate (i.e. £3.75 per hour). The basic rate will of course vary from firm to firm.

The ***advantages*** of a time rate system of payment are:

1.   It is easy for the firm to calculate wages.
2.   The worker knows exactly what he is to receive for spending a certain period of time at work.

The ***disadvantages*** are that:

1.   Good and bad workers are paid the same.
2.   There has to be a 'clocking in' system to determine the hours worked.
3.   There needs to be supervision to make sure that the quantity and quality of the work produced is maintained.

B. PIECE RATE

With a piece rate system, employees are paid on the basis of the quantity of work produced. This type of payment is usually used when quality is not very important. The employees will normally receive a basic rate to which is added an extra payment based on the amount produced.

The *advantages* of a piece rate system are that:
1.   The workers who are quicker get rewarded for their effort.
2.   It provides an incentive to work harder.
3.   The workforce will need less supervision, at least as regards the quantity of work produced.

The *disadvantages* are that:
1.   The work may be rushed, which means that quality may suffer.
2.   Careful employees will earn less.
3.   The employees may be tempted to work too quickly, which may result in accidents.
4.   It can be difficult to fix a piece rate.

Instead of being paid entirely on a piece rate system, workers can be paid partly on a time rate basis and partly on a piece rate basis, through a bonus scheme linked to results.

C. STANDARD RATE

This can be called a 'flat rate' and is the same payment to all workers engaged in similar work. This normally applies to salaried staff, who are paid the same annual amount if they are on the same grade as other workers in that occupation.

The *advantage* is that it is easy for employers to calculate. The *disadvantage* is that it may mean that employees lack the incentive to work extra hours or to provide a better quality product or service.

D. PROFIT SHARING

The company may distribute a part of the profits in the form of cash, or shares in the company, on a yearly basis to the employees. This is a profit sharing scheme and a well-known company involved in this is the John Lewis Partnership.

The benefit to the employees is that they obtain a share of the wealth they helped to create and may, therefore, feel greater commitment to the company. The benefit to the company is that, hopefully, it will persuade the employees to work harder.

E. BONUS SYSTEMS

The company may make cash payments to their employees at particular times of the year. This could be at Christmas or just before the summer-holiday period. Such bonus payments may be linked to a particular standard, such as the length of service, in order to encourage loyalty and to improve motivation. Alternatively, the bonus may be linked to merit (i.e. a merit bonus) perhaps for salesmen who have exceeded a certain sales target.

6 ▶ THE WAGE SLIP

Figure 15.1 shows a typical wage/payslip for an individual, Mrs S. Jones, who works for Zavros Office Supplies PLC, as a personnel assistant.

7 ▶ GROSS AND NET PAY

The wage slip can be quite complicated to understand, so read this section carefully.

You will note from the pay slip that Mrs Jones' gross pay for February 1992 was £599.15. The gross pay is the amount earned for February before any deductions have been made. The net pay or take-home pay is the amount the employee actually obtains after the various deductions have been taken into account. This will be the £417.17 noted in Fig. 15.1, after deducting pension contributions, tax and national insurance contributions. The net pay will be paid straight into the bank account of Mrs Jones at Northwich Bank PLC, York. On the other hand, the net pay could be paid in the form of a pay packet, containing cash or a cheque, at the end of each week.

GROSS PAY − DEDUCTIONS = NET PAY

As can be seen from the pay slip in Fig. 15.1, there is a running total of gross pay (£6518.00) and of tax deductions so far (£1197.12) for the tax year, which starts on April 6th and ends on April 5th the following year. This is so that the company and the Inland Revenue can keep a check on whether the correct tax has been paid throughout the year.

8 ▷ DEDUCTIONS FROM PAY

There are both *compulsory* and *voluntary deductions* from pay.

A. COMPULSORY DEDUCTIONS

These are enforced by law and include *income tax* and *national insurance contributions*.

i Income tax

Income tax is almost always deducted from gross pay before the employee actually receives any payment. It is organised automatically under a system known as *Pay as You Earn* (PAYE). In Fig. 15.1, the income tax is £113.39, almost 20% of the gross salary. The income tax goes to the Inland Revenue and forms part of the Government's finances to provide goods and services. There are certain tax allowances which employees are entitled to and these can be found in the section entitled 'Allowances' (see p 145). After deducting tax allowances from gross pay we get *net taxable pay*. In Fig. 15.1 this was £585.13 for the month in question.

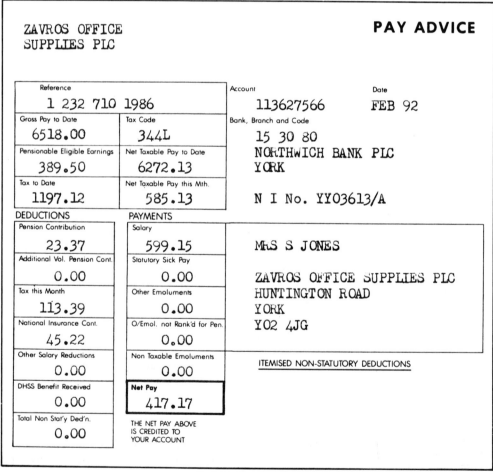

Fig.15.1. The payslip

ii National Insurance Contributions (NIC)

This is also a compulsory deduction which is paid to the Government Department of Health and Social Security. These contributions go mainly towards providing the state pension when we retire, and the sickness benefits to which we are entitled during our working lives. In Fig. 15.1 the NIC is £45.22 per month, approximately 8% of the gross salary. As can be seen from Fig. 15.1, the pay slip includes a National Insurance Number,

Mrs Jones has the Number YY703613/A, and everyone will be given a number if they are paying National Insurance contributions. The number is given so that a record can be kept of who has paid and exactly how much. A school leaver will normally receive a National Insurance Number on starting work and this number will remain with the employee throughout his or her life.

B. VOLUNTARY DEDUCTIONS

These are *not* enforced by law.

i Union Membership Subscriptions
You may be a member of a union and rather than pay your membership subscription on a yearly basis you may decide to pay it monthly. So, for example, if your union membership subscription is £54 per year you may make twelve monthly payments of £4.50. Your employer may pay this directly to the union and deduct the amount from your gross pay.

ii Contractual Saving Scheme
Save as You Earn (SAYE) has been set up by the Government as a way of regular saving. You contract to save so much per month for a period of five years, on which you receive a rate of interest. It is linked to the rate of inflation (which means that your money still keeps its purchasing power) and is tax free. You can pay into the state scheme by having your employer transfer part of your income directly into the scheme.

iii Company Pension
You may obtain a company (occupational) pension, in addition to a state pension, if you make contributions on a yearly basis (out of your gross pay) into a pension fund. The money in the pension fund is then invested and goes towards providing pensions for those who have contributed to the fund. Your contributions to the pension fund can be taken out of your pay before you receive it. It is a voluntary deduction and in Fig. 15.1 is shown as £23.37. Pension contributions are made free of tax.

9 ALLOWANCES AND OUTGOINGS

A. ALLOWANCES
You are entitled to earn a certain amount of money before you pay taxes. These are called tax free (or personal) allowances. The personal allowances for the 1992–1993 tax year were:
▶ personal £3445
▶ married couple £1720 (additional allowance)
▶ single parent £1720 (additional allowance)
There are other allowances, such as the dependent relative allowance, the blind person's allowance and the housekeeper allowance. All these allowances are deducted from the gross pay before tax is taken off.

B. OUTGOINGS
These are *expenditures* which the Inland Revenue will accept as valid for tax relief. They can, therefore, be deducted from gross pay (as well as personal allowances) when calculating taxable pay. For example, for certain jobs it is necessary to be a member of a trade union or a professional body, as with accountants and solicitors. You can obtain tax relief on the subscription, provided the trade union or the professional bodies are recognised by the Inland Revenue and are seen as being relevant to the job.

C. ALLOWABLE BUSINESS EXPENSES
These also qualify for tax relief. If business expenses are seen as an important part of the job then they can be allowed for in the tax calculation. Business expenses normally relate to those who are self-employed and could cover such things as advertising and rent. A written record of all expenses will be needed, which means that receipts must be kept.

10 > TAX CODES

The Inland Revenue can keep a check on an invidual's earnings through the returns made by his employer and through the annual Tax Return filled out by the individual. For most people those earnings come from a single job and they will only be asked to fill in a tax return every two or three years. Others with earnings from several sources will be asked to fill one in every year. Individuals are sent tax forms in April each year. The forms require details of their income, allowances, and outgoings. The allowances and outgoings are then set against gross income to give net taxable income for the year. When this has been calculated, a tax code is issued by the Inland Revenue. This makes sure that the employer deducts the correct amount of tax each month.

The tax code in Fig. 15.1 is 344L. The letter L means that the individual is taxed as a single person. As stated, the personal allowance is £3445 and 344 in the tax code represents the first three numbers of the allowance. For Mrs Jones, there are no other allowances or outgoings; if there were, the code would be higher than 344. A tax code of 516H would mean that the individual receives not only the personal allowance but also the married couple's allowance (total £5165) and 516 in the tax code represents the first three numbers of the allowance. H represents the code for a married person.

Any other allowances, as stated in the last section, will also be added on to the personal allowance and will be included in the code. So if a married man pays union fees of £100 per annum, and these have been agreed by the Inland Revenue, then his code will be 526H.

11 > FRINGE BENEFITS

An employee can obtain benefits from the company which are extra to the wage or salary. Mrs Jones works for Zavros Office Supplies PLC and she may be able to receive a number of fringe benefits.

A. SUBSIDISED CANTEEN

Zavros Office Supplies may be large enough to provide meals either at a reduced rate or free of charge to their employees.

B. COMPANY CARS

A company car may be provided with the job. This could be to employees at a senior level in the company and is a major fringe benefit. This benefit is, however, subject to income tax. Mrs Jones works as a personnel assistant and she may not be senior enough to be allocated a company car.

C. LOWER PRICES PAID FOR COMPANY GOODS

In many manufacturing companies the employees are allowed to purchase the company products at a discount. This is also true for many stores which allow discounts to their staff on the products they sell. Companies which provide a service may also allow discounts to employees. Mrs Jones is probably able to obtain stationery, i.e. paper, envelopes, cards, etc., at a reduced rate.

D. REDUCED INTEREST ON LOANS

Financial institutions may allow their employees to obtain loans at reduced rates of interest. Many banks and building societies offer their staff reduced rates on mortgages and personal loans.

E. CHILDREN'S EDUCATION

An employee may have to work abroad for a certain period of time and whilst abroad the company may provide for their employee's children to attend private schools in the UK.

F. REMOVAL EXPENSES AND LEGAL FEES

If an employee moves within the country, for example with promotion, then the company will normally help with the removal expenses and the legal costs of buying and selling property.

G. HEALTH BENEFITS

The company may provide membership of a private medical insurance scheme free or at a reduced rate. This will allow the employee and perhaps his or her family to receive private medical care.

---

12 ▷ JOB SATISFACTION

Individuals will have different ideas as to what makes a job satisfying, including:

A. PAY

Pay is of key significance to job satisfaction and is covered in detail in this chapter.

B. PROMOTION PROSPECTS

Good promotion prospects are likely to increase job satisfaction. Mrs Jones is undertaking The Institute of Personnel Management course on a day-release basis at the local college. If she passes the examinations then there is a strong possibility she will be promoted to be a personnel manager.

C. ENVIRONMENT

❝ **Note that job satisfaction is about much more than pay.** ❞

The environment the employees have to work in can affect their job satisfaction. The levels of noise, heating, ventilation and dirt and the presence or absence of facilities such as changing rooms and canteens, are all seen as important. Here Mrs Jones is fortunate because the office she works in has only recently been built and is an ideal working environment, being quiet, centrally heated, well-ventilated and clean.

D. COLLEAGUES

If you find it difficult to get on with your colleagues at work then it will obviously affect your job satisfaction. Mrs Jones works closely with eight people in the personnel department and, although she works well with most of them, there is one she finds very difficult to work with. This personality clash tends to upset her from time to time, and reduces her effectiveness at work.

E. FRINGE BENEFITS

The job may provide 'perks' (perquisites) which are extra to pay and can take a number of different forms.

F. MANAGEMENT STYLE

Management style, whether autocratic or democratic may influence a person's satisfaction at work. Management style is dealt with in more detail in Ch.5.

G. WORKING HOURS

'Working hours' refers not only to the hours the employee actually works but also the times of day or night the hours are worked. Many people work a fixed day, say from 9.00 am to 5.00 pm, but others work shifts or flexitime.

(i)   *Shift work*: this is used extensively in manufacturing industries, when it is less expensive to keep machinery going through the night. So as one group of workers (a shift) finishes then another shift starts. Many individuals do not enjoy working on the night shift and this may affect job satisfaction. Hours worked outside a period from 8 am to 5 pm are called 'unsocial hours' and are paid at a higher rate.

(ii) *Flexitime*: a flexible working hours scheme may increase job satisfaction because it allows employees to vary their hours of work, within limits. Flexitime normally operates on the basis that employees have to be at work between 10.00 am and 12 noon and 2.00 pm and 4.00 pm (known as the core time) but that they can arrive at work early (usually not before 8.00 am) and leave late (usually up to 6.30 pm). Employees will have to work a certain number of hours per week but have flexibility in deciding how those hours are made up. Zavros Office Supplies PLC operates flexitime, which pleases Mrs Jones as it allows her to build up extra hours which she can use to take a half-day holiday every so often.

H. JOB CONTENT

There is no substitute for an interesting job. If you work in a factory on a mass-production line, putting chocolates into boxes for example, then you may find it boring and frustrating. Here the lack of job satisfaction may in some way be compensated by higher pay. Attempts to give varied experience to employees may increase job satisfaction.

I. RECOGNITION

Employees may feel a greater degree of satisfaction in their job if recognition is shown of the work they have undertaken. This again refers to the style of management and how those in managerial positions relate to their work force.

J. LEVEL OF RESPONSIBILITY

The greater the level of responsibility given to the employee the greater may be his or her feeling of worth and as a result the greater the job satisfaction.

13 ► MANAGEMENT AND JOB SATISFACTION

Management can attempt to deal with the problem of a lack of job satisfaction and motivation by:

     ► Job enlargement   ► Job enrichment   ► Job rotation

1. A job may be *enlarged* to allow the employee to undertake a wider range of different tasks but all with the same level of difficulty and responsibility. This may reduce the level of boredom and frustration.
2. A job may be *enriched* by giving the employee a greater range of tasks to do, with variations in the level of difficulty and responsibility. This will obviously demand more of the employee and, hopefully, increase job satisfaction.
3. With *job rotation* the employees all learn a number of basic skills and exchange jobs at regular intervals, perhaps working as a team. Job rotation reduces boredom and can help increase job satisfaction.

EXAMINATION QUESTIONS

QUESTION 1

A firm pays its employees by piece-rates.
(a) State ONE advantage to the firm. (3 lines for answer)
(b) State ONE advantage to the employees. (3 lines for answer)
Specimen question: London & East Anglian Group.

PAY SLIP		Location	Pay No.	Name		Month	N.I. Number
		247	9090021	J BROWN		SEP 1982	ZT 128578C

Pay to Date (excl. Supn.)	Pay with other Employment	Tax to Date	Tax with other Employment	Supn. to Date	N.I. to Date	Tax Code
3668.09		804.90		234.16	124.86	156L

Gross Pay	Overtime etc.	Sick Benefit Adjustment	Sup'n Addit Pay	Gross Pay After Adjustment	Superann.	Income Tax	Nat. Ins
671.00				671.00	40.26	150.00	21.47

Advances	Other Deductions	Round up last month	Non Taxable Allowances		Net Pay	Round up this month
	20.00					

QUESTION 2

The Monthly pay slip of John Brown, an office worker, is shown on page 148. Unfortunately the computer has left out the figure for net pay.

(a)   What is John Brown's Pay Number?   **(1 mark)**

(b)   What do the initials N.I. on the pay slip stand for?   **(1 mark)**

(c)   State how much John Brown paid in September towards his pension scheme.   **(1 mark)**

(d)   How much tax had John Brown paid BEFORE receiving his September pay slip?   **(1 mark)**

(e)   Calculate John Brown's net pay for September.   **(2 marks)**

(f)   State:
      (i)   John Brown's tax code number.
                                                                             (1 mark)
      (ii) How this number is arrived at.
      (3 lines for answer)   **(2 marks)**
      (iii)   How John Brown is informed each year of his tax code.
      (2 lines for answer)   **(1 mark)**
Specimen question: London & East Anglian Group.

TUTOR'S ANSWER TO QUESTION 2

(a)   9090021
(b)   N.I. stand for National Insurance.
(c)   £40.26. Superannuation. *Take your time over these questions because it is very easy to write down the wrong figure.*
(d)   £804.90.
(e)   *Again you need to be careful when working out these calculation questions.*
      Gross pay minus Deductions = Net pay.
      So Gross pay = £671.00

Income Tax	£150.00
National Insurance	£21.47
Pension	£40.26
Other Deductions	20.00
Total Deductions =	£231.73

So £671.00 *minus* £231.73 = Net Pay £439.27.
(f)   (i)   Tax code 156L.
      (ii)   This number is arrived at by taking into account his personal allowances. He will be able to earn a certain amount before he is taxed and because he is single (denoted by the letter L in the code) then he is eligible for the single person's allowance. He may also be entitled to other allowances.
      (iii)   The Inland Revenue will inform John Brown of his tax code.

C O U R S E W O R K

ASSIGNMENT – WORKING FOR A LIVING

In this assignment you should describe how a selection of your family and/or friends are motivated in their work. (Be sure to tell them that any information will be treated confidentially and that their names will not be revealed in the assignment.)

You might divide your questions into pay, conditions at work, job satisfaction and fringe benefits.

The following questions will give you a start to the assignment but there may be others you can think of.

1. Find out from members of your family or from friends, which method they are paid by:
    (a)   Time Rate
    (b)   Piece Rate
    (c)   Standard Rate

2. What do the individuals you have chosen see as the advantages and disadvantages of their method of pay? Do these match the advantages and disadvantages given by this chapter?

3. Are the individuals you have chosen, members of any profit-sharing or bonus scheme? If they are, what do they see as the advantages or disadvantages of such schemes?

4. In this chapter, we listed on page 147 the factors which influence job satisfaction. Ask your chosen friends/family to give a list of factors which *they* feel affect their job satisfaction. Do they agree or disagree with the list?

    Are there any other influences on job satisfaction (for example, closeness to home) which are not on the list?

5. Are there any fringe benefits obtained with their jobs? If so what are they? Are they a major factor in job satisfaction and motivation?

    Use any illustrations and examples you feel are relevant.

STUDENT'S ANSWER – EXAMINER'S COMMENTS

QUESTION

A firm pays its employees by piece-rates.
- (a)   State ONE advantage to the firm.
- (b)   State ONE advantage to the employees.

> **Good. You can also mention that the firm will benefit from having less need to supervise its workforce.**

2. a)   One advantage to the firm:-
         The firm can see the amount of work individual staff are producing, and can compare the efficiency between members of staff.

> **Good. The answer gets across the idea that wages are directly linked to the amount produced.**

b)   One advantage to the employees:-
     Gives them an incentive to work faster and more efficiently. The more they produce, the larger wage packet they will receive at the end of the day.

> **A good answer overall, showing that the student understands what is meant by piece rates. Make sure that you can distinguish between piece rates and a standard rate.**

16

COMMUNICATION

INTERNAL COMMUNICATIONS
EXTERNAL COMMUNICATIONS
EFFECTIVE COMMUNICATIONS

GETTING STARTED

There are many different ways in which communications are important for today's businesses. Modern firms need to communicate with a large number of different groups of people:

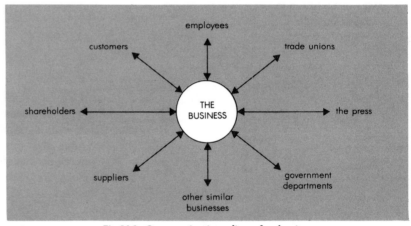

Fig.16.1. Communications lines for business

All these groups communicate with business in different ways. At one end of the scale there is the humble letter while, at the other end, are all the very high-speed links between modern computers, which pass millions of pieces of information every minute.

There are written forms of communication (like letters and reports), visual forms (such as charts, diagrams and television), oral forms (such as speeches, interviews, and telephone) and electronic forms (like telex, fax and computers). A further type of communication is usually ignored or forgotten – human communication on a *non-verbal* basis. This type of communication is normally called *body language* but it really uses our faces more than our bodies.

Types of communication
▶ Written
▶ Oral
▶ Visual
▶ Electronic
▶ Non-verbal
Remember: WOVEN

In order to simplify the extremely complex subject of communications it is best to divide it into those forms of communication which take place *within* the business and those which take place *between* the business and the outside world.

ESSENTIAL PRINCIPLES

A. WRITTEN COMMUNICATIONS

i. Letters

The letter is a form of written communication which is rarely used *within* companies except in special circumstances:

    (a)   between separate parts of the same company which happen to be situated in different parts of the country or in different parts of the world.

THE SICK PARROT RECORD COMPANY LTD
15 High Street
Hollywoodville
HD15 9FN

14 February 1992

Mr L.J. Silver,
The Ship Inn,   Our ref: AB87/0
Treasure Island,   Your reference: SP/LJS
TI5 8PE

Dear Mr Silver,

RECORDING PROPOSAL

Thank you for your letter of 24 January and for the demonstration tape enclosed with it.

I am afraid that our record company does not normally publish sea-shanties and, even if we were to change our policy, we do not think that "Yo, Ho, Ho, and a bottle of rum" is a suitable lyric for the younger audience today.

I am returning your tape with this letter and wish you luck in finding a publisher.

Yours sincerely,

Brian Opstein,
Managing Director.

Fig.16.2. A business letter

MEMORANDUM

To: Post Clerk,   Date: 14 February 1992

From: B. Opstein

Subject: Letters from Mr L.J. Silver

Please note that I have received yet another demo tape from this character. That makes three hundred and seventy two to date!
I am thoroughly tired of sea-shanties and promises of maps of buried treasure and chests full of pieces of eight. In future, please intercept these letters (you will recognise them by the parrot beak marks on the envelope) and return them, unopened, to the sender.

Fig.16.3. A Business Memo

     (b)   between managers and employees in a formal matter, such as employment (the letter of appointment), changes in conditions of service (e.g. promotion or an increase in holiday entitlement) or dismissal.

The letter is treated in greater detail under **external communications** below.

ii. Memos

Almost all of the written communication within businesses is in the form of **memorandums**, **memos** for short. A memo is an informal type of letter which, because it is only sent to people in the same company, does not need to be fully addressed. Figures 16.2 and 16.3 demonstrate the headings of both letters and memos. Memos are not usually signed and they are relatively informal but this does not mean that they do not matter. Memos are part of the official communications of the business and must be treated seriously – in court actions the memos betwen members of staff in a business can be used as evidence.

iii. Reports

Reports are used where a much longer piece of work has to be communicated within the company or by outsiders who are working for the business on a temporary basis. It is generally a detailed written statement on a particular subject. It can be compiled by an individual or by a group and usually contains specific elements, although the shape and order of these elements can differ between companies:

     (a)   A section stating the **objectives** of the report usually in the form of **terms of reference** (the limits which are placed on the investigation needed to compile the report).

     (b)   A section detailing the **findings** of the report – that is, the results of the investigations which were carried out.

     (c)   A conclusion which will usually also contain **recommendations** about the subject of the report.

iv. Agendas

Meetings are a form of oral communication but they need to have some written elements so that people can know what the meeting is supposed to cover and, after it has happened, what the meeting decided. Before every meeting, therefore, the secretary of the committee will send out an **agenda** – a list of points to be discussed which are usually given in a set order:

> ▶ **Apologies for absence** – from anyone who cannot attend
> ▶ **Matters arising** – any matter which a member might want to bring up concerning anything which happened at the last meeting
> ▶ **Main points for discussion**
> ▶ **Any other business** – any relevant subject which may not have been announced on the agenda
> ▶ **Date of the next meeting** – date, place and time.

v. Minutes

Following a meeting, the secretary of the committee, or someone who is nominated, will draw up and issue a record of what was decided by the meeting. This record is called the Minutes of the Meeting.

They are **not** a word-by-word account of exactly what was said (that would be a **transcript**) but are an account of the main matters which were covered, together with the decisions which were taken and a list of who is responsible for carrying out those decisions (see Fig. 16.4).

vi. In-House Journals or Magazines

Many companies communicate with their staff through regular newsletters or newspapers which are usually called **in-house magazines**.

They are magazines produced by the firm itself, circulated purely within the company and will contain news about new products, new employees, special trips being organised, and so on. The magazines are intended to help make staff feel more a part of the organisation and make sure that they know more about what is happening.

There will, of course, be many other forms of written communication within a company, including rule books for the pension fund and sickness scheme, and brochures explaining any discount schemes which may be available. Most large companies also produce an **Annual Report** for their employees which tells them, often in a very colourful and graphic way, how the company is progressing and what its plans for the future are.

MINUTES OF A MEETING OF THE BOARD OF DIRECTORS OF THE SICK PARROT RECORD COMPANY LTD. HELD AT 15, HIGH STREET, HOLLYWOODVILLE ON 30 MARCH 1992

ACTION

Present: Lord Carrott of Cockleton, Chairman.
B. Opstein, Managing Director
Lady Carrot,
P. McCourtney
M. Jogger
Apologies for absence: were received from Sir Eric Whipsnade.

Minutes: The minutes of the last meeting were agreed.

Matters Arising: Lady Carrott reminded the Board that the gold record for Mr Elton Frank had still not been delivered to his mansion in Chelsea.

Mr L.J. Silver: Mr Opstein brought the Board up to date on the matter of the large quantities of demo tapes submitted by Mr Silver, and asked the Board for advice as to how to discourage future supplies of sea-shanties.
It was decided, following a suggestion by Lady Carrot, that Mr P. McCourtney would ask Mr Silver to join him for a re-recording of the old favourite 'The Skye Boat Song'.   P.M.

Any Other Business: Mr Jogger asked the Board why the company had not yet re-released his hit-album "This is the Perambulating Boulders No 37". It was agreed that Mr Opstein would look into the matter.   B.O.

Next Meeting: It was agreed that the next meeting would be held at the Board's premises on 4 April 1992.

Fig.16.4. Minutes of a Board Meeting

B. ORAL COMMUNICATIONS

i. The Telephone

A great deal of oral contact within companies is conducted on the telephone these days and many firms now have internal telephone systems which allow the employees to have conferences with other staff by phone. Up to five or six members of staff can speak together and have a 'meeting' on the phone, without leaving their own individual offices.

ii. Meetings

Meetings are an important form of internal communication. Some are held by telephone or even by video-link (see below) but most are still held on a face-to-face basis in a single room.

iii. Interviews and Assessments

Staff can usually communicate with their bosses in an informal oral way at any time, but firms now have formal ways of communicating as well. If a member of staff is seriously concerned about something, they can request a formal interview with their superior in order to try to sort the matter out. In a similar way, the boss might request a formal interview with the employee in order to bring a serious matter to their attention.

Many companies these days also use formal staff assessment interviews in order to make sure that staff are happy with their work (and that their boss is happy with *them*), to set objectives for the next year and to investigate ways of helping the member of staff to further their career (through further training or education).

iv. Works Committees

Although still not very common, some companies have Works Committees which are attended by representatives of both management and employees. The objective of these committees is to try to make sure that any ideas or problems which might be identified by either management or staff can be discussed.

C. VISUAL AND ELECTRONIC COMMUNICATIONS

Companies use many visual forms of communications internally including posters – for safety information or to let employees know about special offers – and even television. An increasing number of companies these days also ensure that any micro-computers which staff have on their desks are linked together so that letters, reports, memos, and other messages can be sent electronically between them without the need for expensive typing and distribution of paper.

D. NON-VERBAL COMMUNICATIONS

We all communicate in non-verbal ways but we are so used to reading the signals that we hardly notice it. Most people know what it means when someone winks at them. Without a word being said, we can distinguish between a wink which means, "Don't say a word, I am kidding your colleague here", and one which means, "I like you and I want to be friends but I don't know where to begin".

Similarly, it does not normally take an expert to tell you how your father, mother, boss, or teacher is feeling, without a single word being necessary. You read their body language – the frown, scowl, smile, raised eyebrow, or slant of the head. These will tell you almost all you need to know but there are many other, more subtle, signs which we also read – such as the way they stand, or hold their hands or the gestures they make.

Non-verbal communication is being studied in many parts of the world and it has become a serious study for many managers. Careful use of an expert knowledge of non-verbal communication can help managers to understand more about how their staff are feeling.

2   EXTERNAL COMMUNICATIONS

A. WRITTEN COMMUNICATIONS

i. Letters

Firms make use of letters, brochures, and reports as their main forms of external communications. The example of a letter on p. 153 is one to a person outside the company. A Memo would never be sent to someone outside the firm unless it is a copy of an internal memo in order to help them in some way. It should be noted that most memos are considered *confidential* to the firm and should *never* be copied to people outside without the permission of senior managers.

ii. Annual Reports

Annual Reports and Accounts are required by law to be sent to all of the shareholders of a limited company. They contain details of the financial performance of the company during the year and details of the directors who will have to be re-elected at the next Annual General Meeting.

B. ORAL COMMUNICATIONS

i. Telephone

The telephone is, today, the most common way in which people outside a company communicate with it. Most companies now recognise the need for special training for staff who have to deal with the public on the phone. Receptionists and telephone switchboard operators usually have quite long courses on how to deal with people on the phone.

ii. Face-to-face

The phone may be very important but face-to-face contact is still a vital aspect of many businesses. Shops, banks, building societies, hotels, etc., all have to train their staff to be able to deal with the public directly.

C. VISUAL

Today's companies are highly skilled in communicating visually with the outside world. We live in a very visual world in which people are subjected to a large amount of visual communication and the most successful companies are those which make best use of this fact with advertising.

In newspapers and magazines, on the television and on posters, the object is to make people take notice of your product or service by presenting them with attractive and interesting visuals. The advertising can be for your product or service, or for jobs which you would like to attract people into, but it will not be successful unless it draws people to look at it and to read the copy (the written words which form the main part of the ad).

D. ELECTRONIC

There is a wide range of electronic forms of communications and it is growing all the time. The simplest of all is the telephone which has been mentioned above. Most of the newer forms of electronic communications rely on computers to send and receive the information.

i. Computers

Computer communications depend upon a business having:
► a computer (usually a *micro* but quite possibly a larger *mini* or *mainframe*)
► a *modem* (which plugs into the telephone network and enables you to dial into it)
► communications *software* (a computer program which tells the computer how to send and receive messages).
If you have all these pieces of equipment – and they are very common these days even amongst private home-computer users – the computer will act as a receiver for all sorts of information and services:

Databases – for a fixed fee your computer can link itself to much larger computers and can let you use the immense amounts of information contained on those larger machines. Prestel is just one of the more common databases but there are many more.

Telex and mail – again, for a separate fee, you can be linked to an electronic telex service and to electronic 'mail-boxes' into which you can put messages for other people and they can do the same for you. The messages are kept in the memory of a large computer and can be 'read' by your computer whenever you wish.

ii. Facsimile Transmission

Usually just called *fax*, this is a way of sending written or printed pages through the telephone system. If your office has a fax machine and you wish to send a document through to another office in a different city the normal way to do it is by post.

Postal services can be quite slow, though, especially if the other office is in a different country. You might be able to use the *telex* but this is more expensive and means that someone has to type the whole document out again onto the telex machine. As long as the other office has a fax machine, however, you need simply to feed your letter into the machine, dial the number of the other office and the machine will send the letter through almost instantly. What really happens is that the other office receives a type of photocopy of the letter (the original stays with you).

Fax is a very fast form of communication and is much cheaper than telex. It is also very useful for sending graphics (something which telex cannot do and which, up to now, had to be done through the post or by an expensive special messenger). Designs, engineering drawings, even photographs, can be faxed almost instantly. It is known as 'Intelpost'. Today some newspapers use a special form of fax system to send whole pages of a newspaper to other printing works around the world.

iii. Video-conferencing

Face-to-face meetings are still the most usual way that firms conduct their business. The telephone is immensely valuable but business people still like to see the faces of the other person when they are trying to do important business. A person's face can tell you a lot about what he or she really means. Consequently many people still drive hundreds of miles or fly thousands of miles in order to have meetings with other people. A great deal of time and money would be saved if all this travel could be avoided.

Video-conferencing attempts to get around the problem by asking a person who wants to have a meeting to walk along the corridor and to sit in front of a bank of screens and a television camera. The camera takes his or her picture to the other people and the screens show all of the other people to him or her. At present video-conferencing is very expensive. The telephone connections for the TV pictures are slow and not of a very high quality, and the cost of these lines is very high. Companies which want to take advantage of video-conferencing have to install expensive suites of TV screens and cameras.

Some large, multinational companies which have factories all over the world, have installed video-conference suites because it is cheaper than sending executives all over the world to meetings.

Before video-conferencing becomes widely available to everybody, however, a cheaper way of transmitting the pictures and the voices will be necessary. Fibre-optic links will be able to do this. In a few years it will begin to be more common for business-people to hold video-meetings than for them to spend large amounts of time travelling to the face-to-face variety.

E. INFORMATION TECHNOLOGY

In the past it was not clearly understood that communications like the postal service, were really part of the storage and retrieval of information for business. Even in Victorian times, however, firms which needed to know something had to send letters and then wait for the answer to be returned in the same way – whether it was to ask the price of a piece of equipment which they wanted to buy, or whether one of their customers wanted to re-order some goods. The answers were then acted upon (we hope) and the letters were stored away for future reference. The price list would be stored so that the firm would be able to find out other prices fairly quickly, and the letter from the customer would be stored just in case they came back at some time and claimed that they had never ordered the goods or that they had ordered a different amount.

> Typist types a letter asking for the price list.
>
> Letter is posted to the supplier.
>
> One or two days later, letter arrives and is sent to the correct department.
>
> Sales department receives letter and posts a full price list back after, say, two days.
>
> Price list arrives through post one or two days later.
>
> Price list is examined, used and then filed in a filing cabinet.
>
> If the list is needed a week later, someone must walk down to the filing room, find the correct file, remove the price list and return it to the executive who requires the information.

Fig.16.5. Elementary Information Technology – getting, storing and retrieving a price list.

Consider what might happen to the same information with today's information technology: the micro-computer on the executive's desk would be used to link him or her to the supplier's computer and, within seconds, the price list would flash up onto the screen. If a record of the list was required it could be printed out on the printer next to the micro-computer and, if needed to be saved for future reference, it could be saved onto a floppy disk. If the executive wanted another price from the list in a week's time the floppy disk could be selected and inserted in seconds and the information retrieved a few seconds later.

Information technology is not just about speed, however. Modern technology also allows us to store very large amounts of information in a very small space – hence saving money on the cost of floor space and on the labour required to file and retrieve information. Rather than rooms full of layers of shelving or rows and rows of filing cabinets the modern company simply has a computer. Most of the book you are now reading was written and stored on a computer. Its twenty chapters, introduction and indexes are actually kept on just one disk. A similar book written several years ago took up three full drawers of files of a filing cabinet (i.e. almost 70 files).

Micro-computer used to request information on prices direct from the supplier's computer.

Within seconds, information appears on screen.

A written copy can be obtained almost immediately from the printer.

The price list can be electronically filed within seconds on disk.

If required, a week later, the information can be retrieved within seconds from the disk.

Fig.16.6. Information Technology in an Electronic Age

No matter how fast or efficient a communications system is, it is totally useless if the people who are at the receiving end of the system do not understand what the person at the other end is trying to tell them. Within a company, communications have to be in *two* directions – from the senior people to those who make the goods or provide the service, and the other way round.

EMPLOYEES: make suggestions
                react to communications from above
                have attitudes
                have problems
                have ideas and views

MANAGERS: make decisions
                have reasons for those decisions
                make policy for the future
                make proposals for discussion
                want to change ideas and attitudes

Fig.16.7. Two-way communications in Business

The most successful companies are those which enable this two-way process to work. Managers cannot run things properly if they do not know what the problems of the workforce are or if they do not listen to suggestions from below; employees cannot work effectively if the decisions of management are not communicated clearly and quickly or if they do not understand where the company is trying to go in the future.

There is no secret to effective communications except that everyone must understand that the process has to be *two-way*.

In order to be effective, communication must also be:

▶ *accurate:* you must tell people exactly what you want – try going into a record shop and saying simply that you 'want some music'. In business the manager who tells his foreman that he wants 'changes in the production times' will also not be very successful.

▶ *confirmed:* it is important that you make sure that your message has been received and understood.

Neither of these is as easy as it sounds. Your memo to your staff may seem perfectly clear to you but may leave them puzzled as to exactly what you want or when you want it. 'Please make sure that the papers are delivered well before the board meeting' could mean many things: Which papers? Delivered to where or to whom? Which board meeting (our company's, someone else's, the next board meeting or the one after that, etc.)?

EXAMINATION QUESTIONS

QUESTION 1
A _____ is an informal means of communication between departments of the same organisation.
Specimen question: London & East Anglian Group.

QUESTION 2
In the following questions there is one group of responses A, B, C and D. Each letter in the group may be used once, more than once, or not at all. For each question select the best response and mark its letter in the space provided:
A   Telephone
B   Postal Service
C   Confravision
D   Intelpost
From the above forms of communication, A to D, select the one which –
(a)   is a means of holding face-to-face meetings between people working in different areas of the country.
      Answer _____
(b)   is used to acknowledge receipt of a routine order from another firm.
      Answer _____
(c)   is a means of transmitting facsimiles of documents and drawings at high speed.
      Answer _____
(d)   is used to discuss a business problem with a colleague at a branch in another town.
      Answer _____
(e)   is used to link individuals or groups of people in different cities by sound and vision
      Answer _____
Specimen question: London & East Anglian Group

TUTOR'S ANSWERS TO QUESTIONS 1 AND 2

1. Memo.
2. a) C   b) B   c) D   d) A   e) C

C O U R S E W O R K

ASSIGNMENT – COMMUNICATION

Compile a report, with diagrams, which describes the way in which an organisation, with which you are familiar, communicates.
► Start by asking the administrators how they communicate with the staff, with the employees or students, and with the outside world.
► What types of communications media do they use? – electronic types, non-electronic types, etc. (Do not forget human contact as well.)
► Draw a diagram which shows all these communications routes and describe how they are used and for what reasons
► Try, also, to find out how the communications for your organisation could be improved.

17

INDUSTRIAL RELATIONS

**TRADE UNIONS
COLLECTIVE BARGAINING
INDUSTRIAL ACTION
RESOLVING DEADLOCK**

G E T T I N G   S T A R T E D

In December 1990 there were 287 trade unions in the UK with a total membership of 9,947,000. Some of the trade unions were small with less than 100 members whereas others were large, with 10 unions having over 250,000 members. Over the period 1980 to 1990 the number of trade unions declined from 438 to 287. This was partly the result of small craft unions joining with larger ones. In fact, 23 trade unions with over 100,000 members accounted for 81% of the total trade union membership in 1990 (see Tables 17.1 and 17.2 overleaf).

Therefore over 9 miliion workers are members of trade unions, out of an employed workforce of approximately 24½ million. What are the main aims of trade unions? What are the reasons for joining a trade union? Are there different types of trade union? What sort of action might a union ask you to take if you are a trade union member? If there is a conflict between the employer you work for and the trade union you are a member of, then how will that conflict be resolved? These are the main questions you will need to ask yourself whilst reading this chapter. One point to note is that, although this chapter concentrates on the *conflict* side of industrial relations, trade unions do have other roles to play. For example, they are involved in discussions on the economy with representatives from business and government, and in providing education and training, legal advice and social facilities for their members.

Table 17.1 Trade unions: numbers and membership 1980–90

Year	Number of unions at end of year	Total membership at end of year (thousands)	Percentage change in membership since previous year
1980	438	12,947	–2.6
1981	414	12,106	–6.5
1982	408	11,593	–4.2
1983	394	11,236	–3.1
1984	375	10,994	–3.2
1985	370	10,821	–1.6
1986	335	10,539	–2.6
1987	330	10,475	–0.6
1988	315	10,376	–0.9
1989	309	10,158	–2.1
1990	287	9,947	–2.1

Source: Employment Gazette April 1992

Table 17.2 Trade unions: numbers and membership December 1990

Number of members	Number of unions	Membership (thousands)	Number of unions (per cent)	Membership of all unions (per cent)
Under 100	44	2	15.3	0.02
100–499	65	17	22.6	0.2
500–999	22	15	7.7	0.2
1,000–2,499	43	72	15	0.7
2,500–4,999	27	98	9.4	1
5,000–9,999	15	104	5.2	1
10,000–14,999	6	71	2.1	0.7
15,000–24,999	9	167	3.1	1.7
25,000–49,999	25	892	8.7	9
50,000–99,999	7	490	2.4	4.9
100,000–249,999	14	2,233	4.9	22.4
250,000 and more	9	5,785	3.1	58.2
*membership unknown	1		0.3	
All	287	9,947	100	100

*There was one newly formed union in 1990 whose membership is not available.

Source: *Employment Gazette* April 1992

E S S E N T I A L   P R I N C I P L E S

1 ▶ TRADE UNIONS

What are trade unions? They can be traced back as far as the Middle Ages but it is only since the nineteenth century that modern trade unions have developed. They are made up of groups of workers who have a common interest, which may be a common skill, a similar job or the same industry. By joining together as a union the workers can act like a pressure group (see Ch. 18). The members of the union will pay a subscription, part of which will go towards employing union officials. These officials will present the views of the union to the employers in a bid to achieve their aims.

A. THE AIMS OF TRADE UNIONS

A trade union will usually seek to be involved in anything which will affect the situation of its members. The main aims of a trade union can be listed as follows:

1. To improve the conditions of employment, such as wages, holidays and hours of work.
2. To improve the working environment, such as lighting, heating, safety, noise and ventilation.
3. To improve the benefits of the members who are sick, retired or who have been made redundant.
4. To take up the cases of those whom the union see as being unfairly dismissed.
5. To improve job satisfaction, which may mean promoting education and training.

6.   To share in the planning and controlling of the company.
7.   To aid job security.
8.   To influence government decisions. With this in mind, a number of trade unions sponsor MPs and make a political levy (charge) on their members to pay for this sponsorship. The aim is to give the union a voice in Parliament.

B. REASONS FOR JOINING A TRADE UNION

When you start your first job you will normally be contacted by the trade union representative (normally the shop steward) who will ask you if you want to join the trade union. If you do join a union you will have to pay a yearly union subscription. This could be paid all at once or as a certain amount per week out of your wages.

You may be able to make a list of the reasons for joining a trade union and it may include some of the following:

1.   To improve your level of pay (basic rate) and working conditions.
2.   To provide support if you think you have been unfairly treated, unfairly dismissed or made redundant. This may be in terms of advice and/or financial help.
3.   To take advantage of sporting and other social facilities.
4.   To benefit from training courses run by the union.
5.   To obtain discounts in certain shops and for certain services such as holidays.
6.   To identify with colleagues at work who are members of the trade union and who might pressure you to join.
7.   To gain employment where a 'closed shop' may be in operation.

In a **closed shop**, only a member of a particular union can be employed by the firm. The trade union may see the benefits of a closed shop as follows:

   (i)   Non-members of the trade union also receive the benefits which a union obtains for its members, such as wage increases, and so should pay union subscriptions.
   (ii) The union may feel that a closed shop improves its 'bargaining power' because all the employees are members of the union.

The main argument against closed shops is that employees should have the freedom to decide whether or not they wish to join a trade union.

It may also be seen as unfair that a person is not allowed to work in a particular job unless he is a member of a particular trade union.

> **Note that the reasons for joining a Trade Union are not just to improve the level of pay.**

C. TYPES OF TRADE UNION

There are four main **types** of trade union, as can be seen in Fig. 17.1.

Fig.17.1. The types of trade union

i. Craft unions

These consist mainly of skilled workers who often undertake long apprenticeships. They are the earliest type of union and there may be several craft unions within a single workplace. This can make it difficult for the management, who often prefer to deal with one large union when negotiating. There can also be disagreements between the craft unions about how the work between the various crafts is allocated (i.e. demarcation disputes) and the relative pay levels (i.e. differentials). The Amalgamated Union of Engineering Workers (AUEW) and the Electrical Electronic and Plumbing Trade Union (EEPTU) are examples of craft unions, although they also accept unskilled workers.

ii. Industrial unions

These unions include all the workers in a particular industry regardless of what job they do in that industry. They tend to be more common in Europe, particularly in West Germany, than they are in the UK. The nearest examples in the UK are the National Union of Mineworkers (NUM) and the National Union of Railwaymen (NUR). Even these cannot be viewed as 'true' industrial unions. Within the coal industry there is also the newly formed Union of Democratic Mineworkers (UDM) and within the railway industry there is also the Associated Society of Locomotive Engineers and Firemen (ASLEF). The benefit of this type of union to the management is that they only have to deal with one trade union, in areas such as pay and working conditions. The benefit to the members is that being larger, they are in a stronger position when negotiating with management.

iii. General unions

General unions cut across industrial boundaries and will include members regardless of skill, type or place of work. They do, however, represent a high proportion of semi- and unskilled workers and are large unions. The Transport and General Workers Union (TGWU), National Union of General and Municipal Workers (NUGMW) and the Union of Shop, Distributive and Allied Workers (USDAW) are examples of general unions. They can be at a disadvantage because of their size, in that the union leaders may find themselves remote from their members. The union may also be very fragmented with their members spread over a large number of industries nationwide.

iv. White collar unions

These unions include non-manual workers in areas such as clerical, professional, management and supervisory occupations. The white collar unions have been the fastest growing unions in recent times as individuals see the benefits which can be obtained from belonging to a trade union. The Association of Scientific, Technical and Managerial Staffs (ASTMS), the National Union of Teachers (NUT) and the National Association of Local Government Officers (NALGO) are examples of white collar unions.

D. THE TRADES UNION CONGRESS (TUC)

Figure 17.1 depicts the TUC as an 'umbrella' over the trade unions. Although there are some unions, mostly small ones, who are not affiliated to the TUC, over 90% of trade unions are affiliated to the TUC. The TUC was formed in 1868 and acts as a pressure group, representing the views of trade unions in trying to influence the employers' associations, such as the Confederation of British Industry (CBI), and the Government itself. The policy of the TUC is decided at the Annual Congress (Conference) which usually lasts for one week in September. Representatives (or delegates) are sent from the various unions. The number of delegates each union sends to the Annual Congress depends on the size of its union membership. Delegates have the right to vote on such things as the election of the General Council which is responsible for promoting TUC policies. These will tend to be policies which seek an improvement in the economic and social conditions of the working population.

E. TRADE UNION REPRESENTATIVES

i. Shop stewards

At the place of work the trade union shop steward will be the union representative you come into contact with the most. The shop steward is elected by the trade union members in the firm, shop or section in which he or she works, although they will still work full-time for the company. They are called shop stewards because they represent the workforce on the 'shopfloor'. (This word originated in the engineering industry which uses the term 'shops' for the various sections of the factory.) The shop steward will form the link between the shopfloor and the union officials. In large companies a worker representative is required because full-time trade union officials are unable to spend sufficient time in all the companies in which they have members. The shop steward therefore has an important role to play, particularly as national wage agreements have declined in importance and plant bargaining has increased. The shop steward will undertake a number of tasks. These include collecting the subscriptions, acting as a voice for the workforce, recruiting new members and distributing information from the union.

ii. Official trade union representatives
Most trade unions will have full-time union officials, who work at the national, regional and district level and have contacts with shop stewards and union members. The top official of the union is often called the General Secretary.

EMPLOYERS' ASSOCIATIONS
In its simplest form an ***employers' association*** is to employers what a trade union is to employees. Most industries have employers' associations which include employers from that particular industry. These associations may be given the power by their members to negotiate with trade unions on matters, such as the wages and working conditions in that industry. They can also provide advice to members, on such things as Employment Law. Examples of employers' associations include the National Farmers Union, the Engineering Employers Association and the National Federation of Retail Newsagents.

As individual firms grow in size through mergers and takeovers, then the need for them to be in an employers' association declines. Some larger firms, for example Ford, have never felt the need to belong to an association.

THE CONFEDERATION OF BRITISH INDUSTRY (CBI)
Just as trade unions are affiliated to the TUC, so employers' associations are members of the CBI. It was formed in 1965 and represents 250,000 companies, from the smallest to the largest, covering primary, secondary and tertiary production. As well as representing the employers point of view in talks with the Government and trade unions, it aims at promoting prosperity in British industry. It effectively acts as the spokesperson for industry and management.

2 ▷ COLLECTIVE BARGAINING

As an individual you may be able to go to your employer (who may be a large organisation) and ask for a wage increase or for better working conditions. However, on your own you may not be successful in your claims, whereas if you were a member of a trade union and they negotiated on your behalf then the result might be different. The negotiations which take place between trade unions and employers or employers' associations are called ***Collective Bargaining***.

This bargaining can take place at a local or national level. With collective bargaining the relevant trade unions and employers meet together to negotiate an agreement, perhaps about pay or working conditions, which could cover the whole industry. In pay negotiations a national agreement will normally refer to basic rates. These can then be improved at local level where aspects such as bonuses may be negotiated. For example, in collective bargaining over wages (see Fig. 17.2 overleaf) the union will normally ask for a wage increase (say a claim of 15%) which may be far higher than the employer would be willing to accept. On the other hand the employer may offer a wage increase (say 5%) which it may later improve upon. The two sides then negotiate to try to find a wage increase which is acceptable by both sides. This may be an agreement for an 8% wage increase.

Suppose, however, there is no agreement, the trade union is not willing to accept an 8% wage increase and the employers are not willing to offer any more. There may be a number of reasons for this. The company profits may be low, or it may feel that it will have to increase the price of its products (and lose custom!) to pay the higher wage increase. In this case a ***deadlock*** is said to occur. In order to make the employer think again and perhaps offer more than 8% the workforce may take industrial action. The industrial action may have the backing of the trade union. If it has the backing of the union, then the union will have to ballot all the union members, getting them to vote for or against industrial action before the action can take place. The action can take a number of forms.

Fig.17.2. The process of collective bargaining

3 ▷ INDUSTRIAL ACTION

The ultimate weapon which is open to many trade unions is to strike, but as shown in Fig. 17.2 there are other types of industrial action.

A. STRIKES
If a worker goes on strike it means that they withdraw their labour and refuse to work. The strike can take a number of different forms.

Token strike
This is when the workers stage a one-day, half-day or even an hour's stoppage of work in support of their claim.

Selective strike
Here only a certain number of workers, perhaps chosen by areas, are called to strike action by their trade union. Those who carry on working will often pay into a fund to help those who are on strike. This can often be a very disruptive form of action.

All-out strike
With an all-out strike normally all members of the union withdraw their labour until the dispute is settled. This sort of strike will usually have trade union support which means that the strike is *official*. Here the union will make available a certain amount of strike pay provided there are sufficient resources to support a 'strike fund'. Part of the trade union subscription made on a monthly basis by members will go towards this fund. An *unofficial* strike on the other hand does not have the unions support or backing and can be called a 'wildcat' strike.

Certain workers may continue to work whilst the strike is in progress. It may be that they disagree with the strike, or cannot afford to strike because of financial commitments such as mortgages and goods bought on credit. These workers may be called 'Blacklegs' by those who are taking strike action.

When calling for strike action, the trade union in question has, under the Trade Union Act 1984, to hold a secret ballot of all its members for the strike to be lawful. The action must be approved by the majority of the union members. If the trade union fails to hold a secret ballot before calling a strike then it loses its legal immunity and the employer could require the strike to be called off and could sue the union for damages.

Picketing

To support their strike action, workers will stand close to the factory gates and try to dissuade other workers and suppliers of goods from entering the factory. You may be aware of picketing in disputes from reports on television or in the newspaper, such as the dispute at the Wapping newspaper plant.

Secondary Picketing

This is picketing which takes place away from the company or industry involved in the dispute. Those involved in secondary picketing can have injunctions issued against them as introduced under the 1980 Employment Act.

Sympathetic Strike

In certain instances a group of workers may take sympathetic strike action in support of another group of workers.

Blacking

A trade union's support of another group of workers may not go as far as strike action but could include 'blacking'. Here they may refuse to handle equipment, goods, etc, of the industry or firm of the workers on strike.

B. WORK-TO-RULE

Here workers stick closely to the rules and regulations which govern their work. These rules can be very detailed and are usually viewed only as guidelines. If, however, the workforce follow them strictly they can bring the company to a standstill.

C. GO-SLOW

Make sure you are aware of the different stages an industrial dispute can go through.

Here the workforce do their jobs more slowly, deliberately taking longer to complete their normal working operations.

D. OVERTIME BAN

This can be very damaging to a company. With this kind of industrial action members of the union only work normal hours and refuse to undertake any overtime.

E. SIT-IN

The workforce may refuse to leave the factory, making sure that no goods enter or leave it. A sit-in might occur if the factory is threatened with closure and is, therefore, a strike against the threat of redundancies. The outcome of this might be that workers take over the business, e.g. as a workers co-operative.

4 RESOLVING A DEADLOCK

The trade union and employers may be in **deadlock**, with neither side being willing to move its position. To help resolve the dispute both sides can call on the Advisory, Conciliation and Arbitration Service (ACAS), see Fig. 17.2. This is an independent body set up by the Employment Protection Act in 1975 with the role of trying to improve industrial relations. It provides its services free and is impartial. It is run by a council made up of a chairperson and nine members nominated by the TUC (3), CBI (3) and 3 independent members.

ACAS provides:

1. ***Advice and information*** on all areas of employment.
2. ***Conciliation***. Here ACAS will be in touch with both sides and will try to find areas which both sides can agree on so that they can come together to start negotiating again.
3. ***Arbitration***. ACAS will, if the two parties agree, refer the dispute to arbitration. An independent group will then listen to the case of both sides and put forward what they view to be a fair settlement. Both sides have to agree in advance to accept the arbitrators' findings.

EXAMINATION QUESTIONS

QUESTION 1

Strikes by workers without trade union support are known as _____
_____ .

Specimen question: London & East Anglian Group

QUESTION 2

An official who acts as a link between trade union members at work and the union's regional office is a _____ .
Specimen question: London & East Anglian Group

QUESTION 3

Collective bargaining is a way of settling wage rates between employers and _____ .
Specimen question: London & East Anglian Group

QUESTION 4

The following article appeared in the 'Daily News'.

Possible Layoffs at XYZ

"We are facing increasing competition from home and abroad". Bob Smith, managing director of XYZ Engineering told our reporter yesterday.

"We must get more up to date machinery and reduce our labour costs. Productivity must improve and we need to become more competitive".

Immediately after the article appeared, Arthur Jones the senior shop steward said, 'This is the first the Union has heard of any changes. I will be calling a meeting of my members tomorrow, and we shall be seeking a meeting with the management as soon as possible. We will resist plans for redundancies'. Bob Smith, when he read the article said, 'They have blown this up out of all proportion. I should have spoken to the unions before letting the press interview me'.

(a) Even before the meeting called by Arthur Jones, many of the members were pressing for immediate strike action. Why might they be suggesting this?

(b) Some members thought that other methods of solving the problem should be tried before taking strike action. What might these methods be and why should the union consider them?

(c) Why do changes at work usually worry the people who will be affected by them?

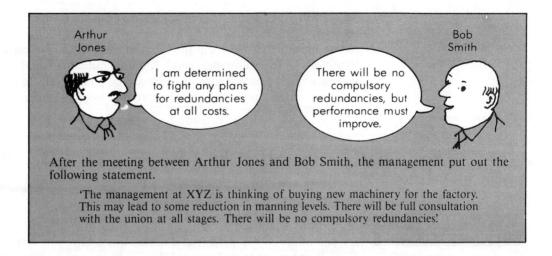

After the meeting between Arthur Jones and Bob Smith, the management put out the following statement.

'The management at XYZ is thinking of buying new machinery for the factory. This may lead to some reduction in manning levels. There will be full consultation with the union at all stages. There will be no compulsory redundancies.'

(d)   What does the management mean by 'There will be full consultation with the union at all stages'? What do you think will be the main points in their discussion?
Specimen question: Northern Examining Association

TUTOR'S ANSWER TO QUESTION 4

(a)   The members of the union may be pressing for strike action for a number of reasons. They will be suspicious that 'up-to-date machinery' will mean less workers, especially since the management want to 'reduce labour costs'. Pressing for strike action will indicate their disapproval of the management proposals for XYZ Engineering and serve as a reminder of what might happen if lay-offs do occur. The members will hope to put pressure on the management at an early stage, by demonstrating their willingness to disrupt the firm's activities if jobs are lost or unacceptable work practices imposed. The union members will probably be unhappy about the fact that the **Daily News** got to hear of the possible lay-offs before they did.

(b)   There are a number of other methods which could be considered in solving the problem. The union members could operate an **overtime ban**, refusing to work more than the normal number of hours per week. This could be very damaging for the company as could a **work-to-rule**, with the workers keeping closely to the rules and regulations laid down by the engineering company. The members may also consider a **go-slow**, undertaking their work as slowly as possible. All of these actions, however, may fail to achieve the desired result for the members of the union. The management may be adamant that lay-offs will have to occur and that productivity will have to improve if the company is to compete with companies at home and abroad. The alternative to industrial action, therefore, could be **negotiation**. Discussions with the management could lead to a satisfactory outcome. The union leaders could agree to voluntary retirement or non-replacement of those who leave. They could also agree to increase productivity (output per person) as a means of becoming more competitive. Increased productivity and a more efficient company could mean that redundancies are avoided or kept to a minimum. ***In answering this question it could be easy to write about the other forms of industrial action and fail to mention negotiation. Be careful that you consider all the possible alternatives, including negotiation.***

(c)   Changes at work usually worry those who will be affected by them because any change involves uncertainty. The workers will have had their security threatened and will be concerned about redundancy and having to find another job. There may be high unemployment in the area and they may have to consider moving to another town. This can create all sorts of problems over their children's education, leaving family and friends and having to move house. The change at work could involve the introduction of new machinery. Here, too, there will be the fear of the unknown with new ways of working and, possibly, training to be undertaken.

(d)   Full consultation means that the management will talk to the union when arriving at their decisions. There will usually be established procedures for management raising issues with the unions *before* a final decision is made. Consultation can involve questions such as: How many workers will be made redundant? What new machinery will be introduced? How will the introduction of the new machinery affect the working conditions of the union members? The final outcome could be redundancies; if so how are these to take place? Are they going to be on the basis of natural wastage, with those over 65 not being replaced, or will there be a need for compulsory redundancies?

C   O   U   R   S   E   W   O   R   K

**ASSIGNMENT –
INDUSTRIAL DISPUTES**

INDUSTRIAL DISPUTES

Are you aware of any industrial disputes which have just started? You may have noticed such disputes on the TV news. More information is likely to be available on these disputes from the national newspapers. Keep an account of the dispute(s), perhaps in the form of newspaper cuttings. Some of the questions you could address are: Why did the dispute start? Did collective bargaining take place? What sort of industrial action has the workforce undertaken? Is the dispute official or unofficial? Is the factory/workplace being picketed? How is the dispute being resolved? Has an outside body such as ACAS been involved?

You can write up your findings as a case study. Is the final result of the dispute the one you expected? If not, why not?

STUDENT'S ANSWER – EXAMINER'S COMMENTS

This is a student's answer to question 4, page 168.

4)   'Possible layoffs at xyz.'

66 **A good start.** 99

a) Many members were pressing for immediate strike action because they feared that they could lose their jobs if more up to date machinery was brought in. Also, because management communication has been poor, and the article in the paper had appeared unexpectedly, the workers probably feared that they would lose their jobs the same way — with no prior warning. Their strike action would stall any redundancies which might occur.

66 **An excellent answer. Uncertainty about the future is an important aspect of this part of the question.** 99

b) Other methods of solving the problem could be to have better communication between the management and the union. If they got together, they may be able to sort out their differences, before anything drastic happened. If they had problems with communication, they could call in an unassociated body, eg an Industrial Tribunal, or ACAS, who may be able to invest-tigate the matter and help to solve the problem.

Good. Better communication may have stopped the problem happening in the first place. Negotiation might help stop the problem becoming more serious. However altenatives to strike action could have been mentioned, such as an overtime ban, work to rule, go slow, etc.

c) Changes at work, both large or small, usually worry the people who will be affected by them, as they can cause unrest, disputes or even job losses. For example, when a company wants to bring in more up to date machinery, it's usually to replace a worker who is inefficient or uneconomical to the company, therefore the worker will lose his job, as the machinery may be more cost-effective.

Some good points. You might also mention that workers may be 'redeployed' to other parts of the company. Perhaps they will have to move areas, uprooting family, etc. This could happen if they had to look for another job after being made redundant.

d) When the management says 'there will be full consultation with the union at all stages', it means that from now on, there will be a high level of communication between the two bodies. Whatever the management decides, the Union will be informed of it, to try to reduce conflict. They will mainly discuss where the new machinery will be, which workers will be affected, and who will have to reduce their hours or be laid-off.

Again, some good points.

Overall a very good answer to this question.

AIDING AND CONTROLLING BUSINESS

LOCAL GOVERNMENT
CENTRAL GOVERNMENT
GOVERNMENT AND
    BUSINESS
THE EUROPEAN ECONOMIC
    COMMUNITY
AID FOR BUSINESS
REGULATING AND
    CONTROLLING BUSINESS

G E T T I N G   S T A R T E D

Business in the United Kingdom is surrounded by a very large number of influences which either try to help it or to control it:

▶ Local Government
▶ Central Government   *plus*
▶ International Organisations

▶ Trade Associations
▶ Professional Bodies
▶ Educational Bodies
▶ Pressure Groups
▶ The Press and TV

Each of these organisations has a role in helping businesses or in trying to control them for the sake of the public and other businesses. They operate in a wide variety of ways:

    Firstly, by *aiding* businesses:
      by providing information;
      by providing money or insurance;
      by helping directly in training;
      by helping with exporting.
    Secondly, by *controlling* business:
      by setting up laws which businesses have to abide by;
      by exerting pressure in different ways.

This chapter will examine the ways in which business is helped or controlled, but it is necessary, first, to set the scene by considering the structure and role of the various systems of government and institutions which can affect businesses – local, national and international.

ESSENTIAL PRINCIPLES

1 ▶ LOCAL GOVERNMENT

The system of local government which exists in the UK today has only been in operation since 1974. The system prior to 1974 (which had been started in 1888) had many more units of local government. There were, for example, 1,750 authorities at the second tier ('Districts') compared to just 422 today.

The most important change since 1974 has been the abolition of the Metropolitan and Greater London Councils (both of which occurred in 1986).

As far as businesses are concerned, local government has a number of important roles. District authorities in England and Wales have the power to levy business rates (property taxes) although this may well change if proposals for new local taxes on individuals (rather than on property) are accepted. Under any new system it seems likely that business taxation will be decided not at local level but by central government.

Table 18.1 shows the responsibilities of the various local government types. The main areas of business interest are:

▶ Rates   ▶ Education
▶ Planning   ▶ Roads

Responsibilities	Metropolitan areas	Non-metropolitan areas
Rates (and rebates) Rent rebates Slum clearance Refuse (collection) Public health Housing (and home improvement) Local planning	District (usually called Boroughs)	District
Libraries Personal social services Education		
Police Fire Waste disposal Structure planning	New separate authorities	County

Table 18.1 Local authority responsibilities in England and Wales

> **Councils are composed of *elected* councillors who receive expenses but do not receive a salary for their work. The new "County level" authorities for fire, police, waste disposal, etc., are not elected but are appointed.**

Both Districts and Counties have responsibility for planning how their areas are going to develop in the future. This usually means setting aside areas for industrial and business growth, making sure that there will be enough houses to house any new workers, ensuring that there will be enough schools, and making sure that the roads will be able to cope with any new industry or housing. All of this is obviously of great concern to the businesses which are either in the area or considering moving to it.

The way in which these plans are presented to the public and approved by the Councils and the Government is in the form of Structure Plans, which state how the authority's area is going to grow, what areas are going to be set aside for house-building and which for business and industry.

Education is provided by the Counties in rural areas but by Districts in the larger cities. Business is always concerned to know that education, especially at the higher levels, is being directed towards the needs of industry and commerce, and that suitable courses are available to train their staff once they have left school or college and joined the firm.

2 ▶ CENTRAL GOVERNMENT

Many services cannot be provided at local level and it is for these that we have ***central*** or ***national*** government. Parliament is responsible for governing the country and the party or parties with the largest number of seats in Parliament form the Government.

Parliament supervises the work of the Government and is responsible for passing laws which the Government wants to put into effect. By tradition, the Prime Minister cannot come from the House of Lords but several Cabinet Ministers (the most senior Ministers) can be drawn from the Lords. The Prime Minister selects the senior Ministers who form the Cabinet (the Committee which runs the UK on a day-to-day basis). The Prime Minister also selects all the other Ministers who make up the rest of the Government but these Junior Ministers do not sit in the Cabinet. Each Minister of Cabinet rank has responsibility for one of the large Departments and has other Ministers and a great many Civil Servants to help.

3 ▷ GOVERNMENT AND BUSINESS

The Government in London – at Westminster – and the large number of local governments, influence business in a great many ways:

The producer – is affected by government rules on planning and location of industry, by laws on conditions of work and on safety of products, and by taxation.

The consumer – is affected by the Government's efforts to protect them from unscrupulous producers – by laws on consumer protection and safety, by standards, and by the work of weights and measures inspectors employed by local governments.

The workforce – is affected by government provision of education and training, by laws on the conditions of employment, by safety regulations, by laws on pay, and by laws affecting trade unions.

Perhaps one of the most significant influences on business in the United Kingdom is outside the **direct** control of central and local government, namely the **European Community** – the EC.

4 ▷ THE EUROPEAN ECONOMIC COMMUNITY

The EC was founded in 1957 by the Treaty of Rome. Its objective is to promote unity among the countries of Europe, at least partly by making trade easier. By 1960 Britain had decided to join the EC but it took three attempts and twelve years before the other EC countries agreed to its admission. Along with the United Kingdom in 1972, Denmark and the Republic of Ireland also joined. Since then, three other members have been admitted: Greece in 1980, and Spain and Portugal in 1986.

All twelve members of the EC have agreed to be bound by decisions taken centrally. They have abolished customs duties between themselves so that goods can be sold more easily and they have established a single set of customs duties between themselves and the rest of the world (called The Common External Tariff).

A. MEMBERSHIP OF THE EC

Original Members 1957	Joined 1972
West Germany	United Kingdom
France	Denmark
Italy	Republic of Ireland
Netherlands	Joined 1980
Belgium	Greece
Luxembourg	Joined 1986
	Spain
	Portugal

The EC is now the largest 'single market' (i.e. without internal tariff barriers) in the western world – around 320 million consumers. Decisions in the EC are taken by the **Council of Ministers** which is made up of government ministers from each of the twelve member-countries. The **European Commission** is responsible for the day-to-day operation of the Community and for recommending new policies.

The 518 European MPs are now directly elected by the people of the 'twelve'. Britain has 81 of those MEPs (*Members of the European Parliament*). In the last election – in 1984 – the Conservatives took by far the largest share of these seats. The parties sit in 'international parties' in the European Parliament (see below).

If there are disputes between member countries or if the European Commission feels that individual governments or companies are not abiding by the rules, the **European Court** will be the place in which the case is heard.

International Political Party Groups in the European Parliament

1. Communist Group
2. Socialist Group (including the British Labour Party)
3. European People's Party
4. European Democrats (including the British Conservatives)
5. Liberal and Democratic Reformist (including the British Liberal and Social Democratic Parties as observers)
6. European Alliance for Renewal and Democracy (including the one Scottish Nationalist MEP)
7. European Right
8. Rainbow Group (most environmental parties)
9. Independent Group

B. THE EC AND BUSINESS

Although one hears very little about the EC in the popular press or on TV and radio, the effect that this organisation has on British business is now extremely important.

▶ *Agricultural business* is affected by EC decisions on food prices, on grants for small farmers, and on future agricultural policy.

▶ *Business in areas of high unemployment* can receive significant grants through the EC's Regional Fund to cover buildings and equipment.

▶ *The EC Social Fund* spends a great deal of money on retraining of young people, women and certain other types of employee; especially in industries such as shipbuilding, textiles, coal and steel.

▶ *The Transport policy* helps business by encouraging faster and more energy efficient forms of transport and by helping to build motorways, tunnels, railways and canals.

▶ *The European Investment Bank* gives loans at good rates of interest to large and small businesses.

▶ *'Competition Policy'* makes sure that business does not co-operate too much against the interests of the consumer.

The EC today, affects almost every aspect of business life and is also involved in trying to improve education on a European-wide basis. One proposal, in 1986, was for funds to be provided to ensure that, by around 1990, 10% of all European students would spend at least part of their course in another EC country.

> **The Common Agricultural Policy (CAP) commands around three-quarters of the whole EEC budget.**

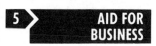

5 AID FOR BUSINESS

There are, today, a bewildering variety of sources of *aid for businesses*. It is easier to understand if they are broken down into two broad areas of help and assistance:

Government Aid for Business, and Aid from Private Organisations.

A. GOVERNMENT AID FOR BUSINESS

This falls under a number of headings:

1. Information for business
2. Finance for business
3. Help in training staff
4. Aid for exporters
5. Advice for business

i Information for Business

The Government collects a great deal of information and most of this is available to businesses to help them plan their products or campaigns. The Central Office of Information (COI) in London has information on almost all aspects of business and most of it is available at the COI Library for researchers to use. In addition, much information is published each year in the form of government statistical booklets. These can be of immense help to business. For example:

Social Trends contains information on such things as population trends, wage levels and growth in wages around the country, and how people use their leisure time.

Annual Abstract of Statistics has a wealth of economic statistics on such topics as employment, health, education, national income, exports.

Balance of Payments (Pink Book) contains details of how much the UK has exported and imported, to and from which countries, and for how much.

Employment Gazette contains information on industrial disputes, employment vacancies, growth in earnings, training, and other employment-related areas.

Regional Trends has a lot of very detailed information and statistics on the economic, social and population changes which have taken place in the UK's regions during the previous year.

ii Finance for Business

The Government provides finance for business in several ways but the most important ones are 'Regional' grants and subsidies (see Ch.6 on Industrial Location), the grants and assistance provided for small businesses which are just starting out, and the special grants for firms which are in 'high-tech' businesses like micro-electronics and automated manufacturing. Grants to help with research costs are also available.

One of the most recent ways in which the Government helps small business is through grants for people to start up their own businesses. These Enterprise Allowances pay the person a weekly amount for about one year in order to help them get started.

There is also a Small Firms Loan Guarantee Scheme which was introduced in 1981. Under this scheme the Government will 'guarantee' up to 70% of bank loans for small businesses in return for strict supervision and the payment of an insurance premium.

iii Help in Training Staff

> **In 1987 these schemes were increased when the government introduced the JOB TRAINING SCHEME (JTS) for the long-term unemployed.**

In these days of very high unemployment the Government has constructed a number of schemes in order to help people in finding a job. The main groups these schemes are aimed at are the young and the long-term unemployed. The schemes include:

▶ YTS   ▶ Action for Jobs   ▶ Restart

iv Aid for Exporters

The United Kingdom relies on trade for almost a third of its annual income and trade is, therefore, taken very seriously by government. The Department of Trade offers a great deal of help to British exporters – from statistical information on overseas markets to help with filling in Customs forms.

UK exporters can sometimes get grants to help them to begin exporting to certain markets, and there are regular trade visits – organised by the British Overseas Trade Board (BOTB), a subsidiary of the Department of Trade – to introduce exporters to certain markets. The BOTB provides a variety of services to exporters and these are added to by an organisation known as SITPRO. This is responsible for helping to simplify the extremely complex task of filling in export forms.

The list of government aids to exporters would include:

▶ publicity for British products through British magazines published by the Government, and through British Embassies abroad;

▶ free advice on market research;

▶ financial aid to businesses in employing marketing consultants;

▶ a well-developed library of books and research findings on export markets which is called the 'Statistics and Market Intelligence Library' (the use of which is free);

▶ an Export Representative service in which an overseas member of an Embassy's staff will make enquiries and business contacts on your behalf;

▶ the chance to travel with British trade missions to markets you are interested in.

Many of these services do not come free of charge but they are considerably subsidised by the UK Government.

v Advice for Business

Through a network of local offices, government departments provide advice for businesses on industrial location, on regional grants for the assisted areas, on Enterprise Zones and Development Areas.

Central government also offers help and advice on a wide range of business problems including production engineering, industrial design, advanced technologies, and research.

Many local councils have also set up offices offering advice to small businesses.

B. PRIVATE AID FOR BUSINESS

Over the years, business has developed a number of ways in which it is able to help itself. In most areas of the country there are Chambers of Commerce which allow business people to meet and to discuss their problems and successes.

Most types of business have their own trade association, such as the Furniture Industry Association. These associations have been established to try to protect their members from laws which they believe will harm them, and to promote the industry with the general public. Examples include the Society of Motor Manufacturers and the Engineering Employers Federation.

At a national level, industry has set up the Confederation of British Industry (the CBI) to look after its interests. The CBI also gives advice to its members and runs regular courses and conferences. (See Ch. 17.)

Education, too, provides aid for business in the form of research and development, as well as consultancy. Many universities and polytechnics have contracts with specific firms to research special areas of science and to provide the firm with the results. A number of such institutions, together with management departments and business schools, also provide consultancy for businesses which need advice. The lecturers are 'hired out' as consultants to the firms to try to solve specific problems which the firms themselves might not be able to solve. The firm receives valuable advice and the university, polytechnic or college receives valuable direct experience for its staff.

6 ▶ REGULATING AND CONTROLLING BUSINESS

Business is heavily surrounded by controls and constraints most of which have developed over the years in order to protect workers, consumers and other businesses. They can best be understood by dealing with them under three headings:
▶ Government regulations
▶ Government control
▶ Non-governmental control

A. GOVERNMENT REGULATIONS

There is now a tremendous amount of law relating to business and it is impossible to deal with it all in the space available. There are, however, a number of very important areas of law which need to be noted:

i The Law of Contract

A *contract* is an agreement between two parties to do something. It does not have to be written down but, in order to be recognised by the Courts, it does have to have certain features:

▶ there has to be an *agreement*, which can be seen by the fact that one party has offered something and the other party has accepted it. In many cases the 'offer' and the 'acceptance' are not the way you would normally expect them to be. For example, in a shop it is not the shop which is making the offer to you. In law the shop is merely opening its doors so that you can examine the goods. The customer then makes an offer for the goods and – if it is acceptable – the shop accepts the offer.

▶ something has to change hands in both directions. A contract does not exist if you get anything for free. The law of contract demands that, in return for the goods or service there must be some *consideration* – that is, something must be given in return, either in money or goods.

▶ there must be an *intention* to create a legal relationship – a bargain between yourself and your father would not normally be called a contract unless it was written down that both of you intended to establish a legal relationship.

▶ the parties to a contract must be legally able to enter into it. The law calls this *capacity* and all adults who are sane have the capacity to enter into a contract.

There are many other aspects to the law of contract but it is important to understand that a contract does not have to be in writing. You are entering into a legal contract every time you buy something from a shop or pay for your ticket on the bus.

Even where large sums of money are concerned the law still recognises and enforces unwritten contracts. If you want to buy or sell shares through a stockbroker you may do this on the telephone. The act of telling the stockbroker to buy or sell a certain number of shares in a specified company is a legal and binding contract. You cannot phone up five minutes later and try to cancel your order.

ii Protecting the Consumer

The law of contract, if applied literally, allows no way for a consumer to take goods back or to complain about their quality. For hundreds of years the law said that the buyer of goods was responsible for making sure that they were fit for the use to which they were to be put. This was summed up in the Latin phrase – *caveat emptor* (Let the buyer beware). Today, however, the law of contract has been amended in certain ways which give the consumer additional protection (except, for sales of goods between private individuals, e.g. for second-hand cars, where the *caveat emptor* rule still applies).

The Sale of Goods Act, 1979. This act gives the customer extra protection when buying certain types of goods. The act effectively says that goods must be the same as they are described on a label or by the shop assistant. The best known provision of the act is that it now is to be assumed that goods are of 'merchantable quality' and 'fit for the purpose for which they were sold'. This means that customers can buy goods on the firm assumption that the quality will be appropriate to the use to which they will be put. This does not mean that the goods will never break down, merely, that they will last for an amount of time which a court would regard as 'reasonable'.

iii Trading Law

The laws by which companies may trade are complex and are divided into those which are established at local level (by-laws governing such things as early-closing days) and the national laws.

Weights and Measures Act, 1979 Local councils have departments of weights and measures whose duty it is to ensure that local tradespeople are treating their customers fairly. In years gone by, it was not unusual for traders to add chalk to their flour or to add water to beer or spirits. Sawdust was often used to give bulk to bread and meat was often sold when it was going rotten. Local shops would often have a wide difference in the weights which they used to weigh out the customer's food. In this way the customer would believe that they were getting a full pound of flour, butter, bread, or potatoes, whereas, in fact the weight had been filed down so that – although it was marked 1lb – it only weighed, say, 13 ounces. The shopkeeper's profit would be increased by the saving of 3 ounces on every pound sold. It was common in public houses well into this century for customers to receive 'short measure' in both beer and spirits. The local Weights and Measures Inspectors are still kept busy making sure that scales and drink measures are accurate.

The Trade Descriptions Act, 1968. This act makes it an offence to falsely describe something which you are selling – whether in writing or orally.

Food and Drugs Act, 1955. An Act which helps to protect consumers from unscrupulous shopkeepers. The Act makes it a criminal offence to sell food which is unfit for consumption. It also sets standards for hygiene in food premises and sets up a number of regulations on what must appear on the labels of food products.

Consumer Credit Act, 1974. This Act requires the Office of Fair Trading (which was set up under the Fair Trading Act, 1973) to license any firm which lends money to the public (usually in the form of credit on purchases). The companies must explain to people what the *true* cost of borrowing is. This is usually given in the form of the APR – or Annual Percentage Rate (of Interest).

Fair Trading Act, 1973. The Office of Fair Trading was established by this Act with the objective of controlling the way firms do business with the public. It seeks to regulate what are known as 'Restrictive Practices' – attempts by firms to 'fix' prices or to 'share' markets. (By agreeing to share a market and not to compete against each other two firms will be able to charge higher prices than they would otherwise.)

Consumer Safety Act, 1978. This Act regulates the construction of most items which can be dangerous in the home such as fires, cookers, electric irons, microwave ovens, and toys.

iv Competition Law

If businesses are allowed to grow they may form what are known as monopolies. A monopoly is a company which is effectively the only company supplying a particular market. In Britain the telephone service is a monopoly (held by British Telecom) and the electricity and gas boards have a monopoly of the supply of electricity and gas into our homes. Monopolies have the disadvantage that, in view of the fact that they are the only supplier in the market, they can charge almost whatever they like. Economists call this the ability to make super-profits and it is usually seen as being against the interests of the consumer. Not only are prices higher than they might otherwise be but the monopoly has no incentive to improve the service of the product.

It is felt, therefore, that wherever possible, the authorities ought to encourage competition and to try to make sure that large companies which control large shares of particular markets are closely watched.

Monopolies and Mergers Act, 1965. This Act attempts to control large companies and to encourage competition by making sure that a firm cannot have too much control over a market. A *monopoly* is defined as existing whenever a firm controls more than a third of any market and the Act set up a Monopolies and Mergers Commission with the power to investigate and report on any situation which gives cause for concern. Under the Act, the Secretary of State has the power to refer any proposed merger to the Commission and, if the Commission decides that the merger would create a firm which was too large and that it was 'against the public interest', the Secretary of State can forbid the merger.

Since the UK joined the EC our firms have also been subject to EC Competition Policy which tries to do the same thing for the whole of Europe. On a number of occasions over the past ten years several very large firms have been fined millions of pounds for trying to restrict competition by 'price fixing' (that is, coming to secret agreements that they would not try to undercut each other's prices).

v Employment Law

In this area there is a great deal of government legislation designed to protect the employee. The need for employment law goes back to the nineteenth century when some workers used to be paid in the form of 'truck'. This meant that the worker did not receive money at the end of the week but, instead, received vouchers which could only be exchanged at the company's store where the food, clothes and other stock were extremely expensive. Several 'Truck' Acts, beginning with one in 1831, were needed to deal with this exploitation of working people. During the nineteenth century the government also began to regulate the hours which women and children could work. Today, there is a very large amount of law concerning the treatment of people at work and every business-person needs to know most of it in some detail.

Factories Act, 1961. This Act is only the most recent of a long series of Factories Acts which govern conditions of work inside manufacturing plants. Most of the original rules contained in the Act come from the nineteenth century and govern such things as the fact that:
► no machine can be cleaned while it is still moving
► women cannot work in a factory within 4 weeks of childbirth
► women are not allowed to work down a mine
► women and young people (under 18) cannot work more than 9 hours per day or more than 48 hours per week.

Health & Safety at Work Act, 1974. This is an extremely important law which, for the first time, makes it a criminal offence to expose either employees or non-employees to risk. It covers all industrial and commercial premises and the products which a firm manufactures. The Act also makes it a duty of every employee to take care of the health and safety of themselves and their work colleagues.

Race Relations Acts, 1968, 1976. These laws make it an offence for an employer to discriminate in any aspects of business on the ground of race, ethnic origin or nationality. These aspects are:
► Recruitment   ► Training
► Promotion   ► Dismissal
► Conditions of Service

Equal Pay Act, 1970. This legislation came into force in December 1975 and requires that women are paid and given the same benefits as men where they are doing the same work.

Sex Discrimination Act, 1975. Although this Act overlaps to a certain extent with the Equal Pay Act, it requires that women are treated equally in other ways too: that they are not discriminated against in recruitment, promotion or training. It should be noted that this Act also applies to men. The law makes it illegal to advertise jobs in such a way that it appears that only one of the sexes will be considered. The only way that it is possible to advertise for a 'sales-girl' or for a 'postman' is if the advertisement also states that either sex will be considered.

Employment Protection Act, 1978. Employees receive certain rights under this Act which requires, for example, that an employer should keep a woman's job open for her if she leaves, temporarily, to have a baby. The Act also requires that staff be given a minimum amount of notice if they are to be dismissed; the actual amount depends on how long the employee has worked for the employer. An employee is also entitled to redundancy payments if his or her job is to be abolished, and to compensation if they are unfairly dismissed.

Sex Discrimination Act, 1987. Employers, under this Act, are not allowed to discriminate between men and women as far as retirement dates are concerned.

In 1980, 1982 and 1984 the Government passed two **Employment Acts (1980 and 1982)** and a **Trade Union Act (1984)** which set out rules by which trade unions are able to conduct their affairs.

B. GOVERNMENT CONTROL

The Government exercises a great deal of *control and influence* over business in other ways.

i Taxation

All companies have to pay tax just like individuals. A firm's profits are taxed under Corporation Tax and it has to account for Value Added Tax (VAT) on the value of everything it sells.

ii National Insurance

All employees must pay a contribution to the benefits they are entitled to receive under the National Insurance regulations. These benefits include such things as medical care, unemployment pay, supplementary benefit, and sickness benefit. The employer also pays an additional amount which is added to the money paid by the employee. The employer's National Insurance payment is regarded by many as a form of tax on employment.

iii Credit Restriction

The Government controls most of the banking system by exercising complicated restrictions on the amount of money that the banks can lend out. Although there are no such laws at the moment it is also possible for the Government to control how much business firms can do by placing limits on the amount of credit they can give. At one time the law stated that, before you could buy a car, you must be able to put at least 33% of the price down in cash.

iv Export Restrictions

These do not affect many companies these days but there are still rules – mainly for defence reasons – about what can be exported to certain countries. It is still quite difficult, for example, to get permission to export computer equipment, if it contains American parts, to the Soviet Union or to Eastern Europe.

v Location of Industry & Regional Policy

The Government tries, through its system of regional grants and loans, to get firms to locate where it wants them to locate (usually in areas of high unemployment) rather than where the firm might have wanted to go.

vi Public Expenditure

The Government spends a very la͟ ͟ amount of money each year – around £160 billion – and the way in which this mon͟y is spent has an effect on UK business. If the Government decides that it has to cut spending and to build fewer roads, schools and houses, then the construction industry will have less orders and will be able to employ fewer people. Similarly, Government decisions on spending can create more demand for almost every type of product. If a new hospital is to be built, business will be created not only for the builders but also for the firms who will provide all the office furniture, typewriters, beds, sheets and blankets, carpets, lights, radios and so on.

C. NON-GOVERNMENT CONTROL OF BUSINESS

There are three main ways in which business is subject to control from private sources.
► from codes of conduct,
► from pressure groups,
► from the media (press, TV, radio, etc.)

i Codes of Conduct

Industry, today, follows many different 'codes of conduct'. These codes are not laws, they have never been passed through Parliament, and they can not be taken to courts. The idea of the codes is that industry is able to set them up and control them themselves rather than having the Government do it for them under an Act of Parliament.

There are two codes which might illustrate how they are used:

Garages have a code of practice which they have drawn up themselves and which all member garages are meant to follow when repairing people's cars. The code says what sort of quotation should be given, how much information it should contain, how the garage should set out the bill for the repairs, and many other things.

Advertisers also have a code of practice which is supervised by the Advertising Standards Authority and which says that all advertisements should be legal, decent and honest.

ii Pressure Groups

Pressure Groups are sometimes called interest groups. They are groups of people who link together to try to influence the way things are run or the way decisions are taken. There are all sorts of pressure groups:

▶ some seek to influence Government, like the Campaign for Nuclear Disarmament or the Campaign for Electoral Reform;
▶ others try to influence both Government and Business, such as the AA and the RAC, the CBI (Confederation of British Industry), trade unions, the Consumers Association, etc.

It is with the second of these two types that we will be concerned with here. The best way to understand the way pressure groups influence business is to look at the way a few of them operate:

The Automobile Association and The Royal Automobile Club. Both the AA and the RAC were set up to try to protect the interests of motorists against both the Government and the car and motorcycle manufacturers. Like most pressure groups they have members who pay an annual fee in order to join. This money is then used by the pressure group to help it to do its job. In the case of the AA and the RAC they try to make sure that any laws which are passed with respect to motorists are good ones and that the products of the car and motorcycle manufacturers are of the right standard.

The Consumer Association. The Consumers' Association is best known for its monthly publication *Which?*. The object of this pressure group is to represent the interests of the buyer of goods and to try to make sure that the consumer gets the best possible value for money. The Association regularly tests all products to find out whether they are safe, how long they will last, and whether there are any problems about using them. Over the years, *Which?* has had a great deal of success in protecting consumers against businesses.

Trade Unions. Trade unions, too, are pressure groups. They seek to protect the interests of their members, the employees, against the firm. They are dealt with more fully in Ch.17. Unions have been quite successful in improving the working conditions and wages of workers.

Environmental Groups. As more and more people become aware of the danger which modern industry can represent for the environment so more environmental pressure groups are established to try to control the activities of both governments and business. Groups such as The Green Alliance, Greenpeace, and Friends of the Earth, spend a great deal of time watching what businesses are doing and opposing them if they feel that their activities will harm the environment or wildlife.

iii The Media

The 'media' means any of the ways in which people receive information. Nowadays it is usual to divide it into the:

▶ paper media
▶ electronic media

The *paper media* includes newspapers, magazines and journals, while the *electronic media* includes radio and television. Almost all of these media have reporters whose job it is to look out for stories which will be of interest to the readers, listeners, or viewers of the medium for which he or she is working. Business topics are not very popular in the tabloid press or on peak-time television (see Ch.9 for more information on what makes up these categories) but such topics can be found in the quality press and on radio and

TV programmes which are designed for 'serious' viewers, and provide very interesting information.

Of course, business is itself influenced by the popular media; Esther Rantzen's programmes which revealed the sharp practices of businesses were very popular and led to many firms having to change their policies, to give refunds, or, even, to go out of business altogether.

C O U R S E W O R K

**ASSIGNMENT 1 –
BUSINESS
AND LOCAL
GOVERNMENT**

Local government has a significant effect on business, and firms pay a large proportion of the income of local councils in the form of rates. Unlike private householders, who also pay rates, businesses do not get a vote at elections and, therefore, have no say about how their rate money is used.

Conduct a survey to find out how local businesses feel about the services they get from local government and how they would like to improve the situation.

You will need to draw up a questionnaire which will give you details of what sort of business it is and how big it is (number of employees is the easiest measure).

1. The questionnaire will need to get the reaction and **comments** of business people on a wide variety of subjects including:
   ▶ Rates   ▶ Public Health
   ▶ Refuse collection   ▶ Weights and Measures
   ▶ Education   ▶ Planning
   ▶ Roads and lighting   ▶ Housing for employees
2. You will need to survey a good range of business; large and small, including shops, offices and factories.
3. Try also to get hold of a copy of the local Structure Plan from the Council offices. It will tell you a lot about where business is growing and what the Council's attitude to the expansion of business is.
4. Write up your results into a final report with illustrations, tables and – if helpful – graphs.

**ASSIGNMENT 2
BUSINESS
AND THE LAW**

In this project you will have to find out how businesspeople feel about the various laws which affect them.

A questionnaire will be necessary, asking for reactions to a wide variety of laws covering:
▶ Employment
▶ Contract and Sales of Goods
▶ Consumer Protection

1. Try to find out whether any single person is responsible for the 'legal side' of things and who that person is.
2. Cover as many different types of business as you can.
3. Try to get hold of and compare firms' terms and conditions of business. These are usually to be found on the back of order forms or invoices.
4. Do the firms (e.g. garages) have to comply with a code of practice and, if so, what is it and who supervises it?
5. Complete the project with a written report which gives the results in the way you think most sensible, for example, by law, by size of business, or by type of business.

CHAPTER

BUSINESS IN A CHANGING WORLD

GETTING STARTED

Just over 100 years ago, in 1885, two German engineers named Benz and Daimler were just beginning to develop the first motor cars and the first petrol engines. Some people are still alive today who were born into that Victorian world at the end of the nineteenth century. In that world business was conducted by letter and by telegraph. Telephones only began to be used in offices very gradually after about 1889. Clerks wrote account books, invoices and statements by hand, by the light of gas lamps and even the typewriter (manufactured by the American company of Remington since 1876) was a rare sight. Documents were methodically filed by hand and cross-referenced with other files using large card indexes. Goods were transported by horse and cart, by steam train, and by steam ships. Factories operated almost entirely on the power provided by steam engines, and the most important energy source was coal.

**CHANGES IN THE BUSINESS
ENVIRONMENT
CHANGES IN TECHNOLOGY
CHANGES FOR HUMANS**

ESSENTIAL PRINCIPLES

1 ▶ CHANGES IN THE BUSINESS ENVIRONMENT

Business transport has developed rapidly from the horse and the steam engine to include motor cars and lorries, aircraft carrying over 100 tonnes of freight, high speed diesel and electric freight trains, and fast cargo ships carrying anything up to 100,000 tonnes.

Business communications have improved. Every company now uses both telephone and telex as standard forms of communication and many are beginning to use facsimile (FAX) machines. The speed and convenience of these methods have been vastly increased by the advent of satellites in orbit around the planet (having partly replaced long-distance telephone cables).

Production of goods has changed from being extremely labour intensive – requiring lots of people to operate all the machines or to make the goods – to being very capital intensive – having many more machines, some of which can operate on their own with only minimal human supervision.

Information storage and handling has changed out of all recognition. The clerks, filing cabinets and card indexes of the turn of the century have been almost completely replaced by complex computer systems which store the same information electronically. The draft chapters of a book such as this would take up an entire drawer of a filing cabinet if they were typed out, placed in individual folders and filed away. Instead, all 20 chapters plus index, introduction and contents can be stored on just one 8 cm computer disc. Rather than the 90cm by 60cm space of the filing cabinet drawer, the disc takes up just 100mm by 75mm. No less than 70 full books could be stored in this way in the space taken up by just one chapter using the old method.

In one lifetime, society has moved from the steam engine to nuclear power and from filing cabinets to computers. Most of this change has been technical and mechanical though. People's lives have been made more comfortable but even as late as the 1960s it was common for people to expect to stay in one job for the whole of their working lives.

From the 1980s into the twenty-first century, change is going to be even more far reaching. The tremendous change that your parents and grandparents have experienced will look very tame beside what is coming!

There are two different aspects to the changes which are coming.

1. There are developments in *technology* which are already beginning to affect our lives. These included *bio-technology*, the science of using man-made organisms to create new chemicals or to change existing ones, *factory automation* and the *information revolution* based on the microprocessor – the computer on a chip.

2. There are the changes which will happen to our lives – the *human* change.

2 ▶ CHANGES IN TECHNOLOGY

We first consider technical changes in the *factory* and then in the *office*.

A. IN THE FACTORY

Change in the factory will involve both *automation* and *expert systems*.

i. Automation

The factories of the near future will certainly have far fewer people working in them. The machines will either be 'intelligent' – that is, they will have their own computers to tell them what to do – or they will be linked up to large central computers which will control the whole manufacturing process.

There are many computer aided machines in operation today. The difference in the future is that Computer Integrated Manufacturing (CIM) will control *all* of the machines, together with the input of raw materials from stores, the warehousing of finished goods and the dispatch of goods which have been sold. Human operators, at least in the early stages, will be required to program the computers, to repair the machines and to repair the electronic components.

Robots are simply computer controlled machines. They are important because, unlike the machines which they replace, they can be reprogrammed at very short notice to do a different job.

For example, machines have been welding motor-car bodies for a very long time. In the past, however, each new design of car had to have a special welding line built for it. The welding machines would have to be positioned exactly right and would then weld the right spots on the car bodies as they were taken past on the conveyor. If the firm decides to change the shape of the car body the whole line of welding machines has to be moved and re-arranged – an extremely expensive and lengthy job.

Robot welding lines are much more flexible. The robots, once installed, can be 'taught' to weld the correct spots on a new car. Each robot usually has a working 'arm' which it uses to reach over and weld exactly the right bits. If the company decides to redesign the car body none of the robots needs to be moved. An operator simply reprograms them ('teaches' them a new set of movements) and the line can get to work on the new shape of the car. Weeks or months of expensive dismantling and moving of machines is avoided. With robots the new car can be going through the production process in a matter of days.

ii. Expert Systems

Computers are going to affect factories in a wide variety of ways. Not only is Computer Integrated Manufacturing going to increase the number of firms which are almost completely automated, but new **Expert Systems** are going to be helping, and possibly replacing, human beings in the areas of the firm where, up to now, humans have felt secure in their jobs.

Up to now computers have been essentially just automatic machines. They have had to be told absolutely everything. They could weld a car body, but they could not **design** it and they could spot a flaw in a piece of metal but they were incapable of **deciding** whether the flaw was dangerous or not.

> **True expert systems are still a long way off. They require immense computing power and speed, improved computer languages, and better ways of acquiring and coding information.**

It seems likely that this will begin to change in the not too distant future. Some computers are already being programmed not with instructions but with rules. The computers then use these rules to design machines and to make their own decisions.

In effect, these expert systems work just like an expert human being. When you go to the doctor to find out why you have got a pain in your back he will use his expert knowledge to narrow down the cause. He will ask you how you think you got the pain: Were you lifting anything? Have you fallen over? Were you playing sport? In most cases the doctor will be able to tell you how you did it and what to do about the pain without even examining you. In doing this diagnosis the doctor is simply applying a large number of complex areas of knowledge, which he learned at medical school, to the problem of your back.

It is, of course, much more complex than this and the doctor would also have to examine you to make a final decision but the essence of an expert system is there. Already, in the United States, expert computers are being used to save doctors' time in giving basic diagnoses of many ailments.

In a similar way, expert systems are now being developed which can design buildings, machines and other computers. The automated factory of the future will probably not require human beings even to analyse faults in the system. The factory and its computers will work out the solutions to problems themselves and then instruct less intelligent robots to put them right.

B. IN THE OFFICE

Change in the factory is going to be very great over the next few decades but change in the **office** is already looking as though it will be even more significant. It will involve:
▶ Information technology
▶ Expert systems
▶ Voice Input
▶ Telecommunications

i. Information Technology – The Information Revolution

Computers have already made the storage and retrieval of information much easier but they have also made all sorts of office work completely different to the way it was only a few years ago.

Software is the instructions which a computer needs in order to do its work. It is the modern term for computer 'programs'. Computers may change – every year we see smaller computers able to do more and more – but the real developments over the next few years are going to be in the field of the software which the computers use. Without software – the programs which tell the computers what to do – a computer is just a mass of useless electronics. The first computers had all these instructions built into them but, today, even the simplest of home computers can 'run' a wide variety of software. In this way, a home computer can be playing a game at one minute and helping you to organise your home finances the next.

In a similar way, most business computers are now almost totally flexible. With the correct software they can help the business to write its letters, design its invoices, keep track of debts, plan future investments, compile the end-of-year accounts, keep long lists of customers or staff, and communicate with other firms or with other computers. There are five important areas of modern 'software'.

Word-processing packages mean that a word-processor can do everything that a typewriter can do but it also enables the user to change what has been written very easily. You can now write a whole report and then swap bits of writing from one place to another and change the style of typeface being used. Modern word-processors can even have spelling checkers added to them and most can be used with what are called 'Mail Merge' programmes to produce personalised letters to many people from one, single standard letter.

Databases: are the computer equivalent of a card index. Any information which has to be stored in some sort of order – lists of customers, of staff, of stock, etc. – can all be kept on a database. The programmes enable the operator to find information quickly and, if they are good enough, to list or print the material in virtually any way they want.

For example, a database of customers could be printed out as:

▶ a list of names in alphabetical order
▶ a list of customers according to which area of the country they live in
▶ a list of customers by sex
▶ a list of telephone numbers of STD-code order.

Spreadsheets: these are really ways of dealing with lots of figures. Where databases keep lists of *words* and can manipulate them, so spreadsheets keep details of *numbers* and can manipulate them in almost any way you wish. Spreadsheets are like a grid of boxes drawn inside the computer. Each box can have a number in it and the computer can handle the number in many ways.

Spreadsheets are normally used for financial information. They can keep details of sales over a period of months and then add them up, divide them by twelve to get an annual average, show them as a graph (in the best spreadsheets) or take them away from figures of costs to get a growth-profit figure.

Accounts packages: almost every business uses some form of computer accounts system these days. It should be noted, however, that they are not the answer to every business's problem. They can be complex to use and, for small businesses they may be more trouble than they are worth. For most medium to large firms, however, computer accounts systems keep their complex financial records and are able to compile everything from a trial balance to a set of final accounts.

Communications software: computers tend to use different languages and they find it difficult to talk to each other. Software engineers have, therefore, developed special programmes which allow computers to talk to one another – often over long distances. In the office, separate computers can be linked together to form networks which allow staff to send information to each other without using paper. By linking a computer to the telephone system and by using the correct software it is possible for even the humblest of home computers to be linked in to a worldwide communications network.

Even at the relatively low level of small businesses and home banking this revolution has meant that it is now possible to pay bills, keep up with your finances and transfer money from account to account without leaving your office or home.

ii. Expert systems

Just as expert systems are set to change the way in which computers help to design products and diagnose problems in industry so similar systems will begin to enter the office of the future. They will be able to analyse marketing problems, suggest solutions to insurance problems, perhaps, even, to run businesses by themselves.

iii. Voices input

Before this comes about, however, the office will almost certainly go through yet another revolution. At present office skills involve typing – in fact, as computers become more important so the need for typing skills has increased. However, typing is really a very awkward and time-consuming way of getting information into a computer. It would be more convenient if the material could be simply spoken into the computer. This is more difficult than it might appear – how, for example, does a computer tell the difference between the words 'pare', 'pear', and 'pair' when spoken to it – but most major computer companies already have voice-computers in the prototype phase and it will not be many years before these machines begin to enter service.

iv. Telecommunications

Many business people are already finding that improved communications means that they need to travel less. Until recently it has been difficult to do the obvious thing – to link several business-people together by phone and television to replace a single meeting. The television and telephone lines needed made this technically difficult and very expensive.

Today, however, optical-fibre communications lines can carry a great deal more information than the old copper electric telephone lines and Video-conferences are beginning to be economic and convenient. Instead of four or five people having to travel hundreds of miles to a meeting they all stay in their own office and pictures and sound from all of the others are transmitted onto screens in front of them. They can see everyone and hold the same meeting without leaving their own offices.

3 ▷ CHANGES FOR HUMANS

► Higher Skills
► Education
► Job Mobility
► Earlier Retirement
► More Leisure Time
► Handicrafts and Human Skills

All around us the machines and what they can do are changing rapidly. It appears that human beings are rapidly being replaced by extremely intelligent robots and that there will soon be nothing for humans to do. This view of the future is not likely to come about quickly even if it happens at all; but there is no doubt that human workers are now less necessary to modern commerce and industry than they have ever been.

There are two ways of looking at this situation:

1. Human beings are being 'robbed' of the work which up to now has given their lives meaning and dignity. There are many people who take this view and who resist the mechanisation of factories and offices. *Or*
2. Computers and robots are now going to release human beings from the back-breaking and boring jobs which they have been tied to in factories and offices. Humans will be released to do jobs or to follow hobbies which will give them far more pleasure in the long run.

The chances are, of course, that neither of these views will turn out to be correct; but it is clear that we humans are going to have to adjust to a very different world over the next twenty years or so. There are a few changes about which we can be fairly certain:

A. HIGHER SKILLS

The first jobs to be taken over by machines are always the easiest and the most repetitive. People used to have to stand all day long just feeding bits of flat metal into machines which stamped them out into pots and pans. Very early in this century those jobs were taken over by an automatic 'arm' which fed the sheets in steadily. Today, it is not just the mechanical jobs which are being replaced by machines. As computers become more skilled they are replacing more and more workers.

Case Study – The Printing Industry

During the nineteenth century newspapers required lots of workers – between the journalist and the printed page stood dozens of people who worked the 'hot-metal' machines which set the journalist's words into metal plates; man-handled the metal impressions of any photographs or drawings down to the presses and placed them on the printing drums; the ink and paper also had to be applied manually and the presses needed constant watching to repair any breakdown.

In the computerised world of today's newspapers there are very few people between a journalist and the printed word. The journalist can type his story directly into the computer which will then allow another person, the sub-editor, to amend it if necessary; the story is then electronically set and photographically printed. Apart from a few highly trained engineers who ensure that the system works smoothly, the paper does not require anything like the staff it had for the old-fashioned process.

The lesson behind all this is that the human beings who *are* required by modern industry are those with *skills*. Most of the unskilled work can now be done by machines. It is the engineers – electronic, production and software – who are needed and will be needed well into the next century. Commerce needs those who have developed skills in a wide variety of areas – such as accounting, marketing, purchasing, sales, communications, and secretarial.

B. EDUCATION

The need for these skills means that the modern worker must be well-educated and – what is more important – prepared to carry on being educated throughout their working life. There are very few areas of business and commerce left in which a worker can leave school, get a job and stay there for the rest of their life without developing their skills or their knowledge. The modern world is one in which education does not end with leaving school or college. In order to keep up with change it is necessary to re-train while at work.

C. JOB MOBILITY (CHANGING JOBS)

As technical change speeds up people will find that the firms they work for may go out of business or change. Even now many people need to have more than one type of job during their working lives and this will almost certainly increase in the future. Having a career has already become an almost old-fashioned idea. It is becoming more and more common for people to change their careers once or twice during their working lives.

D. EARLIER RETIREMENT

With high unemployment likely to be with us for some time to come, firms are able to let employees retire earlier. This trend is being increased by the new law on equality between men and women with respect to the retirement age (The Sex Discrimination Act, 1987). More and more men are opting to retire at 60 or even at 55.

From a business point of view there are two important results from this trend:
(i)   There will be an increase in the demand for all the goods and services which these retired people will need – everything from education in subjects they never had the time to study whilst at work, to holidays.
(ii)   People will have to be taught how to make best use of their leisure time. A person who retires at fifty-five, these days, has many years of life to fill up with interesting things to do.

E. MORE LEISURE TIME

More leisure time is going to be a problem for almost all of us, not simply for those who retire earlier. As the working week becomes shorter the amount of free time we have becomes much greater. Up to now, very few people have ever had the chance to learn how to use this leisure or to try out different hobbies. For many people 'leisure' simply means watching TV or visiting the local pub for a drink. With more time at our disposal we will need more to occupy us and will need to consider all sorts of ways to fill up our leisure hours with interesting hobbies and activities.

F. HANDICRAFTS AND HUMAN SKILLS

Luckily there appears to be a tremendous variety of things to do. If you look around your own area today you will see that there are many types of business which simply did not exist twenty years ago. Many of these firms are providing high quality handicrafts which are now in demand again.

Case Study – Hand-Knitted Woollens

In the 1960s the increase in the supply of machine-knitted woollens seemed to mean that there would never again be a demand for hand-knitted clothes. The machine-made clothes were much cheaper, of reasonable quality, and could be made quickly in immense quantities. Today people are buying hand-knitted clothes again as a type of status symbol and many small businesses are making a good living out of this return to the old crafts.

Craft industries are sprouting up in all sorts of areas and in most trades. At one time it seemed, for example, that the old-fashioned craft of thatching was going to die out altogether. In the late 1960s there were probably only a few people in the entire country who knew the old skills. It was thought that, because tiles were cheaper and easier to maintain, they would replace thatched roofs completely. It has not turned out that way. In areas of the country like Suffolk and Oxfordshire, thatched cottages have been renovated and repaired and this has provided work for an increasing number of thatching companies.

C O U R S E W O R K

ASSIGNMENT – TECHNOLOGY

Technology is changing all our lives all the time. Advanced technology may not interfere with our everyday lives but lots of technological change is occurring in our homes, schools, colleges and workplaces.

Put together a file which describes how technology is changing your life and that of your parents and friends. You should divide it into sections such as:
► Work (in shops, offices and factories)
► School or college
► Home
► Leisure.

You might begin by listing the various ways in which technology is changing your life and then find photographs or advertisements to go with the description you have written.

Alternatively you might look at specific types of technology and find out how they are affecting our lives:
► the computer
► new forms of transport
► new types of telecommunications
► new household gadgets or electronic equipment.

One way of approaching such an assignment might be to ask yourself how modern technology has made ordinary household tasks easier or improved our entertainment.

CHAPTER

20

PUTTING IT ALL TOGETHER

(INTEGRATED EXAMINATION QUESTIONS)

At the end of each chapter, this book has included specimen examination questions to give you an idea of the types of questions you can expect when you undertake the GCSE Business Studies Examination. You will find that the examination papers set by a number of the Examination Groups, will include what are known as integrated questions. This means that the questions asked may each cover more than one area of the syllabus. As you will see from the questions below, they may take the form of a short passage followed by a series of questions drawn from various areas of the syllabus. Note that although these questions include a short passage they could include a piece of visual information or a table instead.

This chapter could, perhaps, be used at the end of your course and before your examinations as a source of revision and examination practice. You could tackle these questions under mock examination conditions. This would mean sitting down in quiet surroundings, maybe in your bedroom or, if this is too noisy then in the local or school library, and trying to answer the questions. The marks allocated for each question are important because they give you a rough guide as to how detailed your answer should be.

A tutor's answer has been given to questions 1 and 2.

INTEGRATED QUESTIONS

QUESTION 1
Read the following passage carefully and answer the questions below.

J Morgan, a private **limited** company producing a cheaper chocolate, is facing considerable **cash flow problems** because of cut price selling from the brand leaders. At an emergency meeting of the Board of Directors it is decided to ask for permission to increase their **overdraft** at the firm's bank, and also discuss with the trade unions the possibility of redundancies for some of the 200 employees.

There has also been a meeting of the local branch of the Trade Union who are aware that the firm is considering some redundancies. The Union are discussing what their attitudes should be towards the problem. The workers are worried about their job security and wish to know what their rights are if they lose their jobs and how the firm is likely to decide who should be sacked.

(a)   State what you understand by the following terms as used above:
  (i)   limited;   **(2 marks)**
  (ii) cash flow problems;   **(2 marks)**
  (iii) overdraft.   **(2 marks)**
(b)   (i)   What is an agenda? What function does it perform for a meeting of the board?   **(2 marks)**
  (ii) Using the information in the passage, state three items that may appear on the agenda.   **(3 marks)**
(c)   Who would be members of the Board of Directors in this firm?   **(2 marks)**
(d)   If the firm made a loss in the financial year, what would be the effect of payments to
  (i)   shareholders;   **(2 marks)**
  (ii) debenture holders.   **(2 marks)**
(e)   As a result of the directors' meeting the Trade Union are informed that 150 employees are to be made redundant.
  (i)   On what basis do you think the firm should decide which employees should be made redundant?   **(4 marks)**
  (ii) What information and advice do you think the unions would offer to those employees being made redundant?   **(4 marks)**

Specimen question: Welsh Joint Education Committee

QUESTION 2
ADC plc is a firm involved in the extraction of sand and gravel. It wishes to increase the size of its business. The Board of Directors have decided to try and take over firms involved in the secondary and tertiary stages of production.

(a)   (i)   Give ONE example of secondary production and ONE example of tertiary production.   **(2 marks)**
  (ii) What is the purpose of the Board of Directors?   **(4 marks)**
  (iii) What is a 'take over'?   **(2 marks)**
  (iv) Explain why ADC plc would wish to become involved in the secondary and tertiary sectors of production.   **(10 marks)**
(b)   The Board of Directors have decided to move their Head Office to another town which is 100 miles away. This would mean that all office staff would also need to move.

   In order to try and stop this, the office workers have decided to hold a union meeting to discuss the problem.
  (i)   Why might the office workers not wish to move to another town? **(8 marks)**
  (ii) What action might the union members decide to take?   **(6 marks)**
  (iii) How would ADC plc overcome the problem of the move for the workers?   **(8 marks)**

Specimen question: Southern Examining Group

QUESTION 3
Read the following passage carefully, and answer the questions below.

Walestran, a successful public limited company specialises in overnight delivery of parcels throughout the United Kingdom. It hopes to expand by taking over a firm that carries bulk goods so that the range of transport services can be diversified. Increasing the size of the business might require a new site for the main transport depot. The Board of Directors are prepared to consider any suitable site within Wales.

Moving to a new site will give the firm a chance to modernise the office and make use of computers. However, several members of the Board think much of the firm's business depends on local customers, who may be lost if the firm moves, and want to expand on the present site.

(a)   Give two advantages to the firm of expanding their range of transport services.   **(4 marks)**

(b)   Explain why each of the following factors might be important in deciding whether a new location is suitable:

     (i)   being close to main roads;   **(2 marks)**

     (ii)   being close to large towns and cities;   **(2 marks)**

     (iii)   the cost of land;   **(2 marks)**

     (iv)   government aid.   **(2 marks)**

(c)   If the company computerises its main office several jobs will be created.

     (i)   What skills and abilities will the firm be looking for?   **(2 marks)**

     (ii)   Draft an advertisement which might attract someone with these skills and abilities.   **(7 marks)**

     (iii)   State two different places where you would expect the firm to advertise the vacancies.   **(2 marks)**

(d)   You wish to object to the firm expanding the existing depot because of the very large number of lorries which will be using the local roads. State and explain three reasons you would give for your objection.   **(6 marks)**

(e)   Why would the people who work in the company's office at the moment be worried about the possibility of the introduction of computers?   **(6 marks)**

Specimen question: Welsh Joint Education Committee

QUESTION 4

Read the following extract from the **Middlebridge Evening Post** and answer the questions below.

EXPANSION PLANS FOR UNITED

United Foods PLC have reported a large increase in profits for the year ending June 1985. The Company has grown rapidly. It manufactures a wide range of canned foods sold under its own brand name as well as supplying several supermarkets who sell under their own labels. The directors have decided to invest part of their profits and diversify into the soft drinks market.

At their last meeting, one of the main decisions concerned the new factory in which the soft drinks would be produced. Most of the workers will be employed on an assembly line and the discussion was about job satisfaction and whether workers should be paid on an hourly rate or on a piece-work system.

(a)   What does the abbreviation PLC stand for? (1 line for answer)   **(1 mark)**

(b)   (i)   Explain what you understand by the term 'brand name' and provide an example to illustrate your answer. (2 lines for answer)   **(2 marks)**

     (ii)   What is 'job satisfaction'? (2 lines for answer)   **(3 marks)**

(c)   United have decided to 'diversify'. Give TWO advantages of diversification to them.

1. _____

_____

2. _____

_____

     (2 marks)

(d)   Suggest how the company might have found that the soft drinks market had room for another competitor. (6 lines for answer)   **(5 marks)**
(e)   At present United sells its food products only to supermarkets. What new and different outlets might be appropriate for the sale of canned drinks? (4 lines for answer.)   **(4 marks)**
(f)   Say, with reasons, whether you think the assembly line workers should be paid on time rate or piece rates. (6 lines for answer)   **(4 marks)**

Reproduced by permission of the Midland Examining Group

QUESTION 5

John Cooke has just been made redundant from his job as a car worker. He has decided to set up a taxi and courier service to provide a service for the public and deliver letters and packages for business.

    He still has to decide whether to work from home or to rent a small office in the town centre.

(a)   Where would John obtain the capital to start up his business?   **(4 marks)**
(b)   (i)   What would be the disadvantages if John worked from home?   **(6 marks)**
       (ii)   What would be the advantages if John decided to rent a small office in the town centre?   **(6 marks)**
(c)   Which place of work would you advise John to choose? Give reasons for your choice.   **(10 marks)**
(d)   John has received a number of applications for jobs as drivers with his business.
       (i)   What qualities would be important for this type of work?   **(4 marks)**
       (ii)   Draw up a contract of employment which could be used for one of John's employees.   **(10 marks)**

Specimen question: Southern Examining Group

TUTOR'S ANSWER TO QUESTION 1

(a)   (i)   ***limited***: a 'limited' company is one which is registered under the Companies Act. There are two types of limited company, the public limited company (PLC) and, as here in the case with J Morgan, a private limited company. The basis of limited companies is 'limited liability' where the owners/ shareholders are only responsible for the debt of the company up to the amount they have put into the company. A private limited company is not able to sell its shares to the general public.

       (ii)   ***cash flow problems***: these happen when a company's cash outgoings exceed (temporarily or permanently) its cash incomings. In the case of J Morgan, the chocolate manufacturer, the cash flow problem stems from a possible reduction in its cash incomings. While it will still have to make regular payments, such as wages, rent, rates and bank interest on loans, it may now be receiving less revenue from the sale of its product. This is because the major producers of chocolate are cutting their price, which will probably make J Morgan's cheaper chocolate less attractive, reducing demand for it. Selling less chocolate at the same price will reduce the revenue of J Morgan.

       (iii)   ***overdraft***: an 'overdraft' is the amount which the bank agrees to let the company take out of its account ***over and above*** what is in it. *Note:* be careful not to confuse an overdraft with a loan (see Ch. 7).

(b)   (i)   An ***agenda*** is a list of items to be discussed at a meeting. At a Board Meeting it lists the matters which will be dealt with by the Directors. A typical agenda will include: (1) ***Apologies*** from those who are unable to attend the meeting. (2) ***Minutes*** or notes from the last meeting which have to be approved. (3) ***Matters arising***, so that those present at the meeting can discuss/comment on the last meeting. (4) ***Reports*** which individuals, such as the Chairman, may want to present as important information to the meeting. (5) ***Special Matters***, Which may have arisen. (6) ***Date of the next meeting*** (7) ***Any other business*** (AOB), so that any matters not included in the agenda can be discussed.

(ii)   The three items that may appear on the agenda for J Morgan under **Reports** or **Special Matters** are: (1) The need for an overdraft (2) The possibility of redundancies (3) How those who might be made redundant should be selected.

(c)   The members of the Board of Directors in this firm are likely to be the members of the Morgan family together with any other major shareholders. This is because it is a 'Private' Limited Company.

(d)   If the firm made a loss in the financial year then the effect on the **shareholders**, who are the owners of the company, might be (1) That a dividend would not be paid. At best the firms reserves might be used to pay a **small** dividend. (2) On the other hand **debenture** holders would be in a different position. These are the creditors of the company, and must be paid or they can force the company into liquidation. Interest payments must still be forwarded to debenture holders.

(e)   (i)   The basis on which the firm should decide which employees to make redundant include (1) The skills still required in the 50 remaining employees. The firm will not want to make employees redundant whose skills are still vital to its operation. (2) The levels of seniority. The firm may want to keep more experienced, senior staff. (3) The nearness to retirement age. Those near to retirement age may be less concerned about redundancy. On the other hand, long-serving employees will qualify for more redundancy pay, and will therefore prove more expensive to dismiss. (4) The nearness to appointment. Those 'last in' may be 'first out'. (5) Those who volunteer for redundancy. Those near to retirement may volunteer for redundancy. Taking volunteers may create less bitterness with the remaining staff and with those leaving.

(ii)   The information and advice the unions would offer to those employees being made redundant include (1) Information on the rights to redundancy pay. (2) Help in finding a new job. (3) Advice on whether **industrial action** would be likely to stop the redundancies. If so, advice on the type of industrial action to take. (4) Advice on the possibilities for **retraining**, the government grants available, the types of retraining suitable to each person.

TUTOR'S ANSWER TO QUESTION 2

(a)   (i)   A secondary producer would be a company involved in the manufacture of goods, for example, a cement producer. A tertiary producer would be a company involved in the provision of services, for example, consultancy service to the building industry.

(ii)   The Board of Directors are a group of individuals who are elected by the shareholders to whom they are accountable. The purpose of the Board of Directors is to run the company. This involves deciding what the company policy is to be and making sure that the policy is carried out. All the major decisions within the company, such as the purchase of expensive machinery, the takeover of another company or the redundancy of employees will also be the responsibility of the Board of Directors. A Managing Director is likely to be on the Board and be the director most actively involved in running the company.

(iii)   **With this question you need to make sure you do not confuse a takeover with a merger**. A takeover is where a company (ADC plc), wants to take control of another company which might otherwise resist its approach. The control of the other company will usually take the form of obtaining sufficient shares in that company. A merger, on the other hand, is where both companies are willing to join together.

(iv)   The extraction of sand and gravel is a **primary** stage of producton. If ADC plc becomes involved with the secondary (manufacturing) and tertiary (service) stages of production, this would be **forward vertical integration**. There could be a number of benefits to the firm from this.

1.   **Less risks**. Being involved in other activities may be helpful if the demand for sand and gravel should decline.

2. ***More secure outlet for its products***. By owning a manufacturing plant which uses sand and gravel, ADC plc can be sure that someone will take its product. ***This reason is similar to 1.***

3. ***Lower costs for the firm***. By adding extra activities, the size of ADC plc will grow. Being a larger firm will help it reduce the average costs of production, i.e. benefit from economies of scale.

4. ***Control over the outlet for the product***. ADC plc might take over retail or wholesale outlets (tertiary stage) as well as manufacturing. It may therefore be able to control the price of products (such as cement) which uses its sand and gravel. By keeping price low, ADC plc can help encourage demand for cement and with it the demand for sand and gravel.

5. ***Extra Profit*** There may be profit that can be made at the secondary and tertiary stages of production. This profit can be added to the profit it is already making at the primary stage.

(b) (i) The office workers may not wish to move to another town 100 miles away for social and economic reasons. In social terms the office workers will have to leave their family and friends. Leaving their 'roots' may prove to be very difficult. Many of the office workers may have children at school and be reluctant to move them, particularly if they are soon to take their examinations. In economic terms moving 100 miles would prove to be very costly. There are removal and legal expenses associated with buying a new house in a new location. If the town is closer to London then the house prices are likely to be much higher. If the office workers live in rented accommodation then they will face a problem if the new town has a shortage of rented accommodation.

(ii) Before any action takes place the unions will want to negotiate with the company. In their negotiations they will want to explore all the possibilities. Is the move the only option open to the company? If so, then they will want to know whether they will be given any financial help with the move. If the union members believe other options are available to the company they may decide to oppose the move. If negotiations break down they may operate an overtime ban or a work-to-rule. As a last resort they may go on strike.

(iii) ADC plc could overcome the problem of the move for the workers by giving them financial assistance with the move. If the house prices are more expensive in the new town then the company may give housing subsidies. Rented accommodation might be provided free of charge for, say, the first six months. Higher salaries could be given to office workers in the new location. Information may also be made available on the new town such as the types of facilities which are available, the schools, shops, and hospitals.

STUDENT'S ANSWER – EXAMINER'S COMMENT

This is an answer to question 5, page 193.

❝ You could also mention that he may have received redundancy pay. ❞

❝ Good points, but more could be made! There would probably be complaints from his neighbours about noise, etc. He would need planning permission to carry on the business at home, which might not be granted, etc. ❞

❝ A good answer. ❞

❝ Good points, which show that you are thinking about John's situation. Perhaps near to the railway station would also help. ❞

5) a) John could obtain his capital in the form of a bank loan or from the government.

b) i) If he worked from home, his business would not be so noticeable or seen by many potential customers. He probably has to travel a costly distance before he'd reach the pick-up destination, normally in the town centre.

ii) to rent a small office in the town centre would be a benefit because it would be more easily recognisable as a business in operation, it is already in (the) a busy town. Therefore, as well as being on the door-step of his customers, more people are likely to see his office and therefore use his services.

c) John would be wise to have his office near to the town centre where organisations wanting taxi or courier services are near-by, and where there is easy access for his vehicles. He needs to be established near potential customers but away from competitors so that he obtains a maximum custom. He needs plenty of parking space so that his service can run efficiently without causing any congestion in the road.

> **Honesty will also be important as drivers will handle money. Being on time is also important.**

d) i)   A clean driving license is essential. Good driving experience. Good knowledge of the area, streets as well as places (businesses).

ii) —

> **A great pity. You will lose all the marks for this part of the question, spoiling what has so far been a very good answer. Always try to make an attempt at every part of the question. Make sure you revise the Contract of Employment.**

INDEX